"**50 Contemporary Artists** is my response to publishers, critics and curators who systematically regurgitate the same list of contemporary artists every season. Being an Artist, the Editor-In-Chief of Artvoices Magazine and the Curator of Artvoices Art Books I view thousands of artists and their works annually. Arguably countless artists are intentionally left out of the conversation because of geography, race, religion and or sexual preference. Art and its function and or appeal to the public-at-large should remain subjective."

TERRENCE SANDERS, CURATOR OF 50 CONTEMPORARY ARTISTS

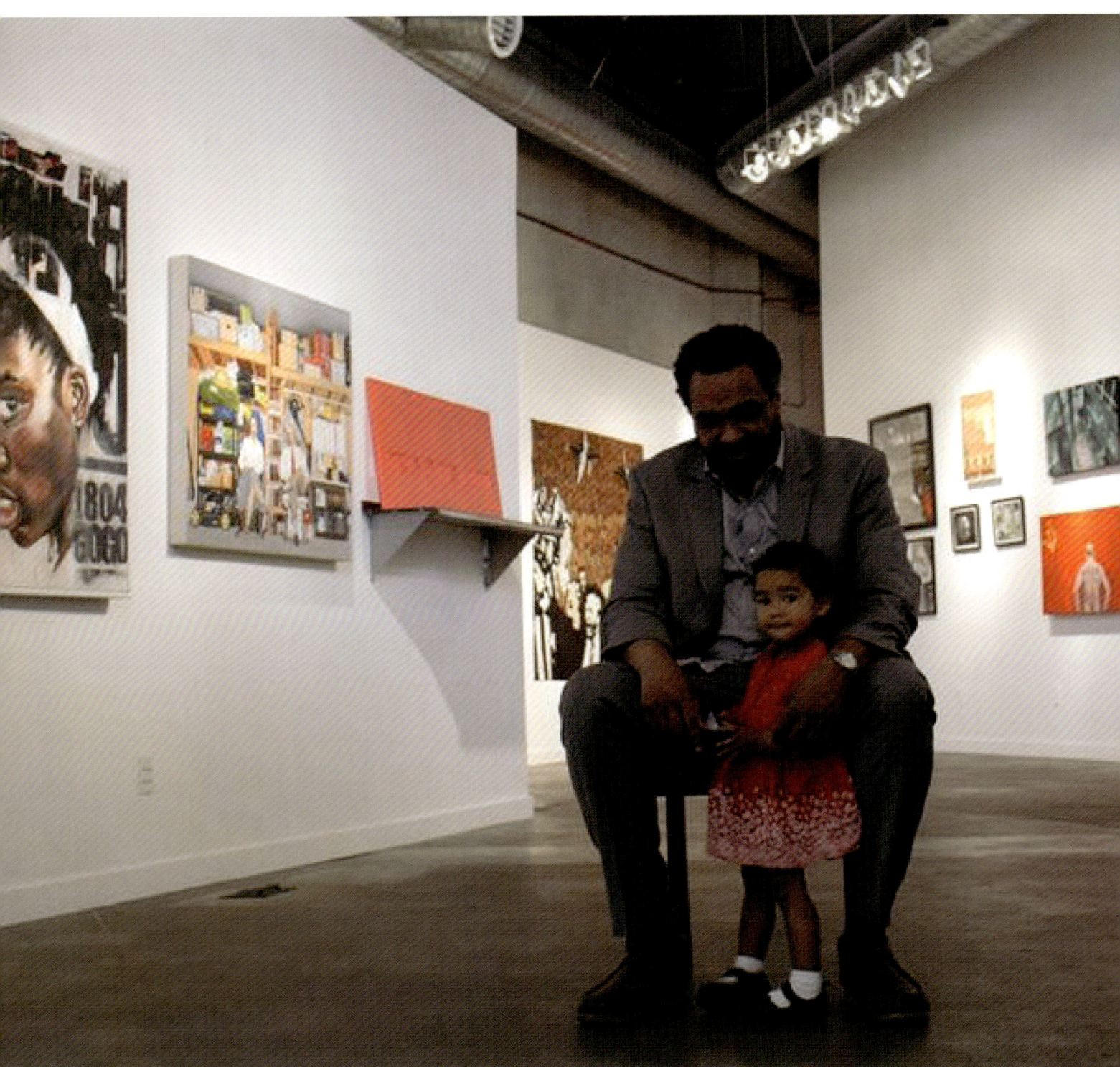

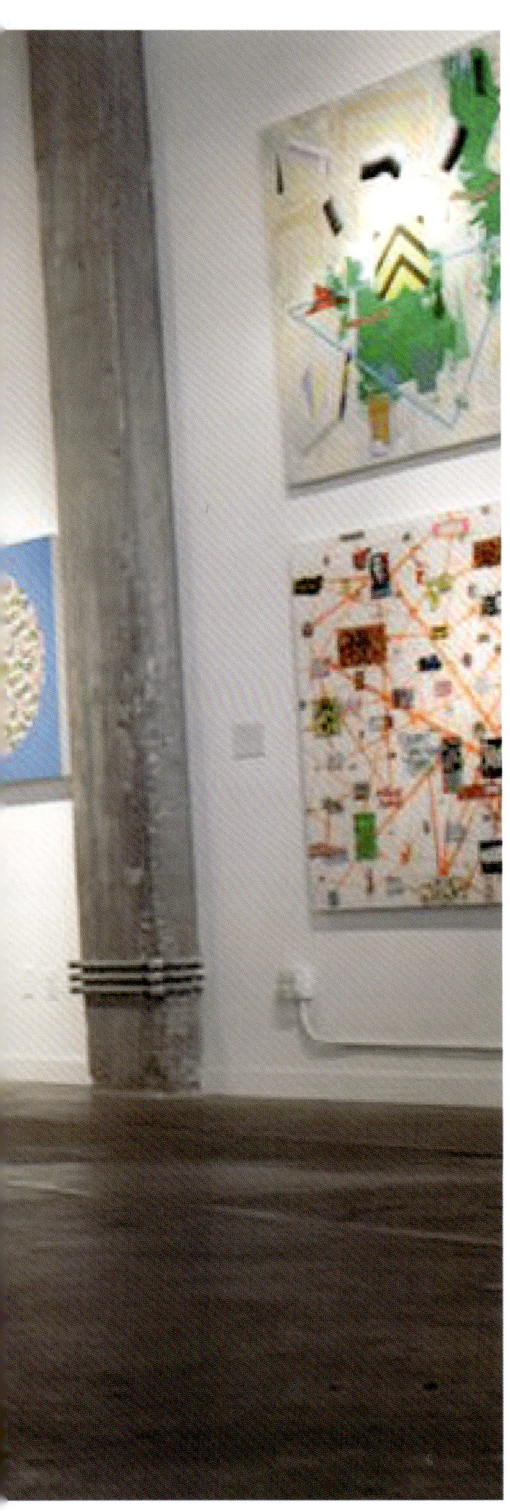

LCCN: 2019952525

ISBN: 978-1-7320048-9-4

Printed in China

Designed by Jen Zhao

First Artvoices Art Books Publishing edition 2022

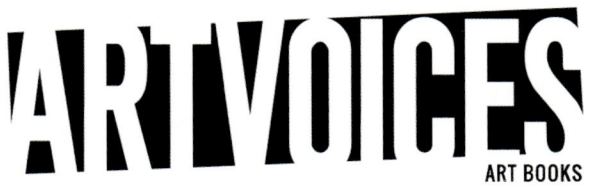

Artvoices Art Books Publishing
www.artvoicesartbooks.com

50 CONTEMPORARY ARTISTS

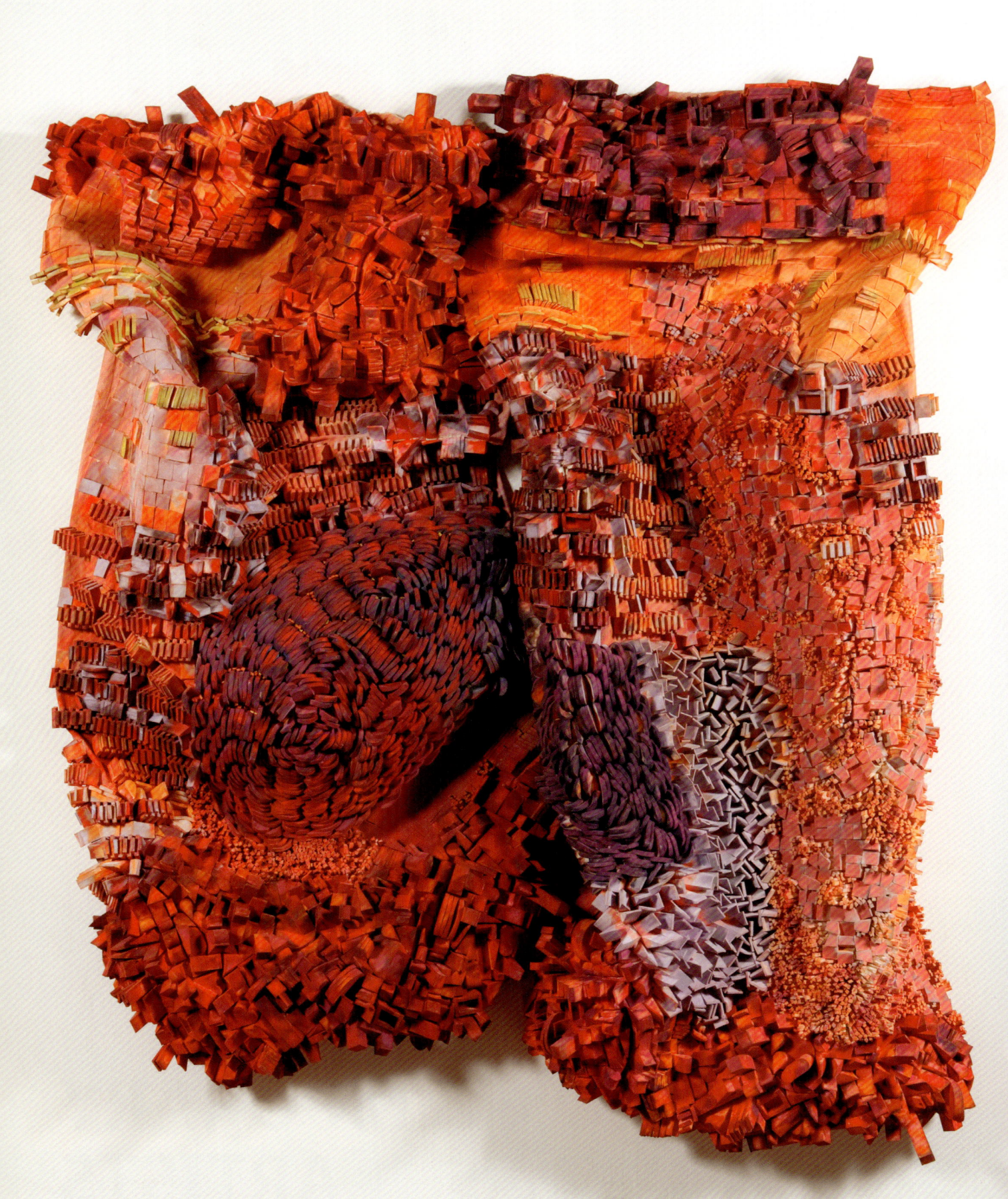

MARGERY AMDUR

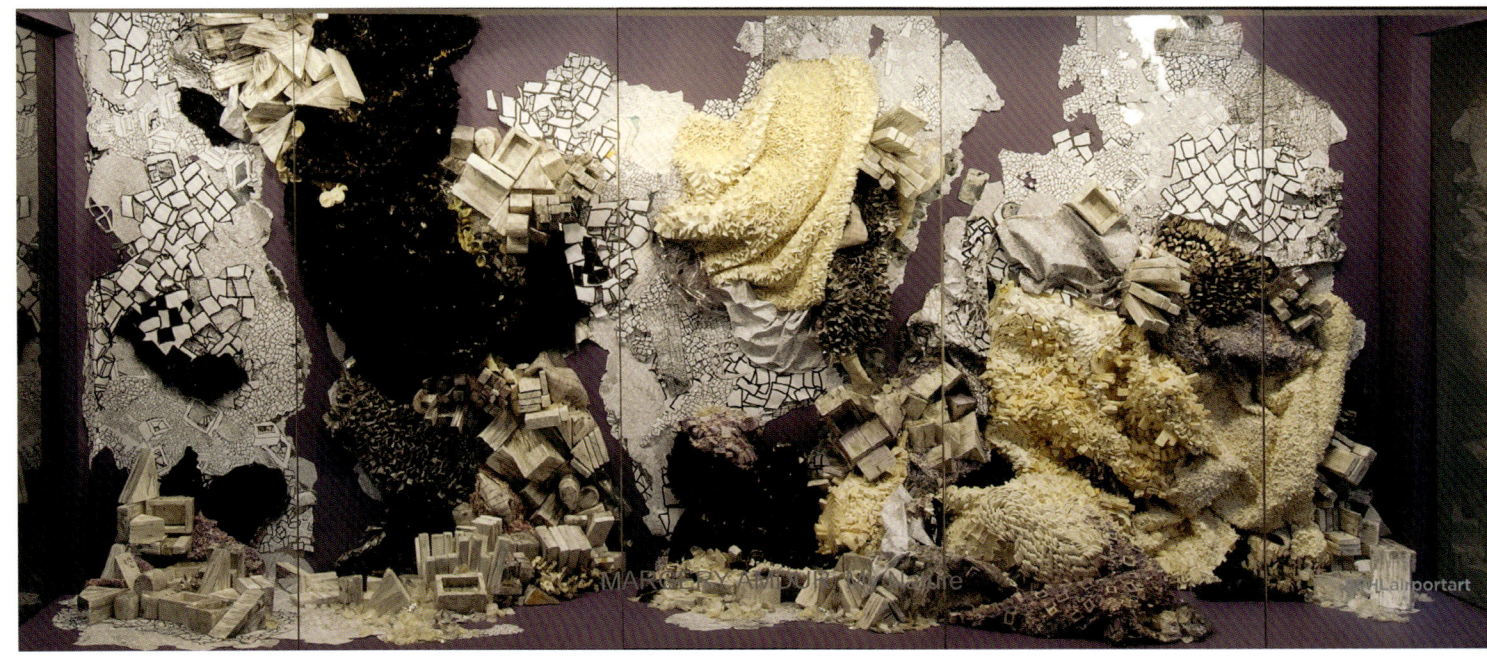

"I am a mark maker-on and off the canvas, and I don't restrict myself to any one material. I like to live in that very fluid space between painting, sculpture, and printmaking, and the idea of an obsessively ritualized process is still very prominent in the work."

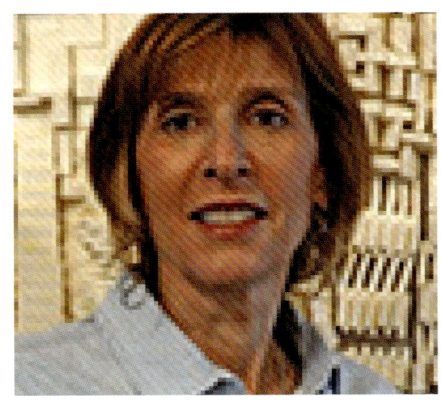

Originally from Pittsburgh, Margery Amdur received her B.F.A. from Carnegie-Mellon University and her M.F.A. from the University of Wisconsin in Madison. Margery has had over 60 solo and two-person exhibitions. Her international exhibitions include Turkey, Hungary, Poland, England, and Iceland. She has been reviewed in national and international publications including Sculpture Magazine, New American Paintings, Fiber Arts, New Art Examiner, Art Papers, and in two of the Manifest International Publications. She was shortlisted in the 2015 International Aesthetica Art Prize, and an interview with the artist can be found on their site. Her next projects include an installation at the Philadelphia International Airport, and an installation at the CEU in Budapest, Hungary.

WWW.MARGERYAMDUR.NET

● **(facing page) Amass #6**
Cosmetic sponges coated in ink, gouache and pastel pigment , 68 x 54 in., 2014

● **My Nature #2**
Cosmetic sponges coated with pastel pigment, digital prints, styro foam, vinyl and glitter., 2015

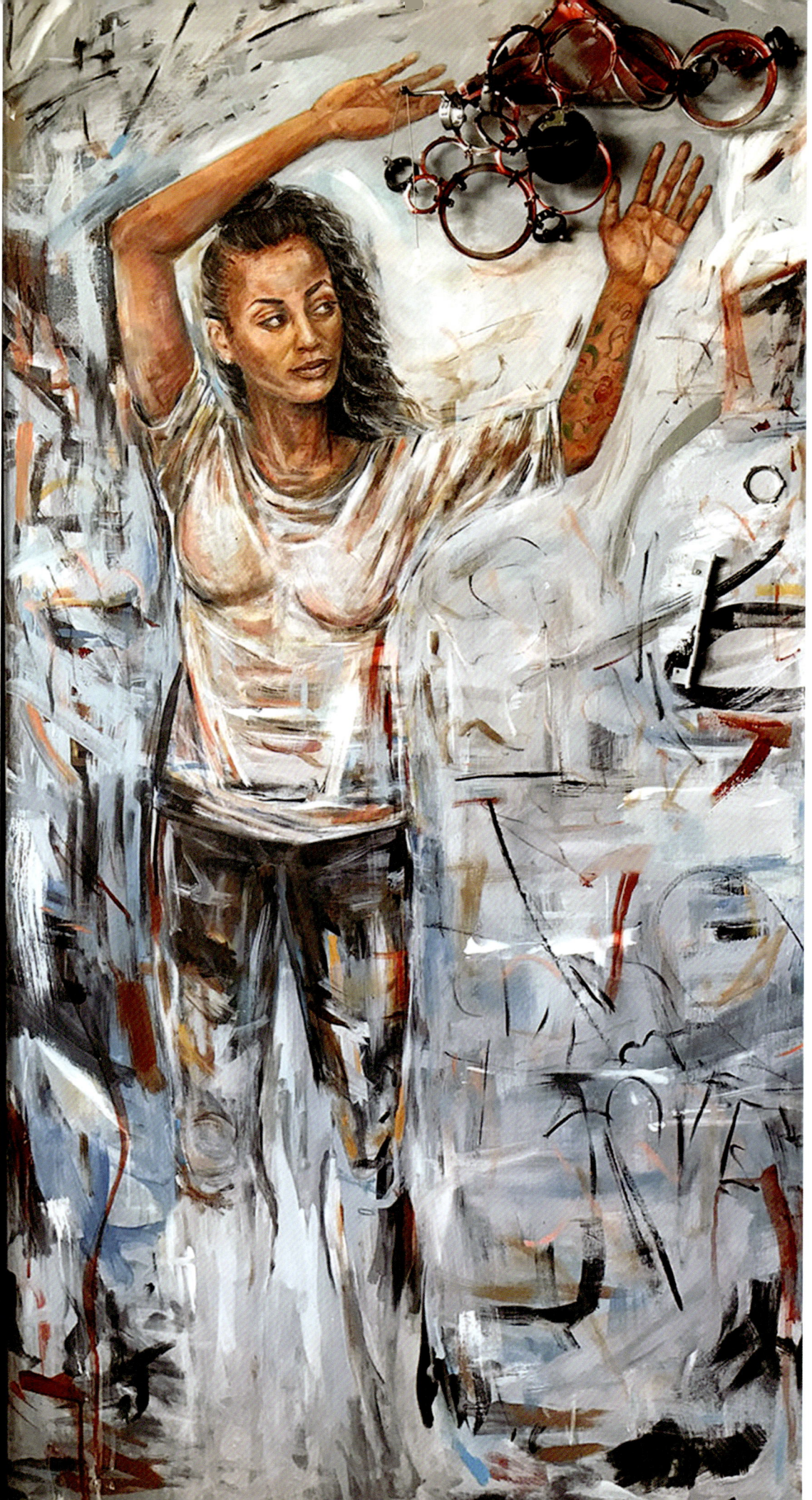

SHARON BARNES

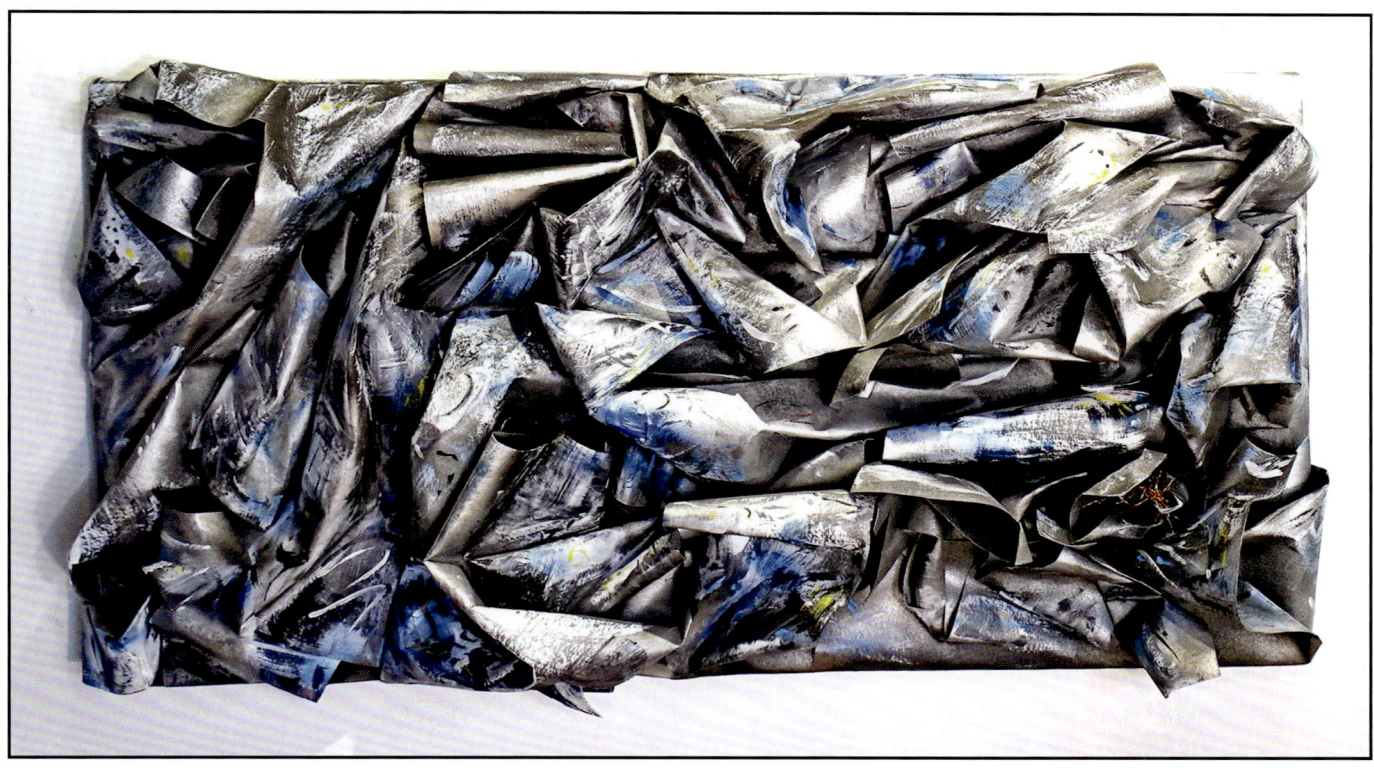

"By manipulating rough, unconventional materials and working through the challenges presented by them, she evokes socio-political metaphors of hope, struggle and change."

Ms. Barnes began her decades long career as a representational painter, but the range of possibilities presented by working in abstraction with hybrid art forms and rough industrial materials, has evolved into her recent bodies of work. By manipulating rough, unconventional materials and working through the challenges presented by them, she evokes socio-political metaphors of hope, struggle and change. Curator Erika Hirugami, MAAB described her work as lying "at the convergence of neo-expressionism, abstraction and deep African American concerns."

Born in Sacramento, CA, Ms. Barnes lives and works in Los Angeles. She has exhibited in major cities of the United States and the Republic of Panama, including "Hard Edged: Geometric Abstraction and Beyond" at the California African American Museum (CAAM) and the 2005 Survey of African American Artists in Los Angeles, also at CAAM.

WWW.SHARONLOUISEBARNES.COM

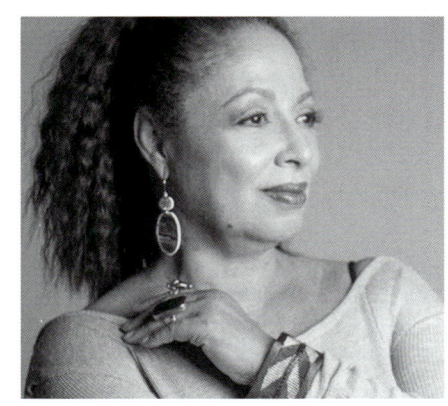

● **(facing page) Woman in Wheelhouse**
Acrylic, graphite, recycled can tops, industrial metals, spray enamel on plywood, 65H x 35W x

● **Playing Fields #2**
Industrial roofing paper, acrylic, gesso, copper, 24H x 48W x 4D in., 2017

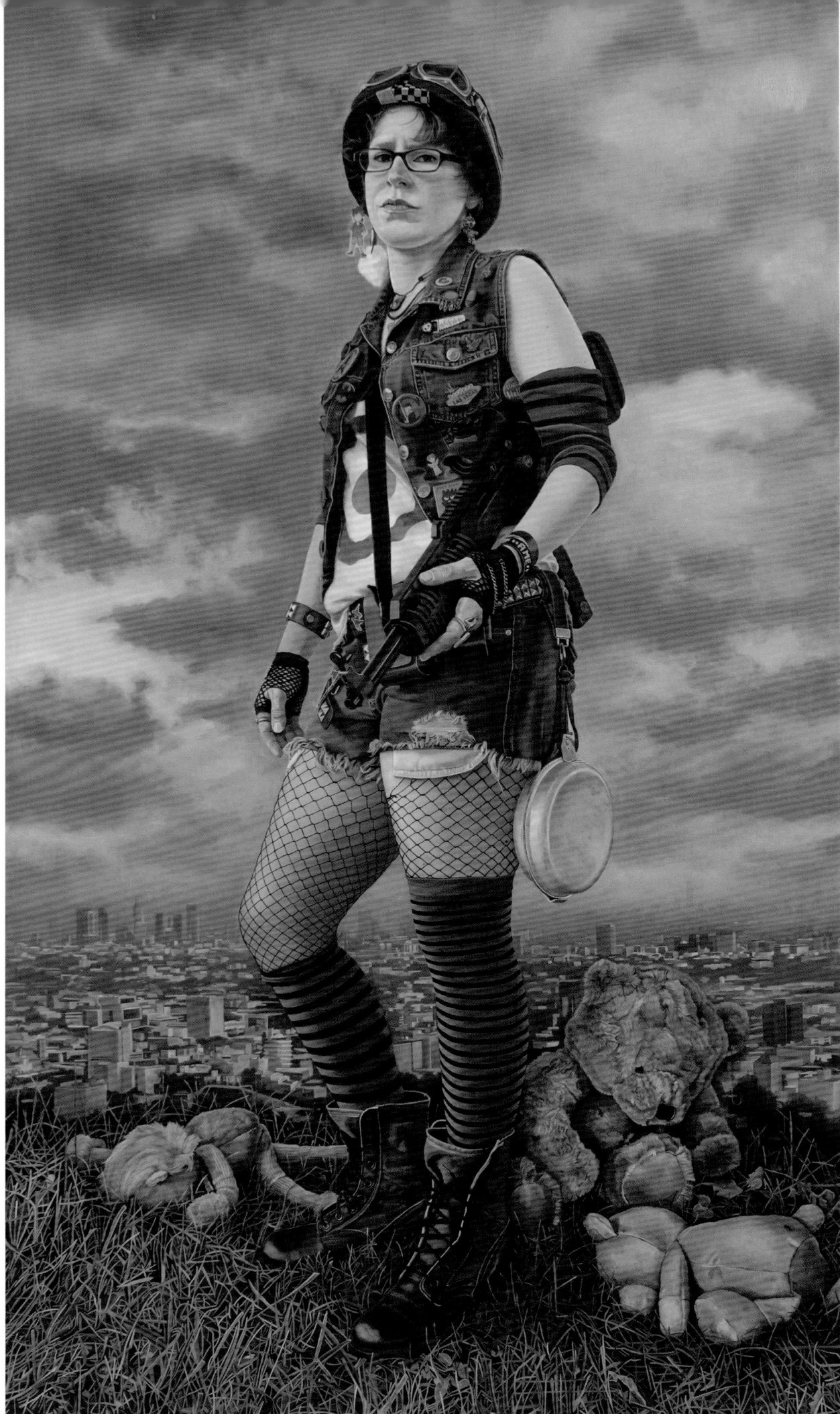

LEIGH BONGIORNO

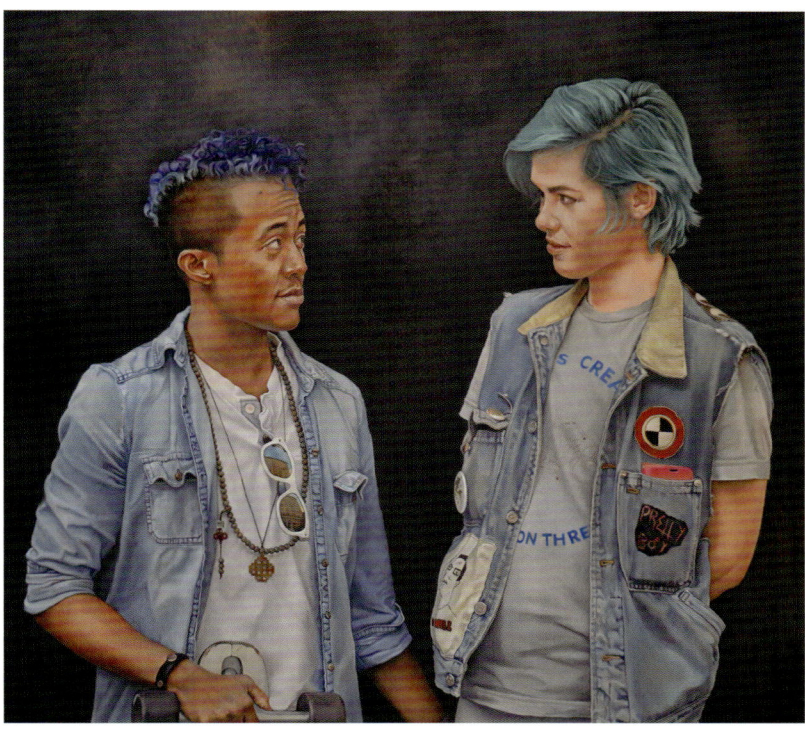

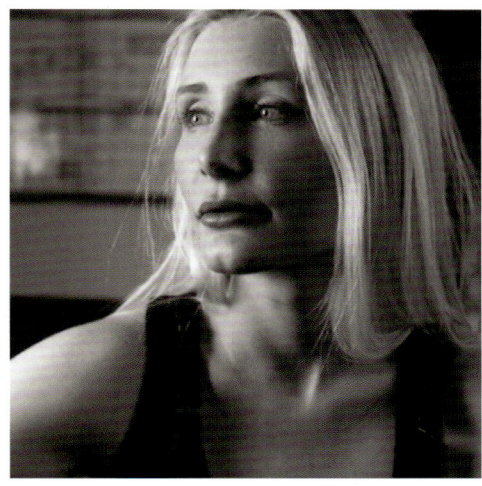

(facing page) **American Portrait**
oil on linen, 72 x 42 in., 2018

Love
oil on canvas, 48 x 48 in., 2017

Born and raised in Cleveland, Ohio, figurative artist Leigh Bongiorno (previously known as Wendy Leigh Knapp) has spent her life dedicated to creating compelling and innovative artworks in a variety of media. Bongiorno began her formal studies in 2005 when she studied with a local portrait artist in Cleveland. During this time, Bongiorno began creating exceptional surrealistic portraits that gained national recognition. Bongiorno enrolled in the Columbus College of Art in 2006 but later transferred to the Cleveland Institute of Art after being inspired by the work of forensic artists who helped officials solve a missing-person's case. Bongiorno earned a degree in Biomedical Illustration in 2011. Bongiorno explored the path of biomedical illustration as a profession and worked with several hospitals, museums, and research facilities including the Cleveland Clinic.

Bongiorno traveled all over the country to try to gain perspective and insight into the vast and varied American lifestyles and cultures. She gained artistic inspiration from various individuals she met along the way, which helped point her career path back to its roots in figurative and portrait-based oil painting. Bongiorno's focus on underrepresented communities and people has since fueled her passion for art even further and has pushed her to become one of the most well-respected figurative artists in the country.

With subjects ranging from transgender individuals to homeless communities, Bongiorno creates artwork to raise awareness and understanding of those living in a marginalized or underrepresented society. Her meticulous creations focus on topics such as race, sex, gender, religion, and poverty. She hopes that her work will inspire others to see the beauty in those around them. Bongiorno has won a variety of awards for her art since 2004, and her work has been displayed in galleries and museums all over the country including the Makeshift Museum in Los Angeles, Cleveland Institute of Art, the U.S. Capitol Building, Corcoran Gallery, Alliance Gallery in New York, Lorain County Community College, and the Diane von Furstenberg Studio.

Bongiorno currently lives and works back in her hometown of Cleveland where she plans to further expand her artistic and humanitarian endeavors in the local, national, and international community.

WWW.LEIGHBONGIORNO.COM

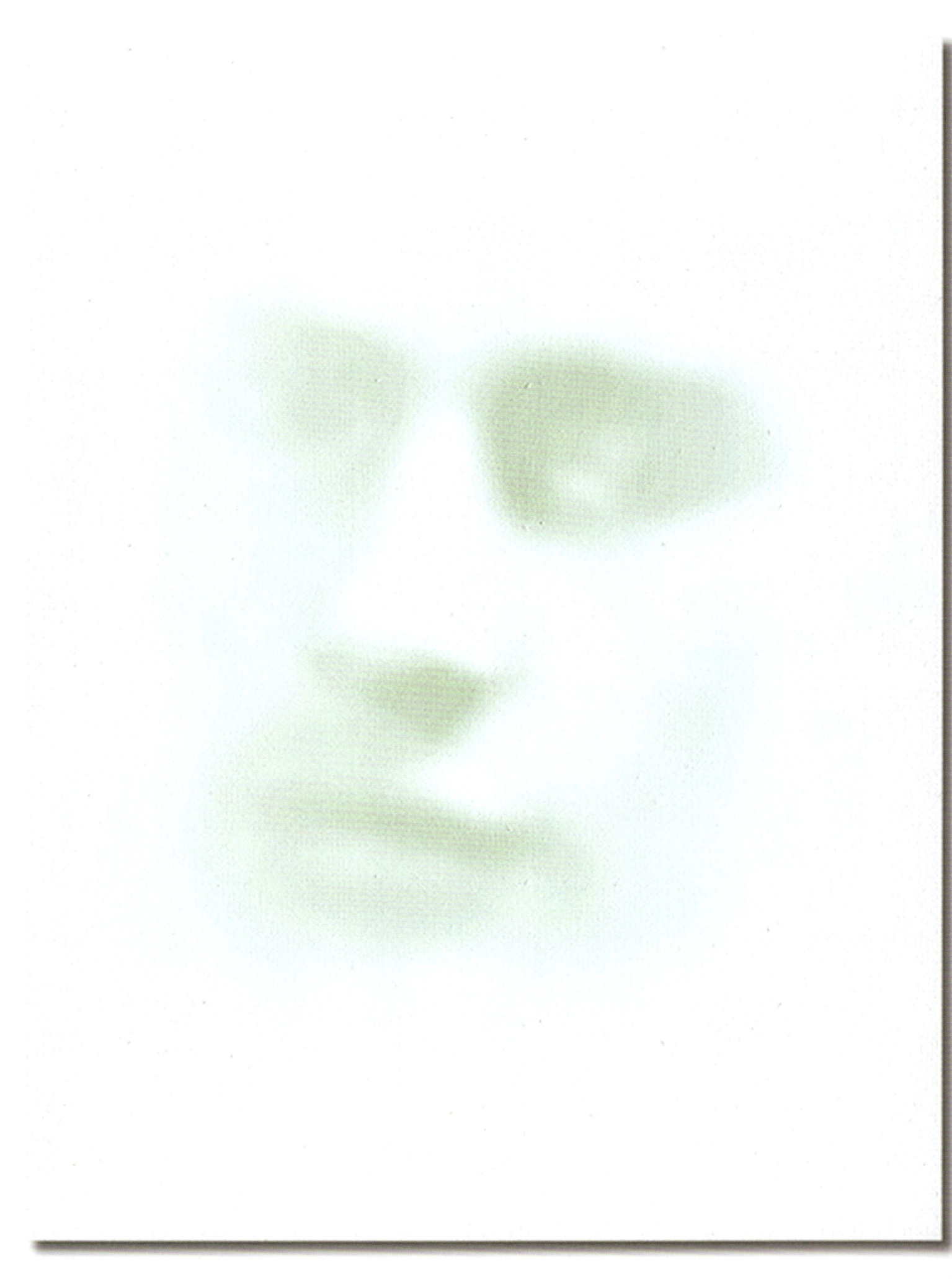

DANIELE BONGIOVANNI

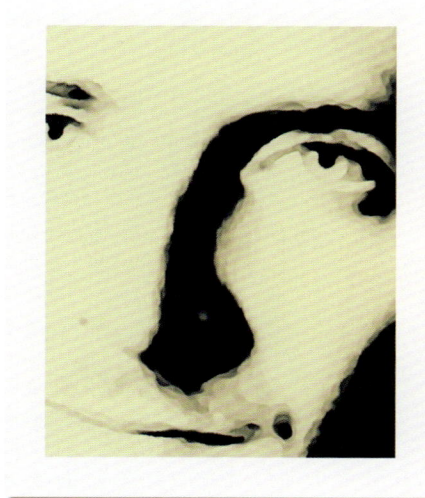 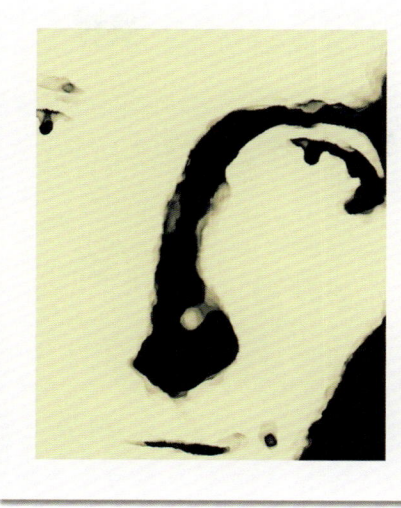 

"A subject painted by me does not necessarily have to laugh or smile but can also take on an apparently relaxed expression that is equally rejoicing. This is because the face has micro features that say much more. To make these micro-features visible, we need to make a careful study that touches both the psychology and the concept of empathy, between our neighbour and us."

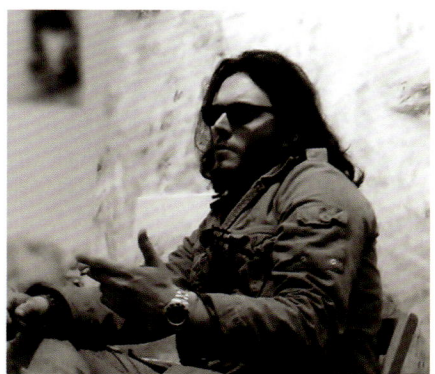

Daniele Bongiovanni is an Italian painter. He works between Palermo, Torino and Lugano. He boasts more than 80 exhibitions all over the world and he took part to major contemporary art events, including two editions of the Venice Biennale d'Arte.

WWW.DANIELEBONGIOVANNI.COM

● **(facing page) Exist**
Oil and mixed techniques on canvas,
70 x 50 in., 2017

● **Mood**
details?

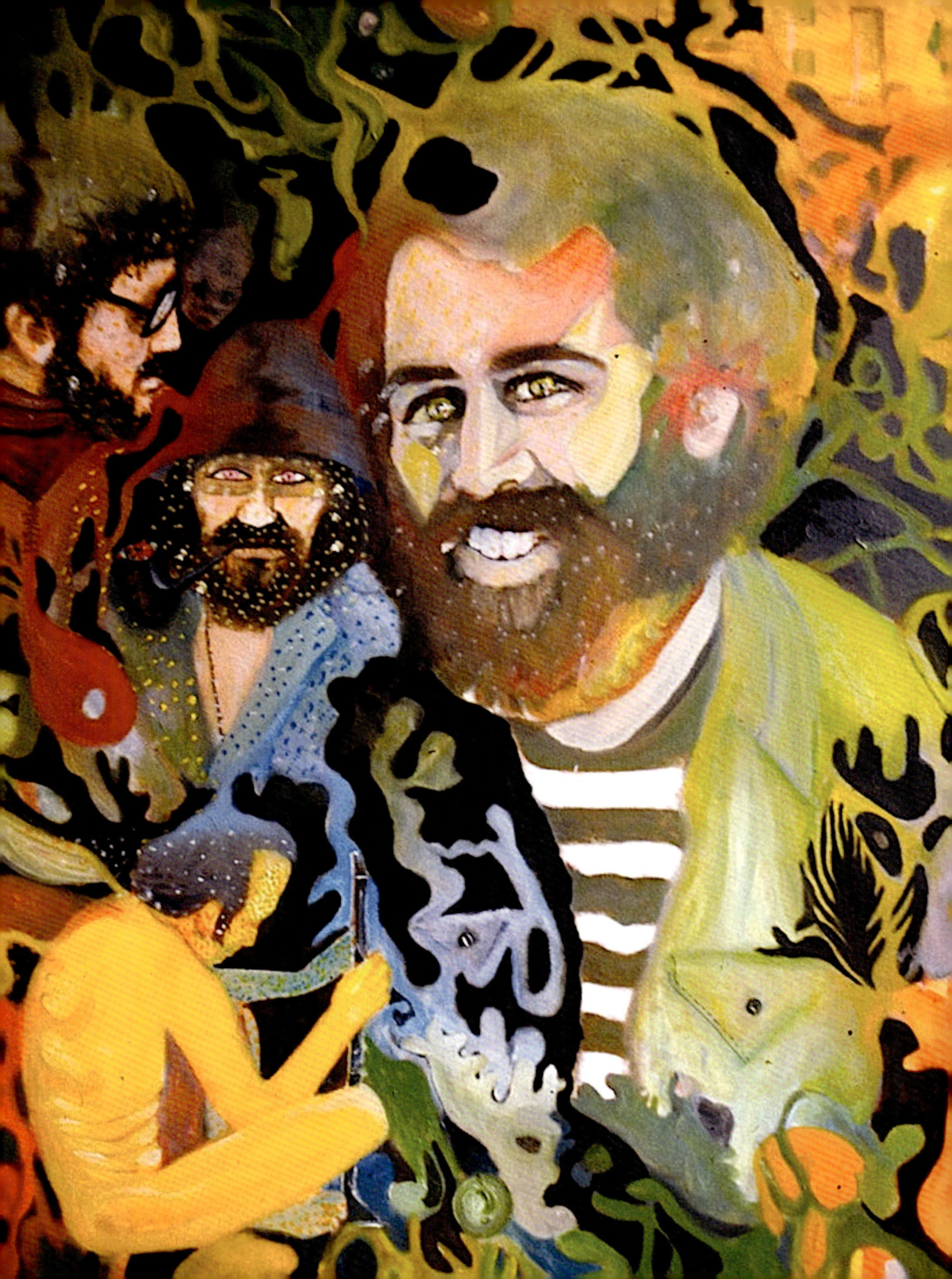

MIKI BONI

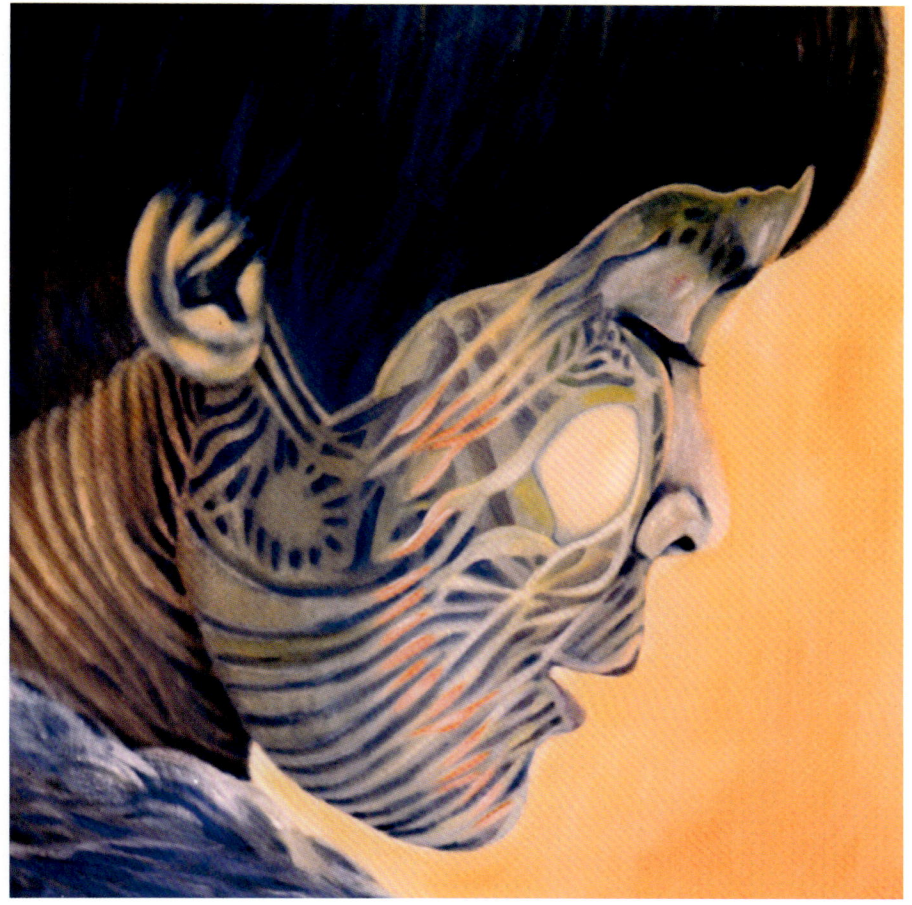

Miki Boni is no ordinary painter. Her background is a varied as the expressionistic works that leap from her canvases. An award-winning painter and Brooklyn NY native, Miki Boni began her career in Manhattan's East Village drawing street portraits. She spent years living in Mexico as a working artist where her art was greatly influenced by that country's muralists as well as several of Mexico's most prolific surrealists. Boni taught Perception, Life Drawing and Painting at the University of Guanajuato while working toward her Masters Degree in Fine Arts. Her work was chosen as one of only a few American artists to be included in the permanent collection of the Museo de Arte Contemporaneo in the State of Nayarit. Working in both in oils and oil pastels, her unique signature is her subtle and sometimes bold use of patterning,

biomorphic in form, creating the illusion of a high-powered microscope probing the inner world of its subject until its molecular structure is revealed. Her imagination is her microscope and the result is juxtaposed on its macro-sized counterpart.

Boni has traveled extensively, gathering image bank material. She has had numerous one-person shows in both the US and Mexico and her works are included in private collections internationally.

Upon her return from Mexico, her work was exhibited at Lincoln Center's Cork Gallery. She was listed in Who's Who of American Women, and was elected to Washington DC's National League of American Pen Women for her accomplishments in the visual arts.

WWW.MIKIBONI.COM

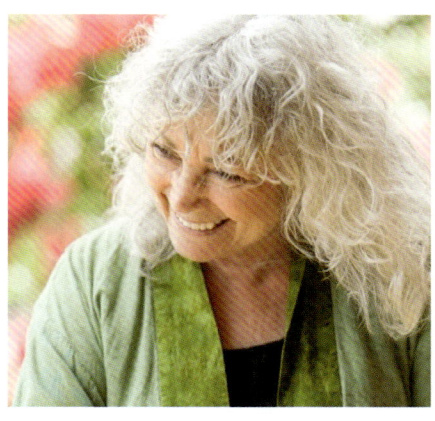

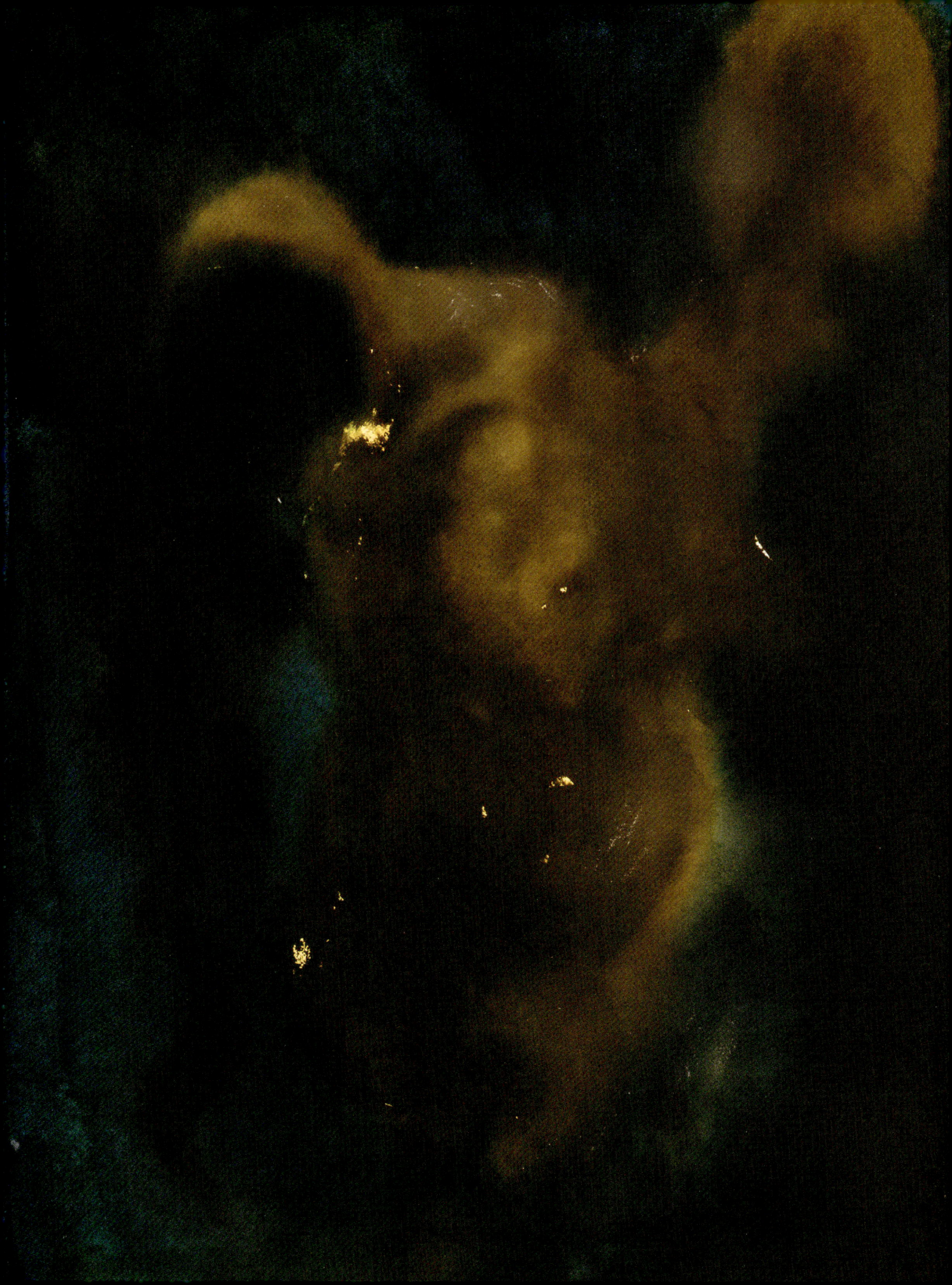

KATHLEEN CAPRARIO

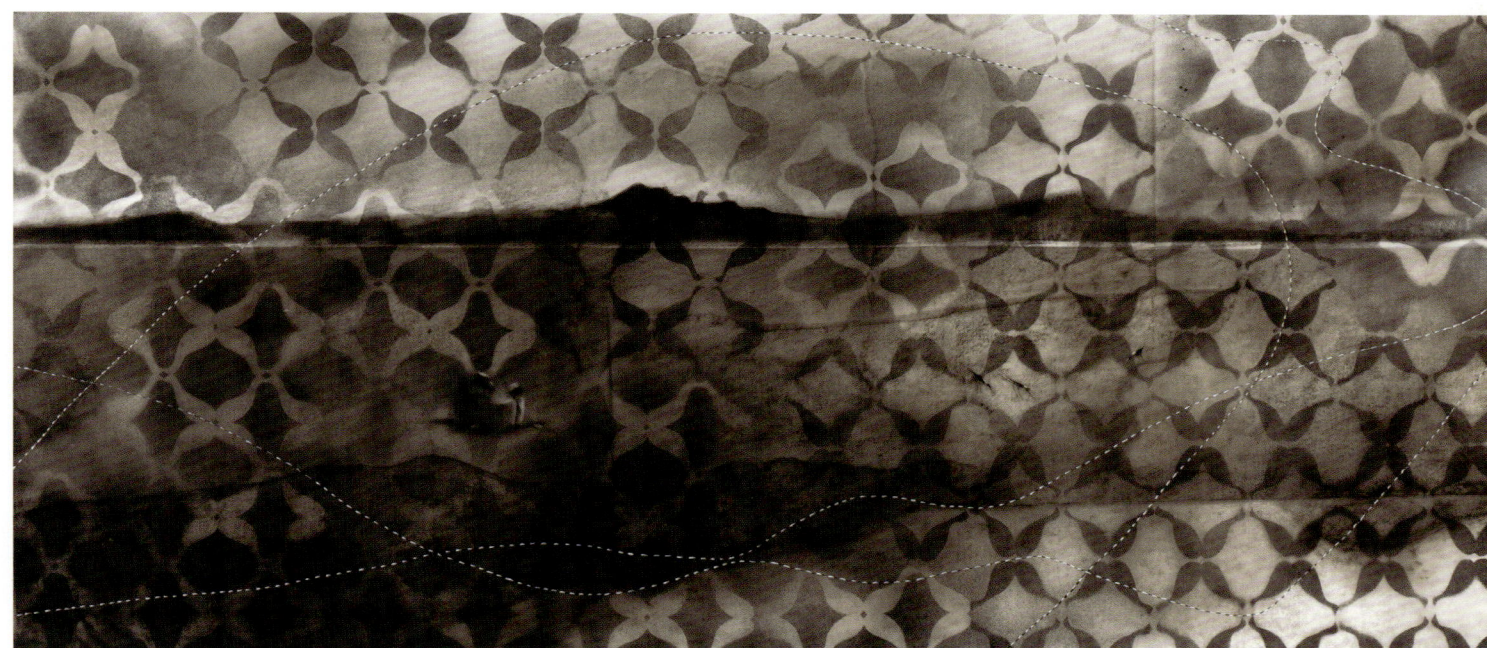

Kathleen Caprario traded the concrete canyons of New York City for the real canyons and broad skies of the Pacific Northwest where she found her life-long subject—the land. Her process is similar to the spontaneous and organic growth of a forest with underlying layers of organizing pattern that metaphorically ground and visually describe the interconnected relationship of self to nature. Caprario's early career in textile design focused her attention on repeated motifs and she developed an interest in pattern and its cultural associations to feminine identity and landscape. Her work continues to evolve from the question, "How am I shaped by my environment?" Caprario's work is exhibited nationally and has received awards including an Oregon Arts Commission Individual Artist Fellowship and the Modesto Lanzone Award. Artist residencies at the Ucross Foundation, Jentel Foundation, Morris Graves' Foundation and Playa Foundation as well as living and working with Aboriginal children in Central Australia (2010), have informed her work.

WWW.CAPRARIOART.COM

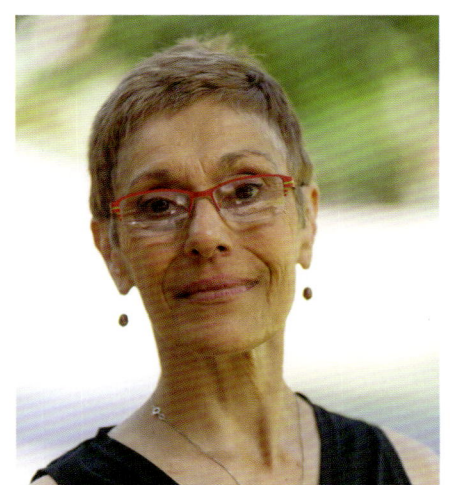

● **(facing page) Waterbodies I**
Watercolor on paper, 30 x 22 in., 2009

● **Avocet Dreaming**
*Graphite, spray paint, chalk on vellum,
42 x 83 in., 2011*

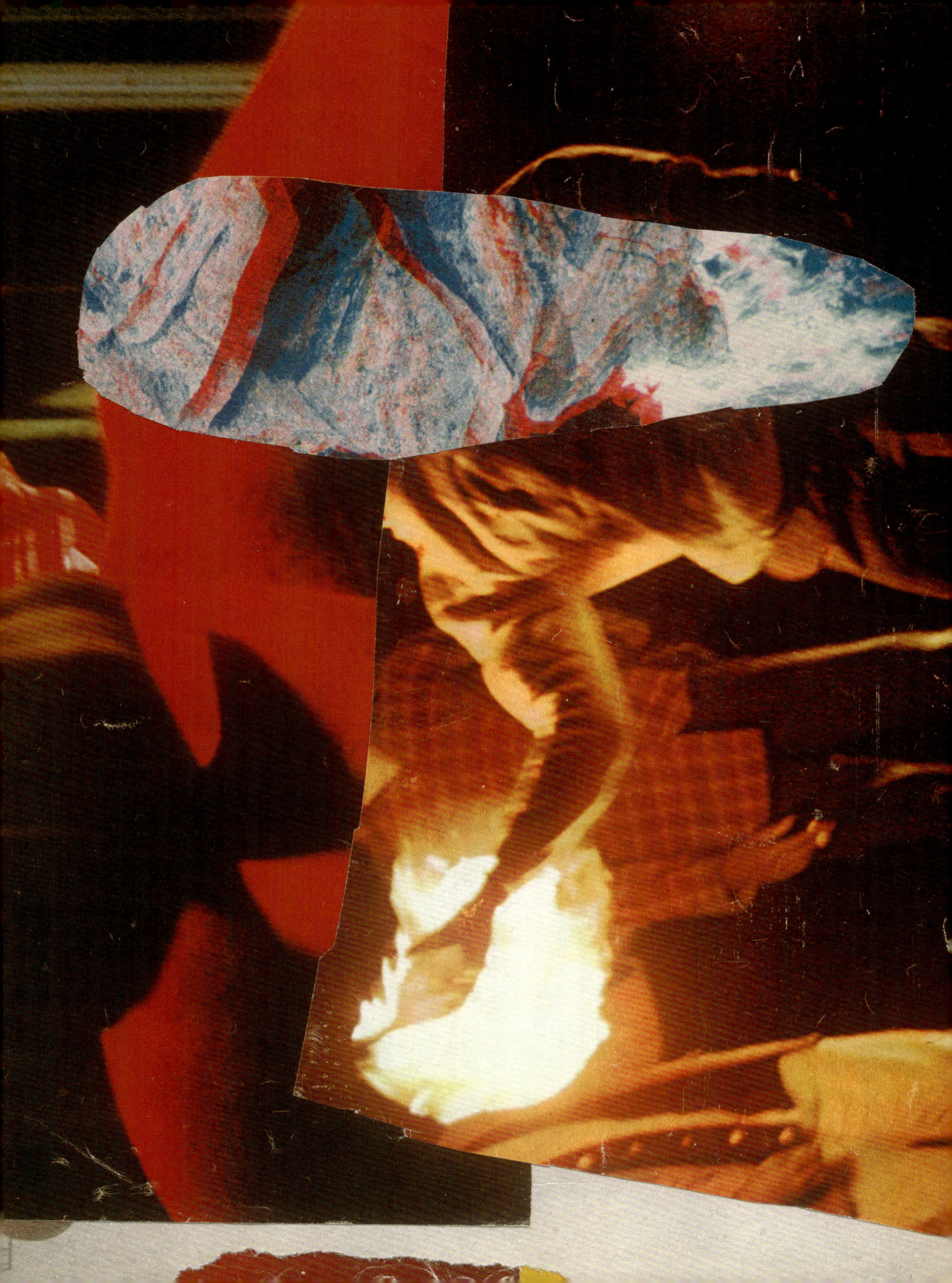

MICHAEL CHANDLER

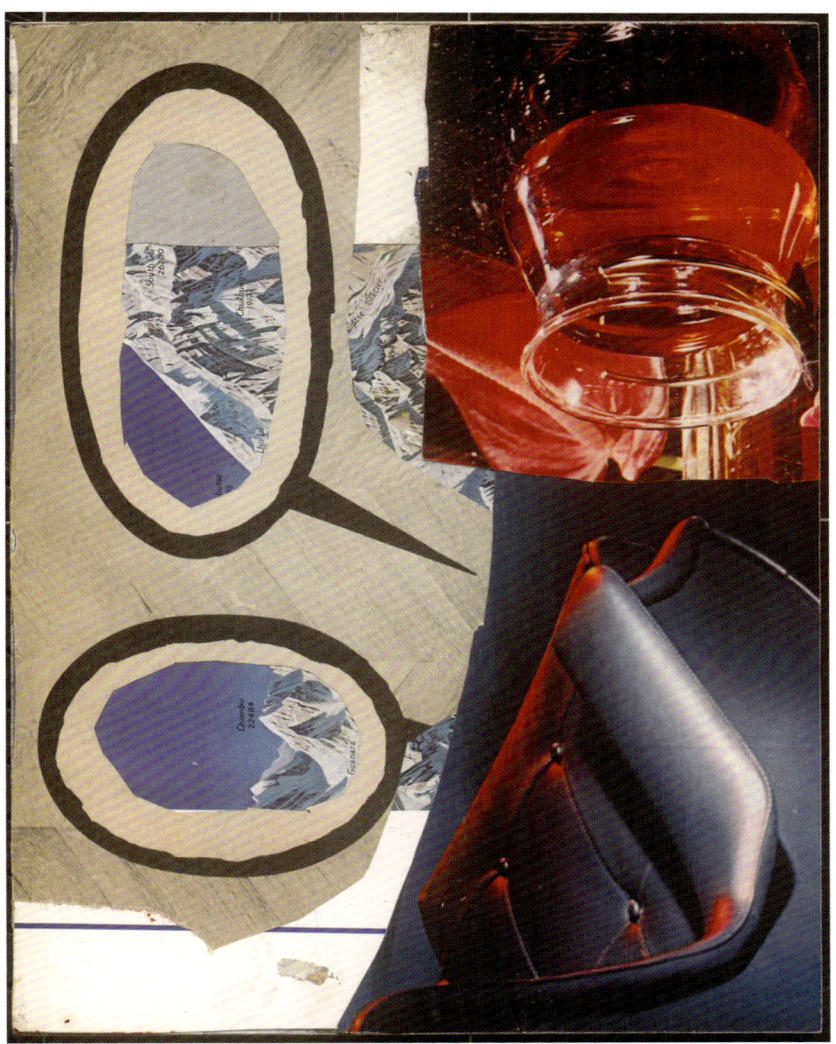

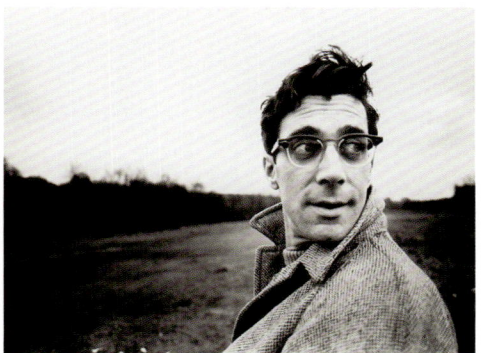

- (facing page) **Fire**
  collage on board, 10 x 8 in., 2018
- **Glacier**
  collage on board, 10 x 8 in., 2017

Born in Denver, Colorado, Michael Chandler was a student of Stan Brakhage at the University Of Colorado in Boulder during the late 60's and attended ArtCenter College of Design in Los Angeles and the Jack Kerouac School of Disembodied Poetics at Naropa. He started showing his artwork in 1972. Chandler has been a gardener in the Hollywood Hills, done mining assessment for the Anaconda Company, worked on Christo and Jeanne-Claude's Rifle Valley Curtain and Running Fence projects in Colorado and Sanoma County, CA, was a surveyor for Contact Logging in Philipsburg, Montana, worked on the production of Walter Hill's movie The Warriors, did installations at the Mudd Club and Club 57 with Mary-Ann Monforton in New York City and was an assistant to Dan Flavin through the Dia Art Foundation. In 1985 he began exhibiting his paintings in New York and Milan at the galleries of Salvatore Ala. Among others, his artwork has been shown in Munich with Galeria Paal, in Bologna at Galleria Comunale d'Arte Moderna, in Seoul at Gallerie Seomi, in Rio de Janeiro at the Museum of Modern Art, with Achille Bonita Oliva's Transavantgardia in Genazanno, Italy, in London with Sandra Higgins Fine Art, at Rhode Island School of Design's Museum of Art and in New York City at P.S.1, the Drawing Center, the American Academy of Arts and Letters, Valentine Gallery in Ridgewood, Queens and John Doe Gallery in Williamsburg, Brooklyn. Mike Chandler lives and works in New York City.

WWW.MIKE-CHANDLER.COM

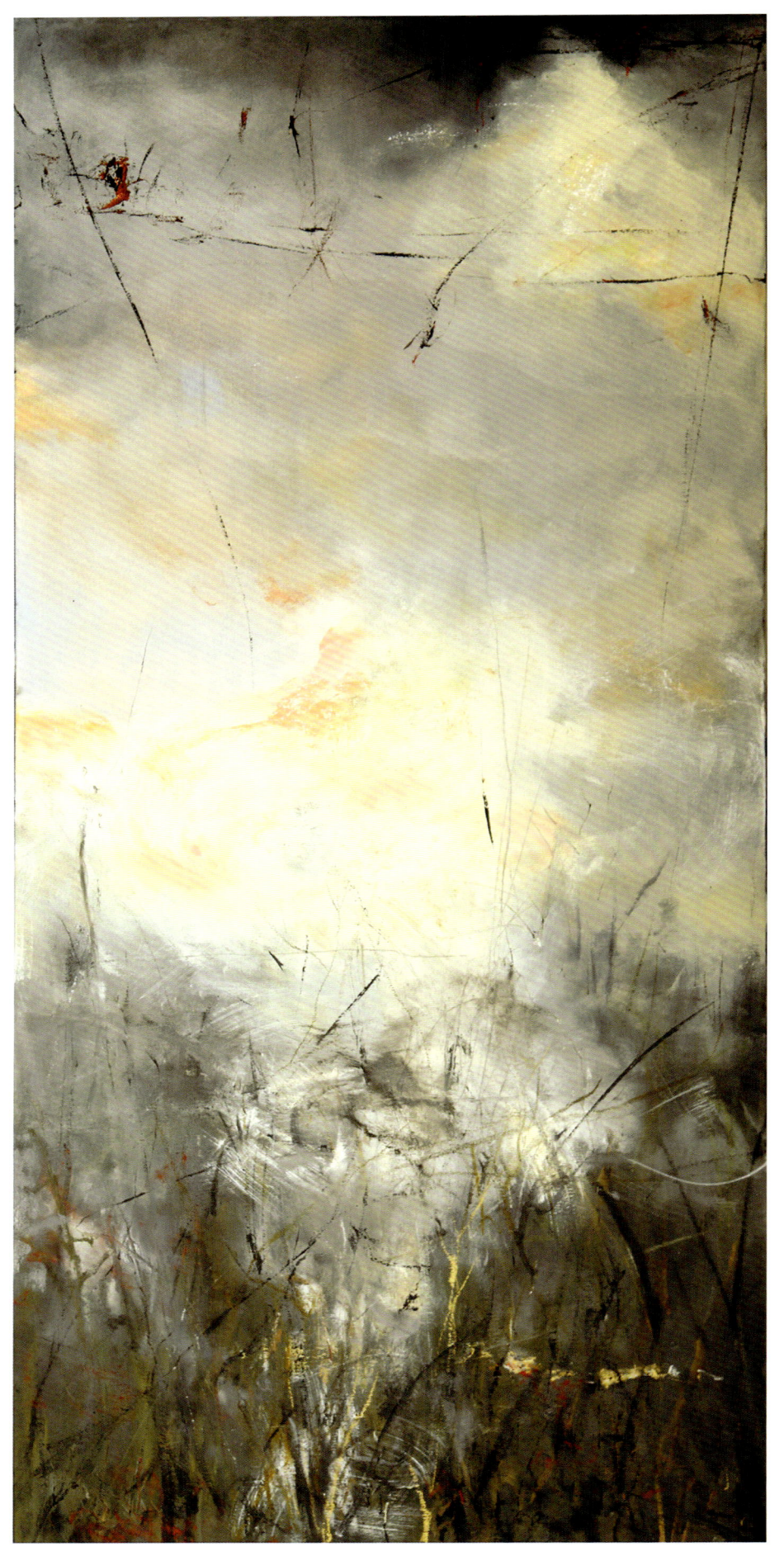

ANDREA CUKIER

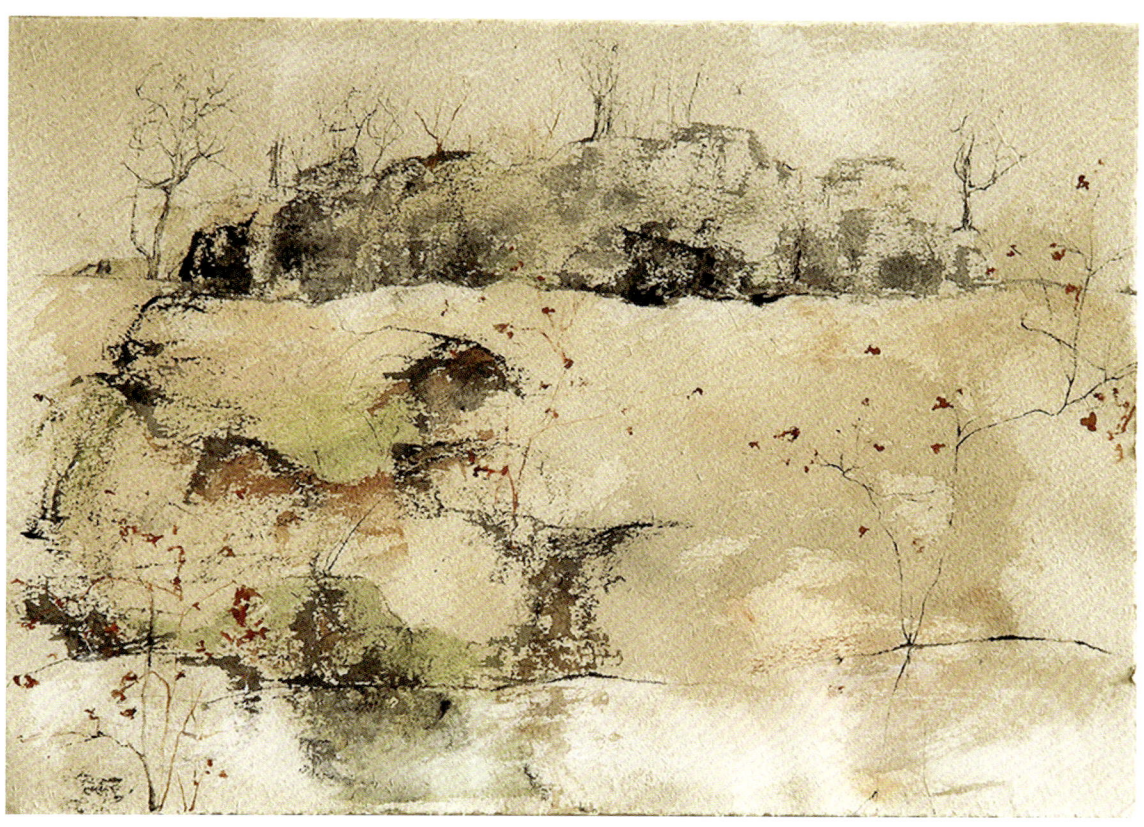

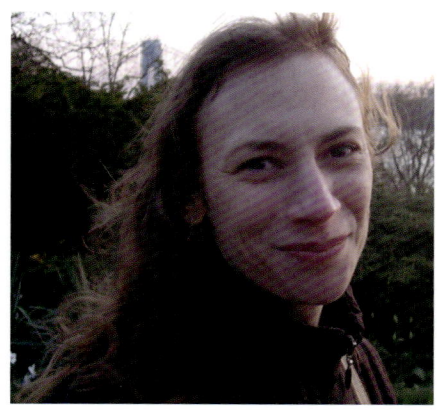

(facing page) Escaoe
Oil on canvas, 48 x 24 in.., 2016

Otoño no Prometedor
*Gouache and ink on handmade paper,
11 x 17 in., 2018*

Andrea Cukier is a New York City – based painter from Argentina, where she graduated as Profesora Superior de Pintura (the result of a 9-year, full time academic career). This degree was accredited in the US as a dual Master's Degree in Fine Arts and Art Education.

She received several awards in Argentina and in the U.S. Among them are: The Northern Manhattan Arts Alliance Grant to Individual Artists, MTA-Artists Unite Subway Elevator Poster Project. She was also selected for and participated in various artist in residency Programs, The Studios at Mass MoCA, among them.

Her work, which focuses on her love of nature and her anxiety about its destruction, was part of several juried exhibitions. The list of group shows includes New York's First Biennale of Women Artists at the Williamsburg Art and Historical Center in Brooklyn, New York.

She had several solo shows in venues such as the Argentine Consulate in New York City, Columbia University, The New York Public Library, The City College of the C.U.N.Y, The Bidwell House Museum in Massachusetts, and Local Project in New York City and Pratt Institute's Manhattan Gallery.

She has collaborated with writers and poets and illustrated a children's book, Hope for Sudan, published by Mirror Publishing.

Some of her paintings are in the permanent collections of the Godwin Ternbach Museum at Queens College, NY; Memorial Sloan Kettering Cancer Center; and the Argentine Consulate in New York City.

WWW.ANDREACUKIER.COM

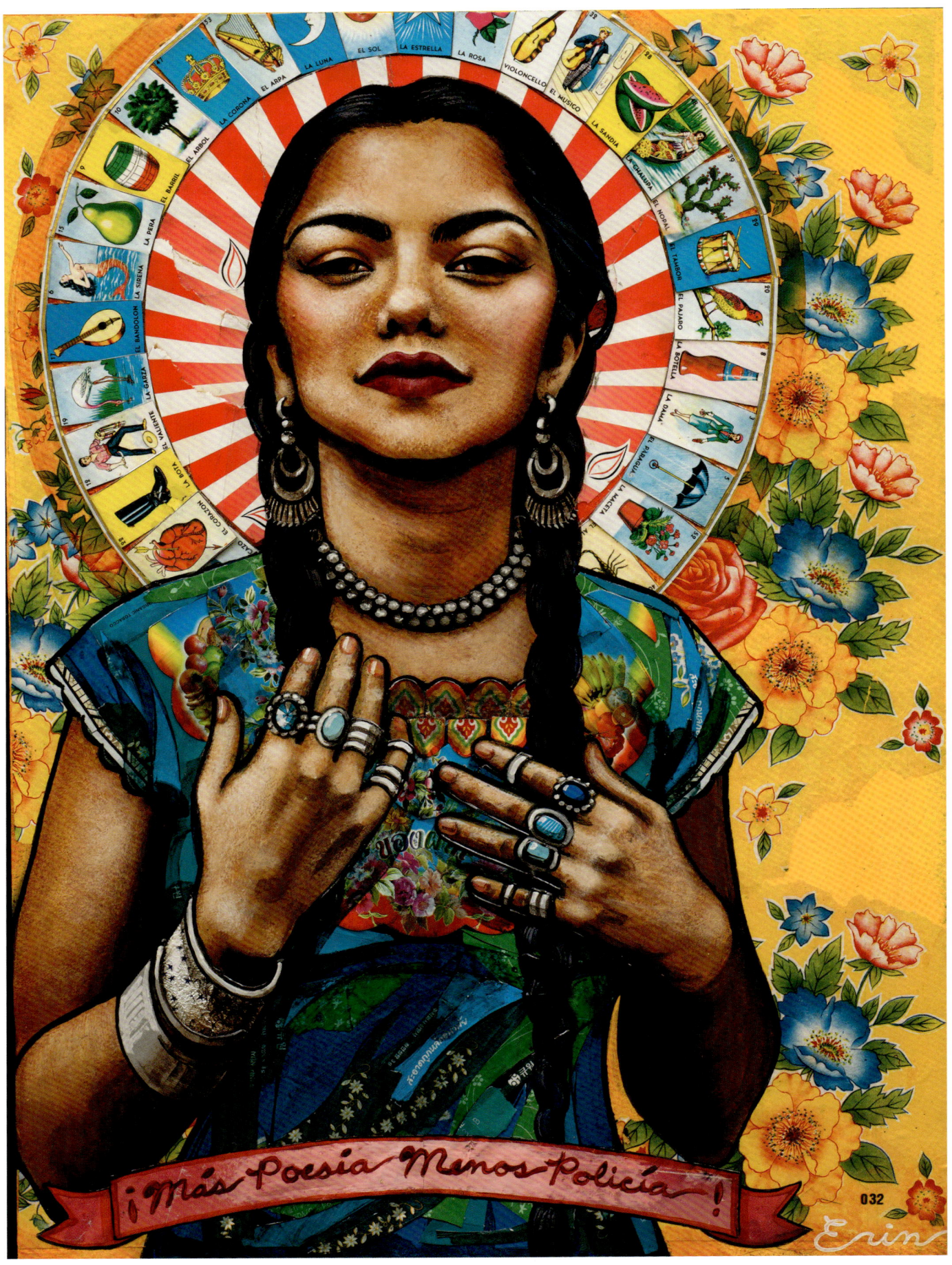

¡Más Poesía Menos Policía!

032

Erin

ERIN CURRIER

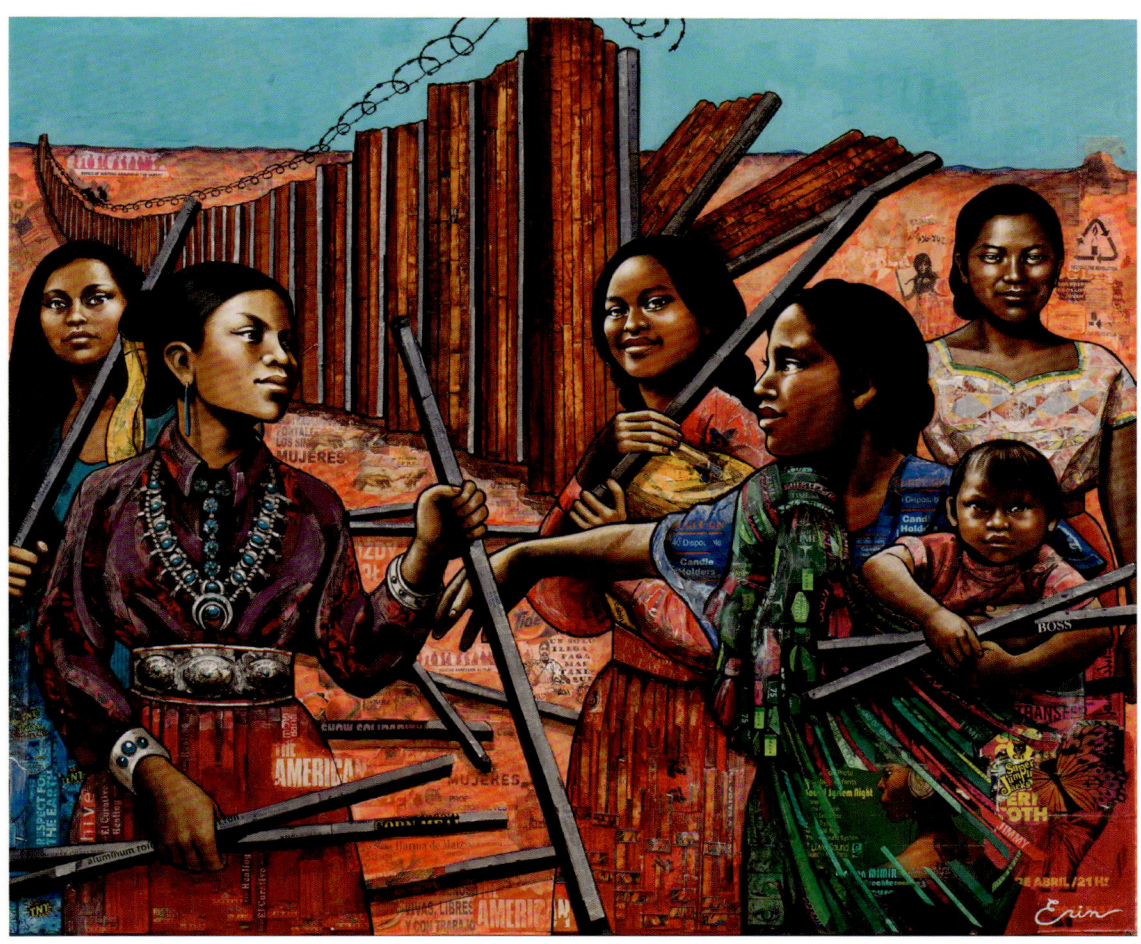

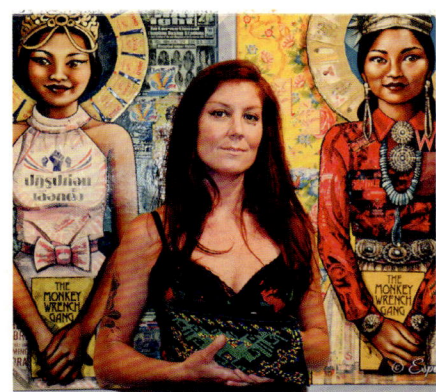

My art-making concerns and process are three fold: first, as a traveling ontographer documenting through drawing the environments that I encounter abroad; secondly, I collect discarded ephemera from the streets of the world; finally, I incorporate the above findings into portraits that celebrate figures who resist or defy authority; as well as people who exist outside of their societies' conventions. My work is comprised of discarded trash I find on my travels as well as acrylic paint and glaze. The discarded waste is re-transfigured into, hopefully, something of beauty; in the same way that discarded human beings, who are the subject of many of my portraits are, themselves, re-contextualized through the privileged position of portraiture,

historically relegated to oil barons and kings. My use of trash is thus a poetic incantation -a call for a counter power rooted in the imagination.

Part portraiture, part collage constructed of disinherited consumer "waste" collected in nearly fifty countries, part sociopolitical archive, but wholly humanist, Currier's work has been featured in numerous solo shows, including a major exhibition at the Bolivarian Republic of Venezuela Embassy in Washington, DC. Her work is exhibited and collected internationally. She lives and works in Santa Fe, New Mexico.

WWW.ERINCURRIERFINEART.COM

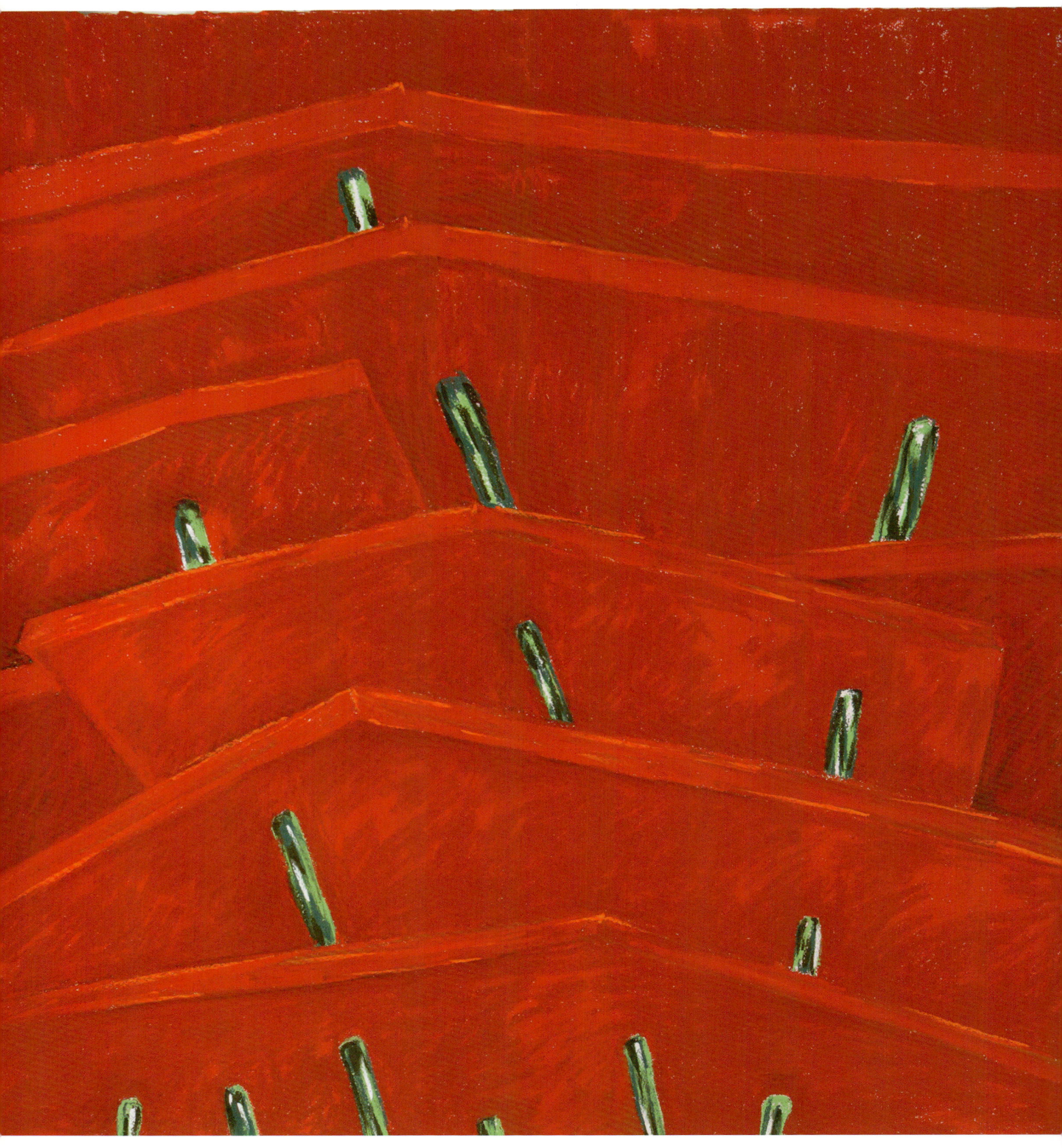

ELVIRA DAYEL

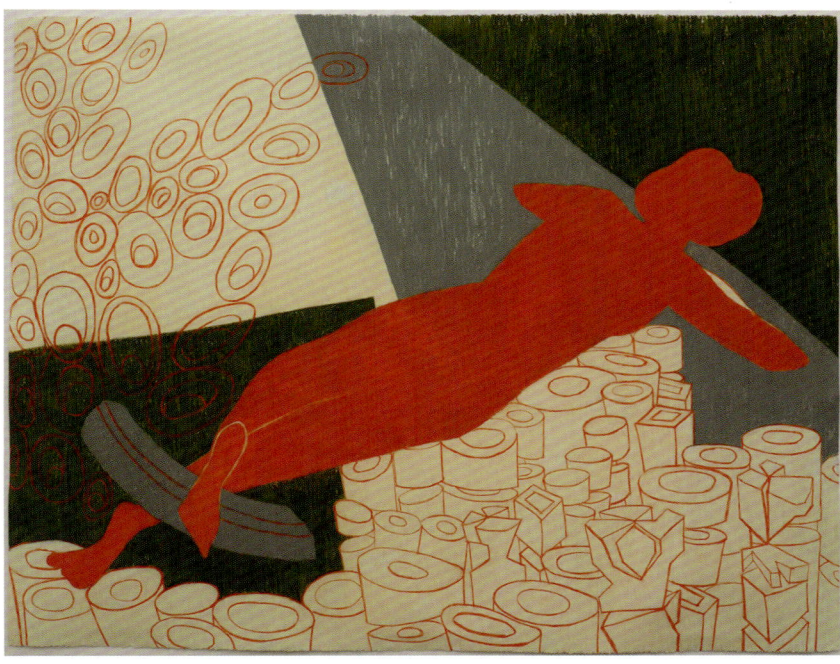

"I see myself as a minimalist using only as much as needed to convey an idea. The color I use carries its own vision. Invented landscapes are new realities, they are constructs."

Elvira m. Dayel was born in summer of 1978 in Ukraine, former Soviet Union. She was raised there and immigrated with her family to the United States in 1994. The wings of immigration brought Dayel family first to Los Angeles. Sunny LA gave family a warm welcome and a reliable shelter. Elvira later pursued career as an artist while initially obtaining two bachelor degrees one in biological sciences and another one in fine arts. She then challenged herself in learning about her deep interest in built environment and city organization, while graduating with a master's degree in Architecture from the University of California, Los Angeles School of Architecture and Urban Design. In 2004 upon successful completion of her studies, Elvira moved to San Francisco Bay Area, where she currently lives and works.

As an artist Dayel works in series of large abstract drawings done in soft/dry pastel on paper as well as 3D-printed mixed media sculpture. Her background in architecture inspires her to use a variety of new media, including digital rendering and paper-cut art.

"Although, I like to think about my work as being idea driven, there is as much reason in my work, as there is intuition. Many a time I unassumingly follow my hand, and while I'm following a feeling, it hopefully, leads somewhere, to make something art & pure.

I see myself as a minimalist using only as much as needed to convey an idea. The color I use carries its own vision. Invented landscapes are new realities, they are constructs. Landscape is re-imagined to provide a new visual space, or an abstracted city/place. My work is a metaphor for searching - my figures, invented landscapes and spaces implicate presence of the unknown, sometimes registering an absence."

WWW.ELVIRADAYEL.COM

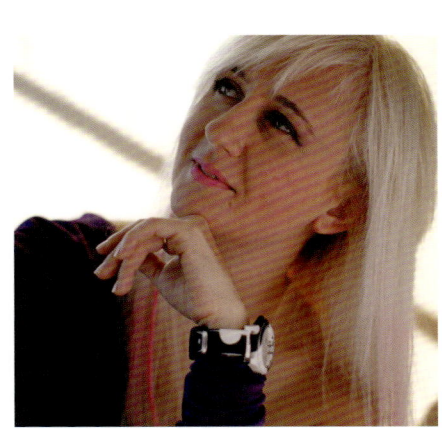

● **(facing page) North Dakota Access Pipeline**
Drawing, soft pastel on watercolor paper, 44 x 30 in. 2012

● **She is Bridge**
Drawing, soft pastel on watercolor paper,, 36 x 51 in., 2018

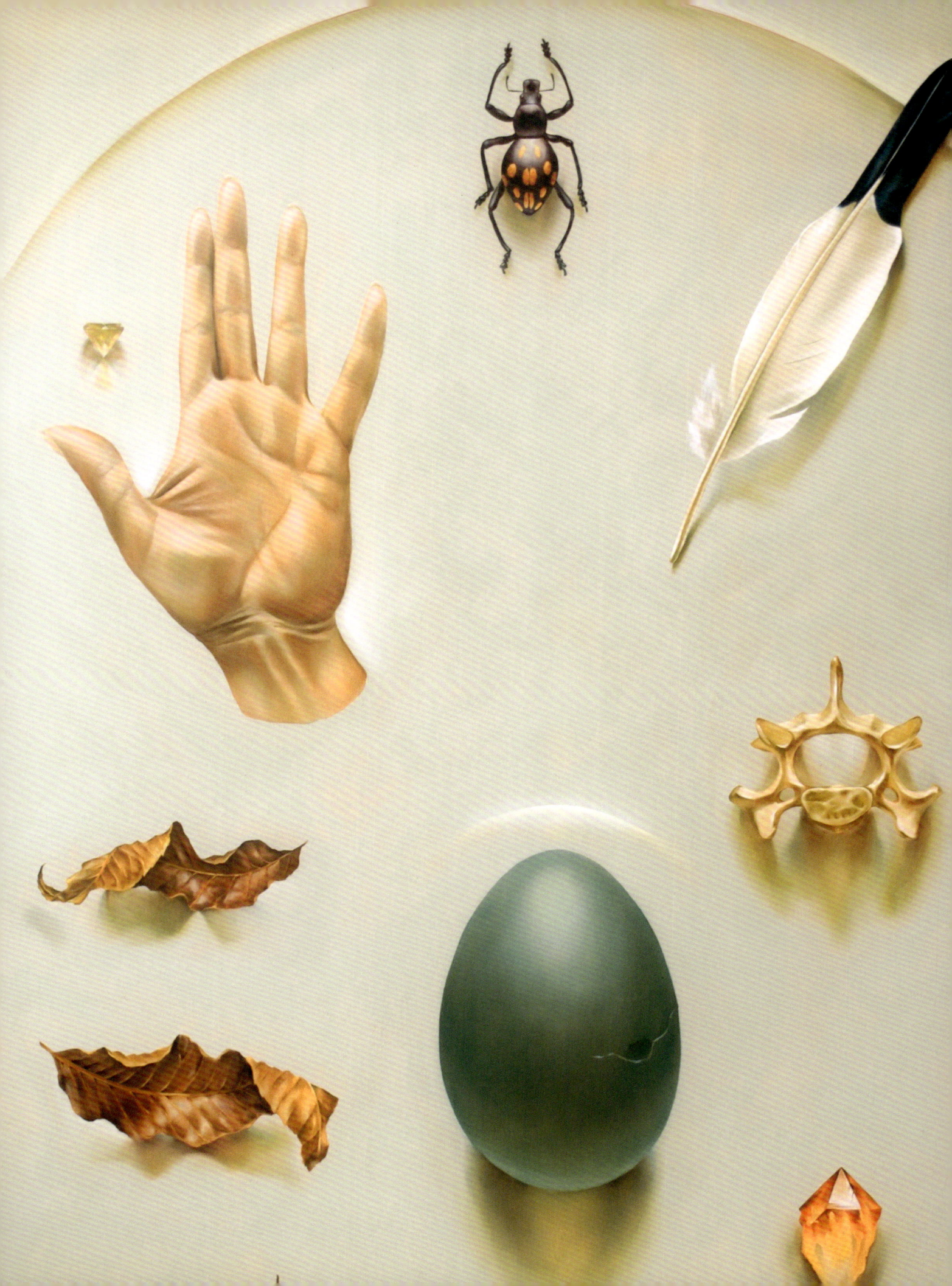

IDA FLOREAK

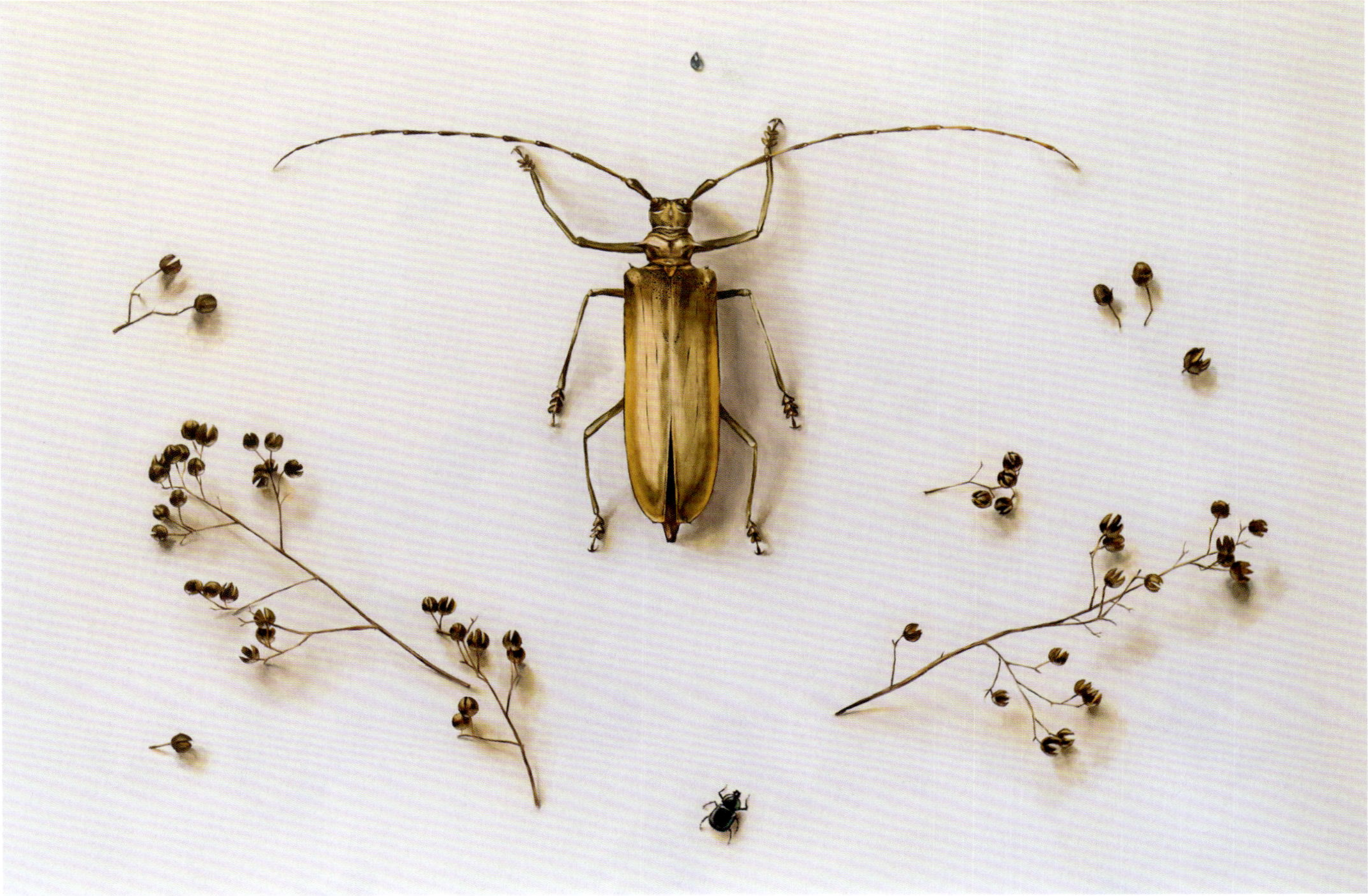

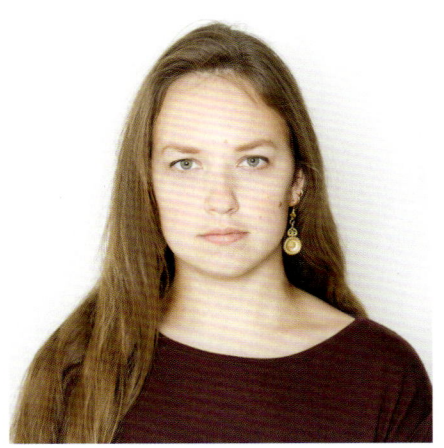

Ida Floreak is a New Orleans-based artist, originally from Cambridge, Massachusetts. She has a BFA from the Rhode Island School of Design where she studied painting and scientific illustration. Ida's work is influenced by her studies in Rome with RISD's European Honors Program and her work as an archaeological illustrator on the Poggio Civitate Archaeological Project in Vescovado di Murlo.

Raised outside of organized religion, Ida turned to science and the natural world to answer questions about our origins and purpose, finding meaning and beauty in the mathematical structure and symmetry of natural objects. Her work explores the tension between scientific study and religiosity and attempts to find a balance between the spirit of inquiry and a sense of awe inspired by the natural world. Ida's paintings emphasize ritual and our search for answers to the unanswerable questions. Pulling from her personal collection, she paints bones, gems, leaves and insects in formations reminiscent of devotional art, shrines and altars. Painting in an over-large scale, Ida attempts to give these small and humble objects a treatment otherwise reserved for saints or deities. Her work aims to bring these disparate elements together with a spirituality that is informed by science, science that is informed by awe, and art that is informed by inquiry

WWW.IDAFLOREAK.COM

● **(facing page) Offering**
Oil on canvas, 48 x 60 n.

● **Askew**
Oil on canvas, 36 x 24 in.

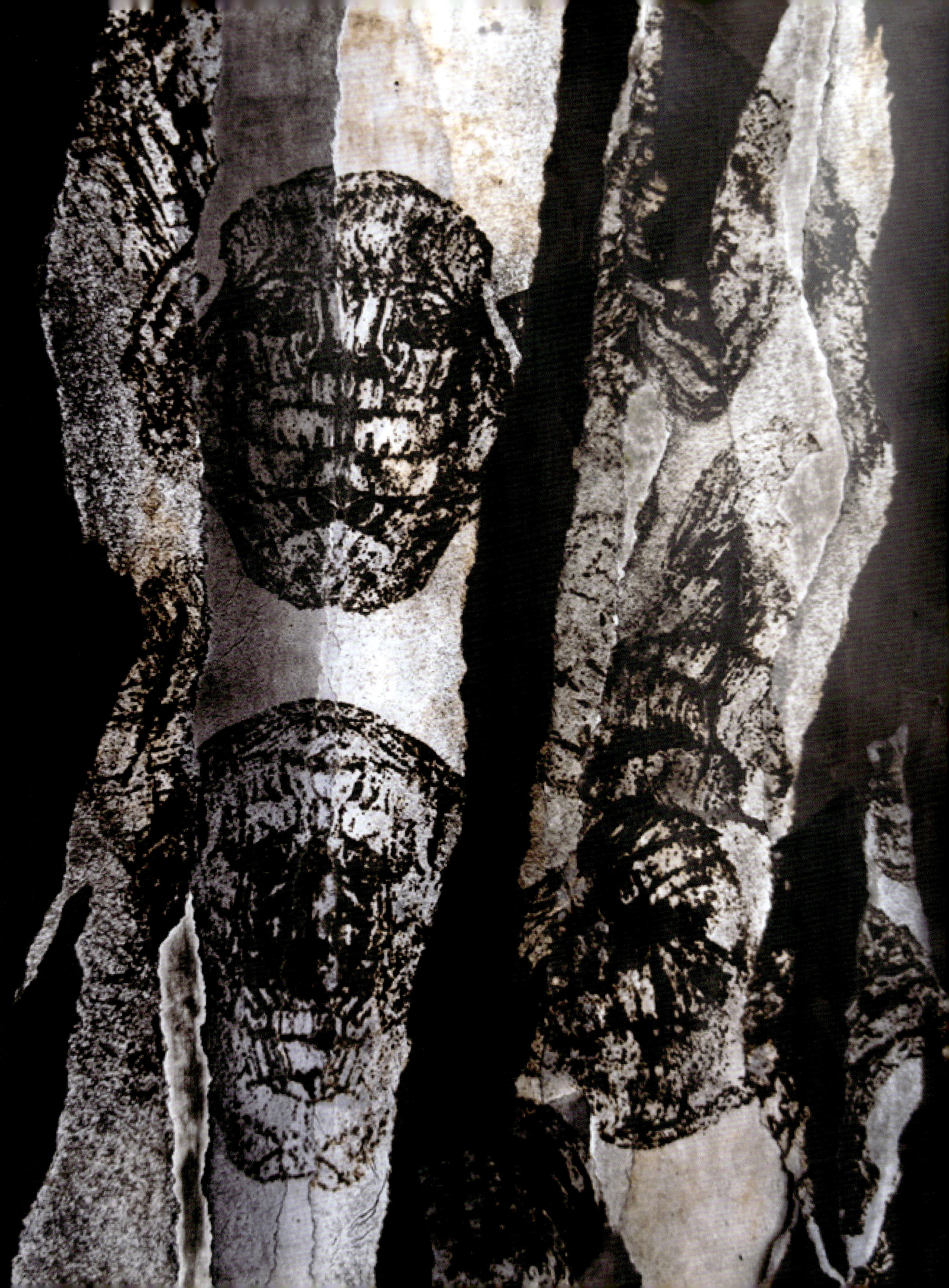

GERARD FRANCES

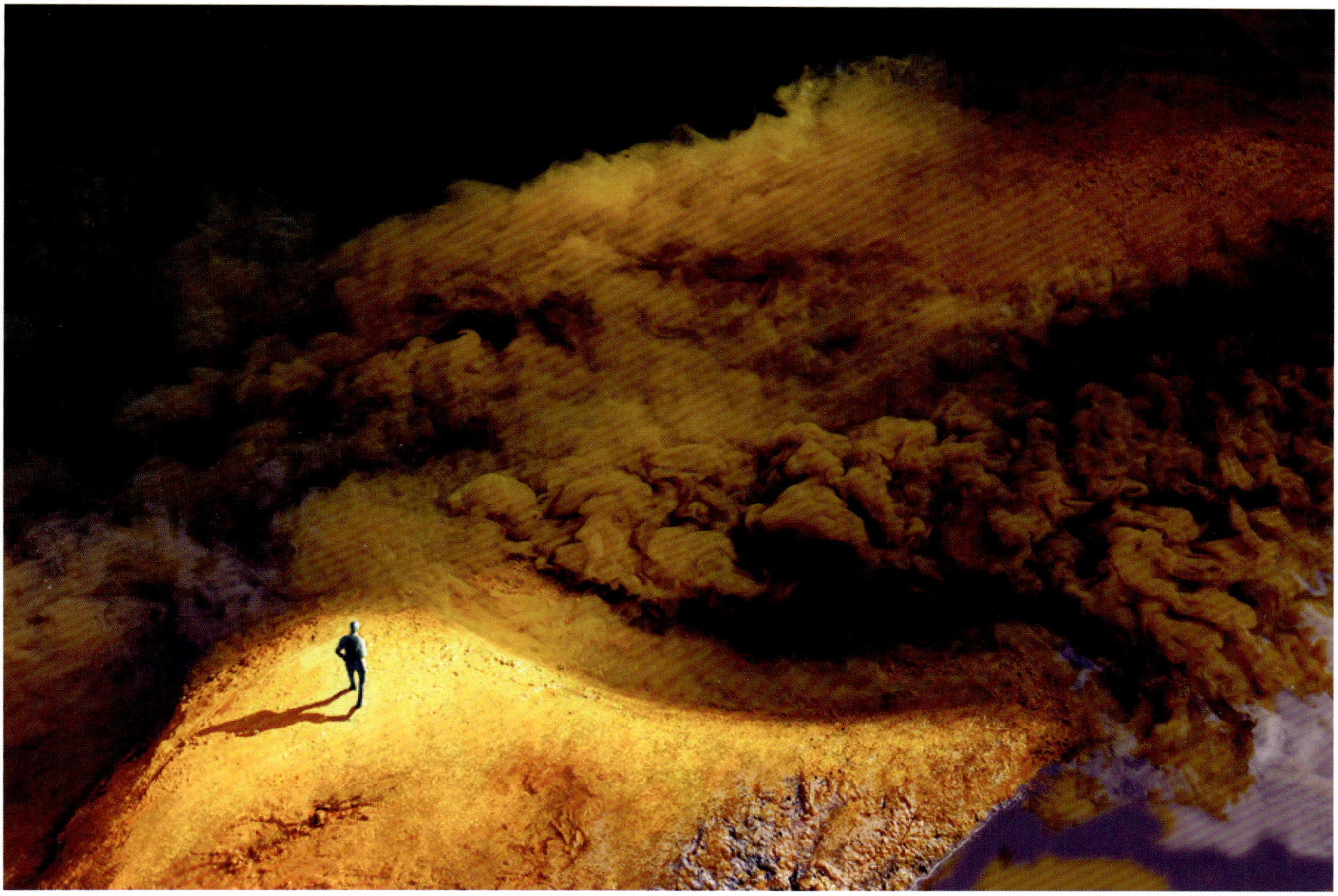

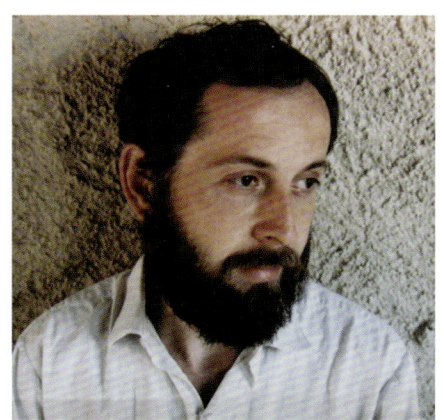

Parisian artist Gerard Frances presents his compelling portfolio of photography, digital art and collage.

"The language of poetry and art is the only way to express certain aspects of our experience of reality in subtle and complex ways. My works, located in my portfolio, are distributed thematically into three parts: The New Landscapes, Abstraction and digital art . Currently the growing success of photography in the world encourages me in my research on digital manipulations. My visual work arises from experimental processes and a desire to develop and explore visual languages inspired by nature. I have practiced the technique of Chinese ink painting extensively for many years. The masters gave me inspiration. I am influenced by the grandiosity of their immortal art . A painting is often represented by its intelligence and its sensitivity. I feel it is very important for an artist to participate in events as it allows him to share his artistic ideas, to express himself and to meet a world of people with an equal passion for art. Art is the expression of all cultures."

WWW.ORI-GERARD.COM

● **(facing page) Origin**
Collage, paper ink

● **Photomanipulation**
details?

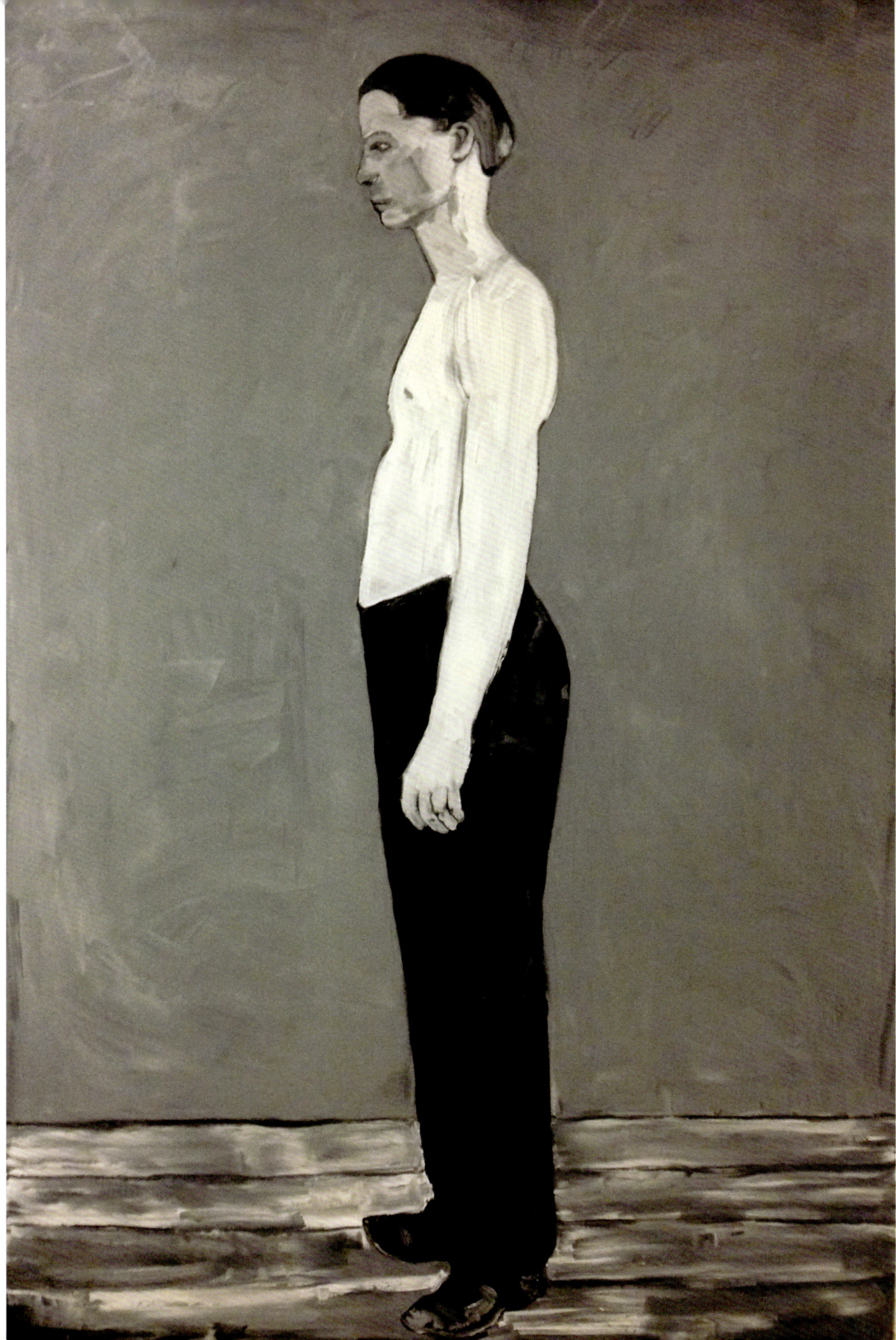

CHRISTOPHER FRASER

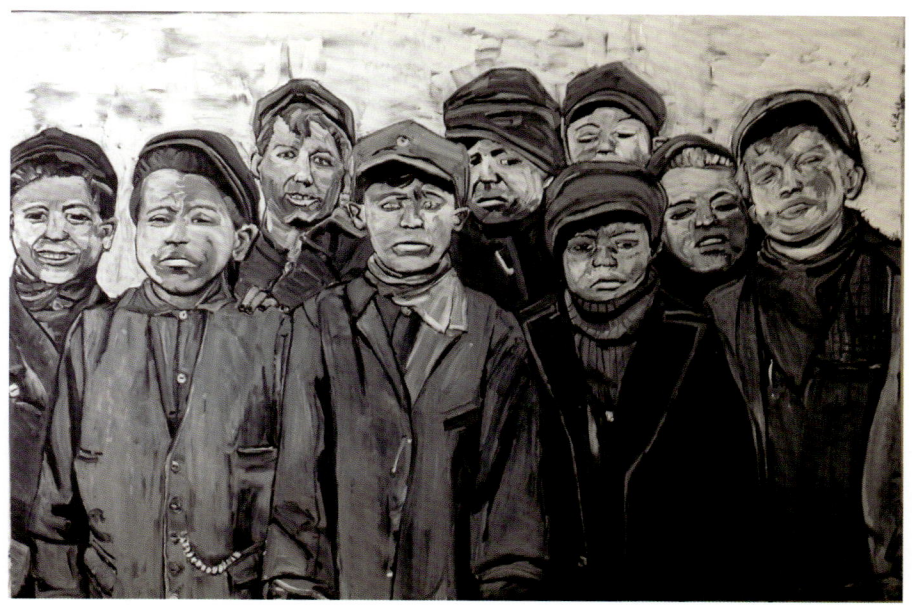

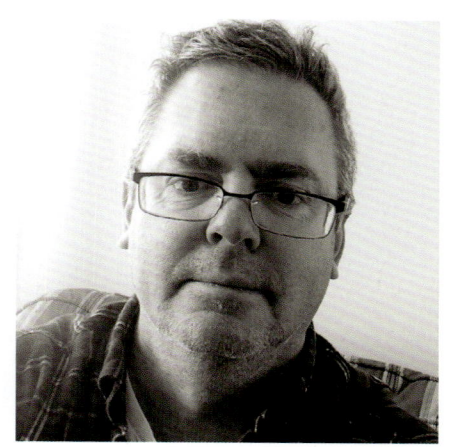

● **(facing page) Origin**
  collage on board, 10 x 8 in., 2018

● **The Industrials**

Christopher Fraser's paintings are figurative, selected from images that incite an emotional response, or effuse an apparent subliminal understanding that is obvious. The paintings are portraits of individual self-awareness, intended to trap the moment in motion, frozen in time, providing a gateway to connect with the subject. Capturing people in a moment in time provides insight into their world. The interaction with the subject is a constant dialogue, an intimate creative connection.

Art is similar to a living being, constantly moving in different directions simultaneously, constantly evolving and expanding, splitting, diverging. Art moves forward with time, and sometimes like in evolution, undergoes modifications, at times with catastrophic fractures and shifts. Cross roads arise, and as a consequence, the destiny of art is the continuation of the new.

Human knowledge of the world is constantly expanding. Expansion is due to the ever-increasing ability to communicate and connect: sharing moments in time, continuing to modify, evolve, transform or become obsolete. The image of humanity is available as it never has been before. The present situation provides an opportunity to look back, and capture the expanse, intricacy, complexity of humanity in painting. Now is an opportunity to capture those images and change art and embrace the new.

Christopher Fraser was born and raised in Vancouver Canada, has lived in Los Altos CA, Chicago IL, and in Boston MA where attended classes at the SMFA. He presently lives and works in Singapore.

www.ccfraserartist.com

The Industrials (After Lewis Hine) , Oil on

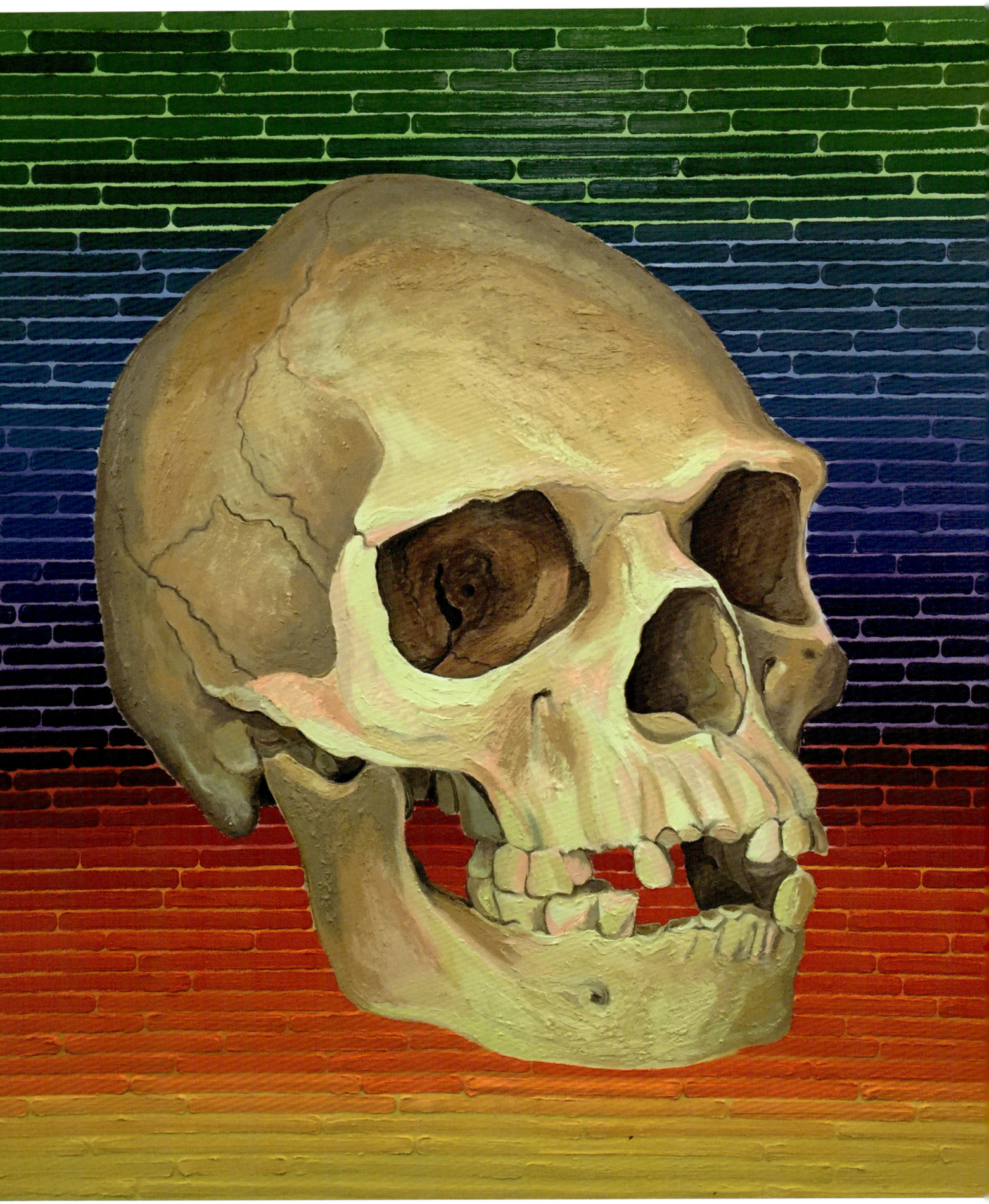

MORGAN FREW

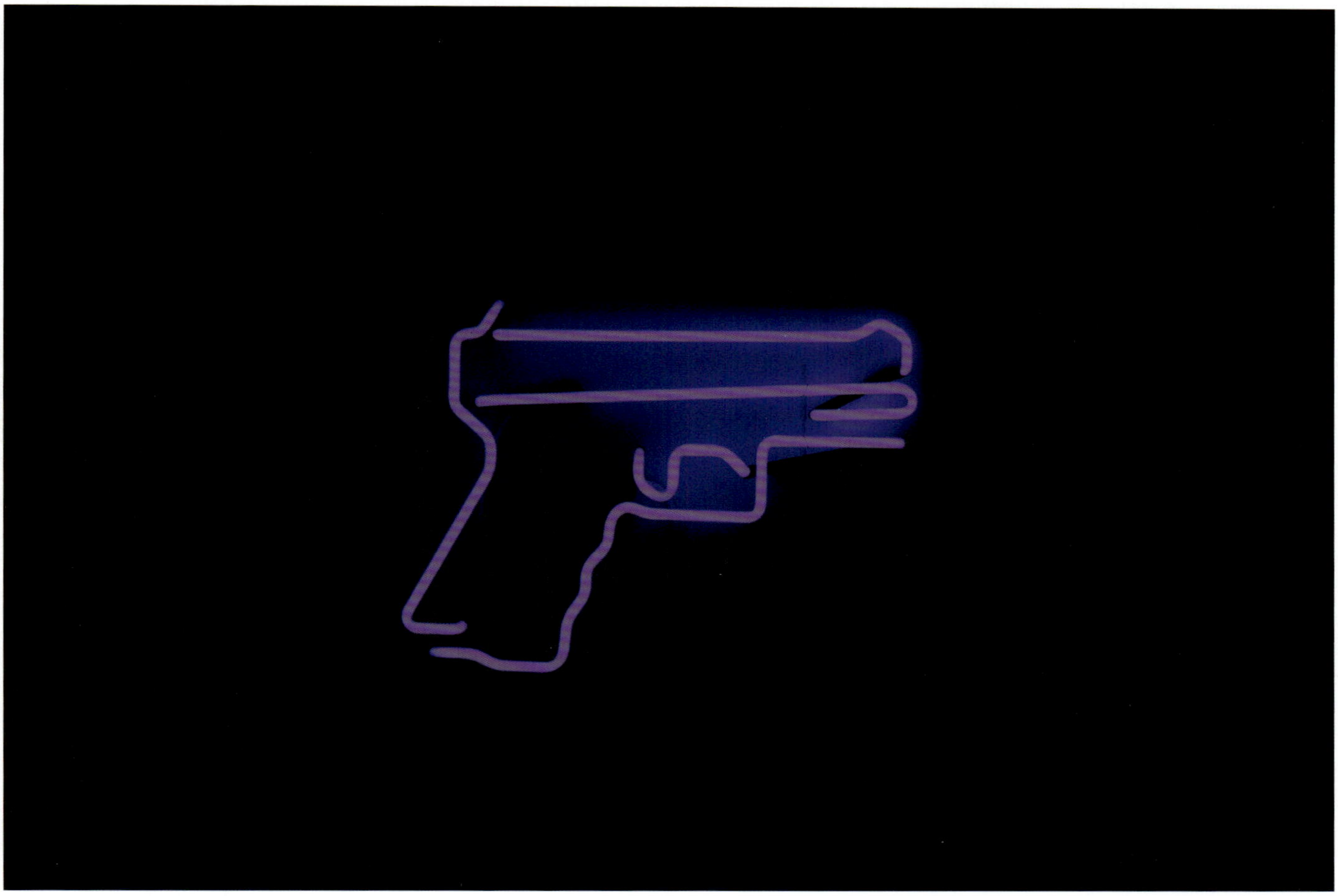

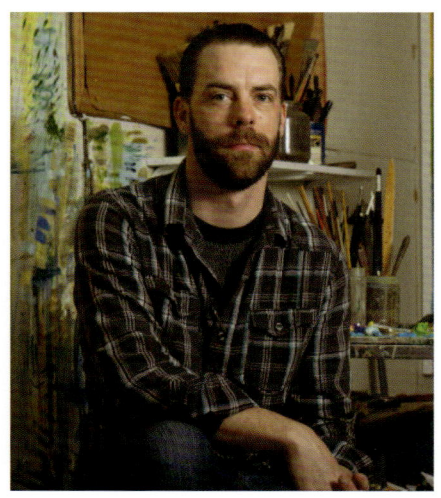

Born in Springfield, Missouri, Morgan Frew received his MFA from Pratt Institute in Brooklyn, New York in 2008, and his BFA from Missouri State University in Springfield, Missouri in 2006. His paintings have been exhibited nationally and internationally, and are held in a number of public and private collections throughout the US. His work deals primarily with the formal challenges of contemporary painting, as well as its psychology and conceptual concerns.

WWW.MORGANFREW.COM

● **(facing page) Aboriginal Skull**
details?

● **Bang Bang Shoot Shoot**
details?

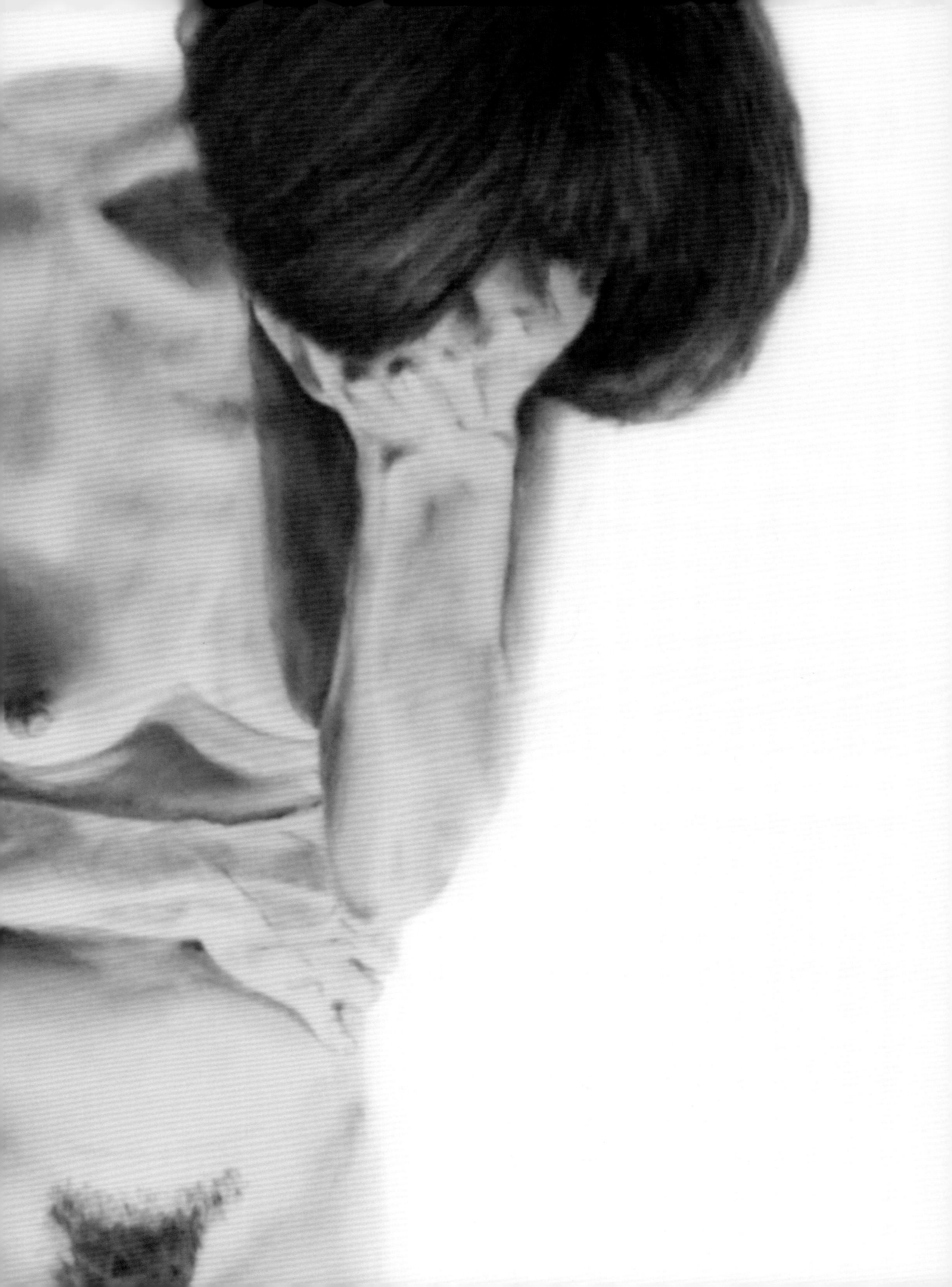

COLLEEN GARIBALDI

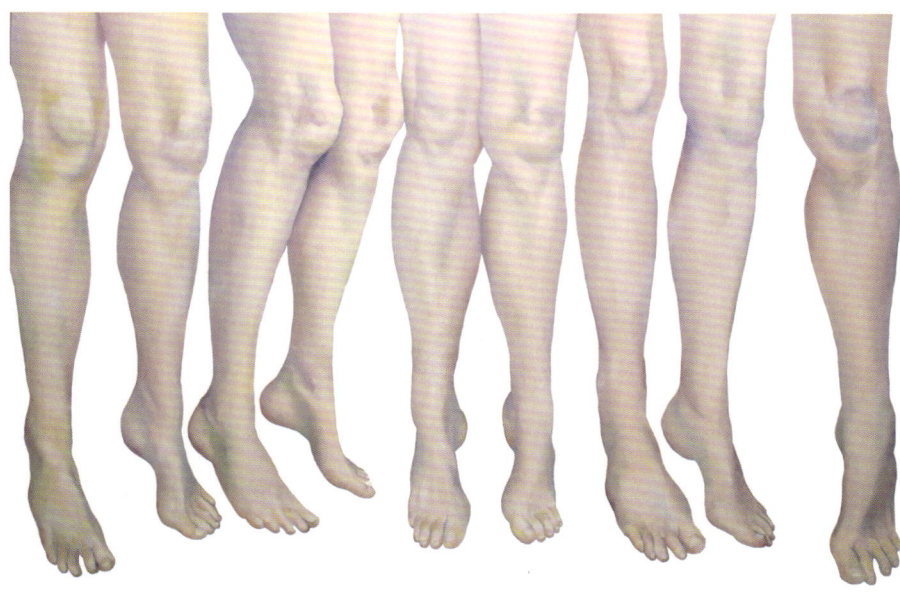

"For me making art leads to awareness, bringing to the surface that which is going on inside. Oftentimes it is a literal journey; for example, an examination of influential patterns in life got transformed into works exploring patternmaking using limbs, pictures of nonsensical and purely graphic configurations devoid of connotation. "

Influenced by the lessons learned as a child traipsing about with my military family of balancing a solid foundation with the enrichment of new challenges and experiences, I've been working in a variety of media, focusing mainly on the figure. Primarily a painter, I've also been exploring 3D, video and stills while maintaining a drawing and photography practice, always pushing my familiarity with materials and methods, trying old and new alike.

Recently I've been looking at the body as object and using it as my tool, exploring my world while questioning cultural norms of viewing the body as mere carnal commodity. For me making art leads to awareness, bringing to the surface that which is going on inside. Oftentimes it is a literal journey; for example, an examination of influential patterns in life got transformed into works

exploring patternmaking using limbs, pictures of nonsensical and purely graphic configurations devoid of connotation. Concurrently, through making work with limbs or the figure in a more narrative manner, such as illustrating feeling like slabs of meat being inspected, I'm ruminating on the omnipresent nature of story, endeavoring to find a way to stay true to my desire to work with abstracted representations of the figure.

My work has been exhibited regionally and nationally and is in multiple private collections. I have been awarded grants and scholarships from the Pennsylvania Academy of the Fine Arts, the Vermont Studio Center and Cloud Farm and was recently in a residency at the Vermont Studio Center.

WWW.COLLEENGARIBALDI.COM

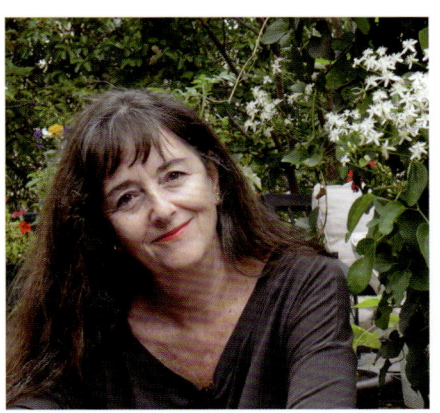

(facing page) Series 1, 4 ●
Graphite on paper, 22 x 30 in., 2015

Being Reviewed ●
Oil on canvas, 30 x 40 in., 2015

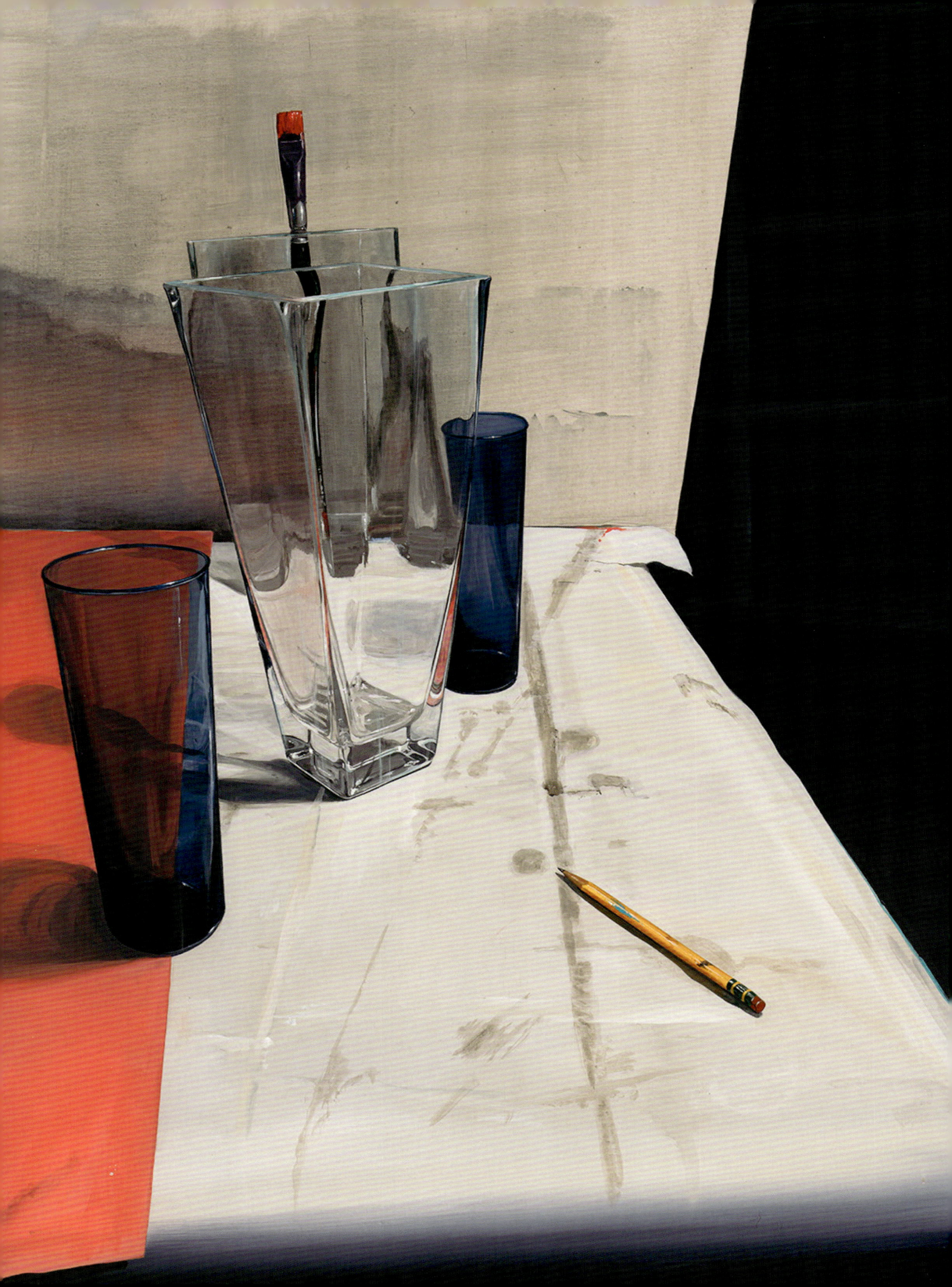

PAUL GIBSON

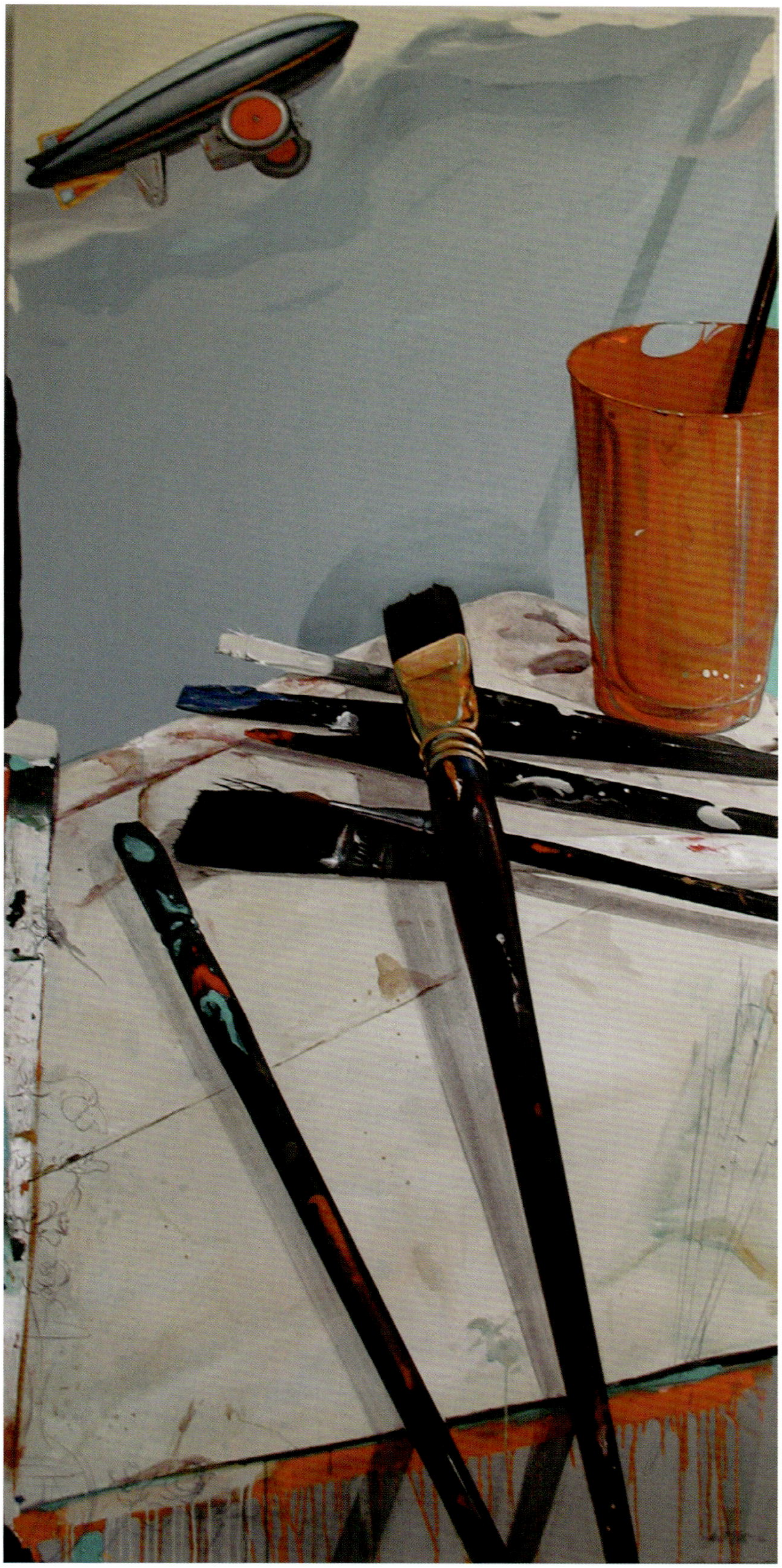

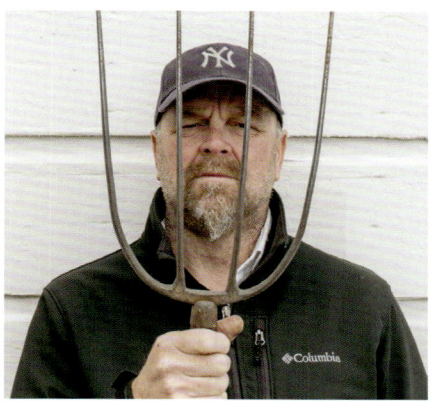

Paul D. Gibson was born 1957 in Los Angeles, California. Paul graduated from Art Center College of Design BFA Pasadena California, Painted at the National Academy of Design , New York, NY on a full scholarship. He's represented by the Desta Gallery, San Anselmo, CA (www.destagallery.com). He now lives with his wife and four children in San Francisco, California and works full time at his studio in the Hunters Points Shipyard art community.

WWW.PDGARTIST.COM/

● **(facing page) Still Art**
Acrylic on Linen , 48 x 36 in., 2018

● **Zefur**
Acrylic on linen, 96 x 48 in., 2016
private collection

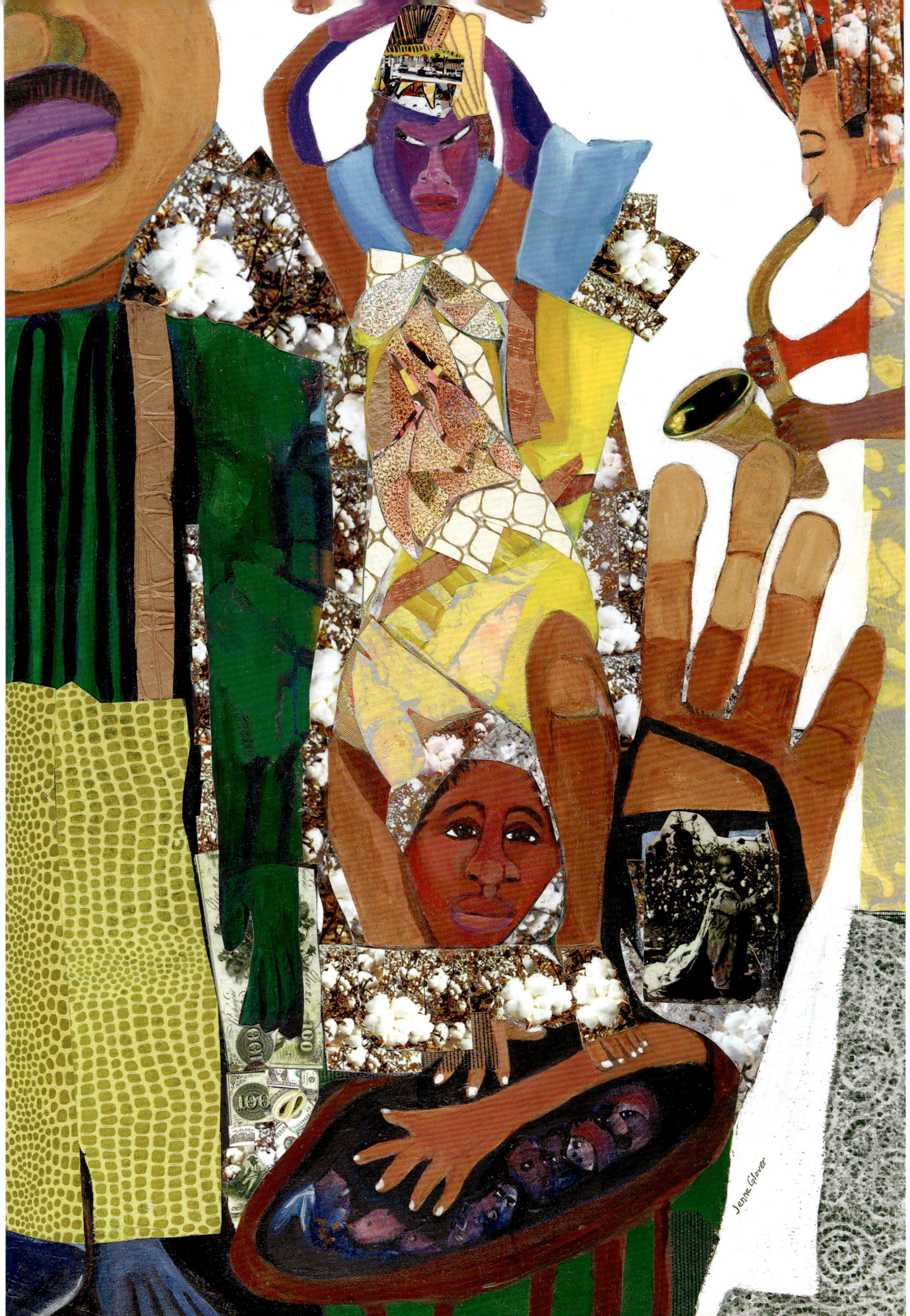

JENNE GLOVER

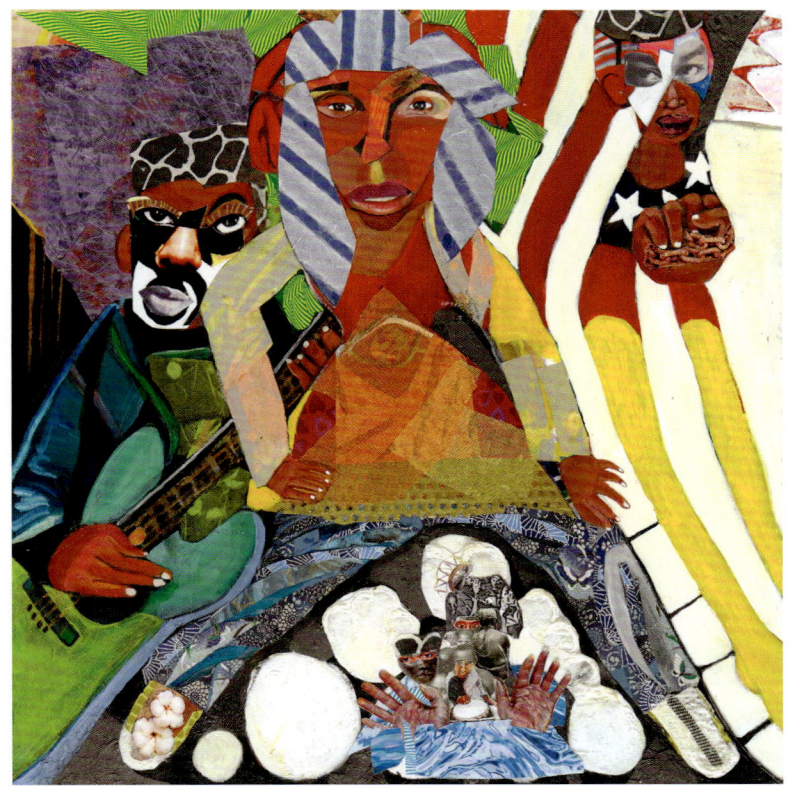

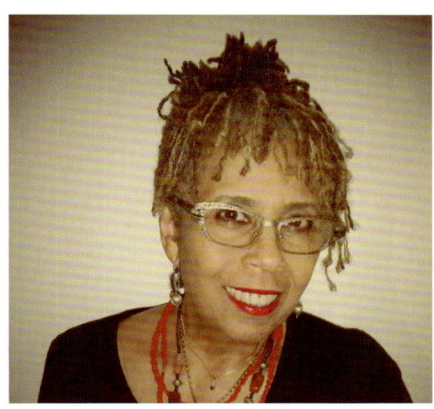

Working from an Afrocentric framework, my evolution from a figurative, expressionist oil painter to a mixed-media collagist has evolved over 40+ years. I have exhibited in over 90 solo, juried, and group exhibitions.

There are many ways my artwork takes life. I may begin by sketching an idea or I may see or hear something that's inspiring. And, I love working out of and over top an artwork that isn't going anywhere because I can incorporate elements of the previous piece into the new work.

My art is colorful, infused with textures, patterns, rhythm, and repetition. It's free-flowing and abstract. Creating mixed-media art is like creating a jazz composition, it's spontaneous and improvisational.

Working without boundaries and restrictions, my challenge is finding the pulse, the beat of the unfolding concept, and going with the flow. My art pays homage to the African Diaspora, humanity and spirit.

Compositions are constructed of magazine cutouts, ready-made materials, paint, photographs, fabric, oil pastels, and images repurposed and altered from earlier works.

My goal is to produce a body of work that is authentic and where each piece feels like the part of a greater whole. Art has peacefully transformed my life and keeps me in touch with the kid inside of me. Art is my passion.

I am currently working on Resilience: Surviving the Middle Passage, Seeking to Live a Privileged Life." This exhibition will be at the Hoyt Art Center in New Castle, Pennsylvania from January 8 through March 28, 2019.

WWW.JENNEGLOVER.COM

INSTAGRAM: @JENNEG2C

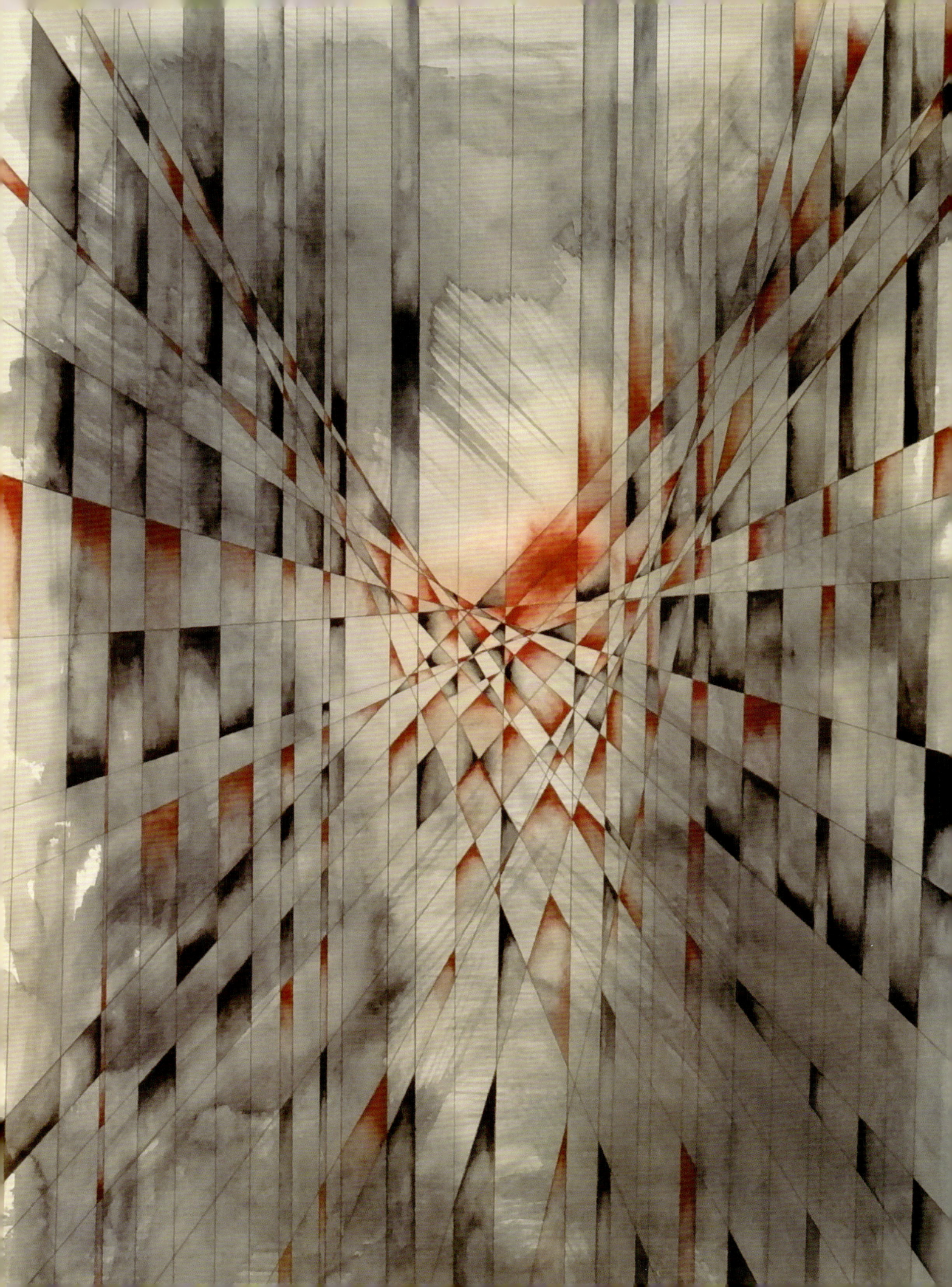

HELGA HOHN-HEIBERG

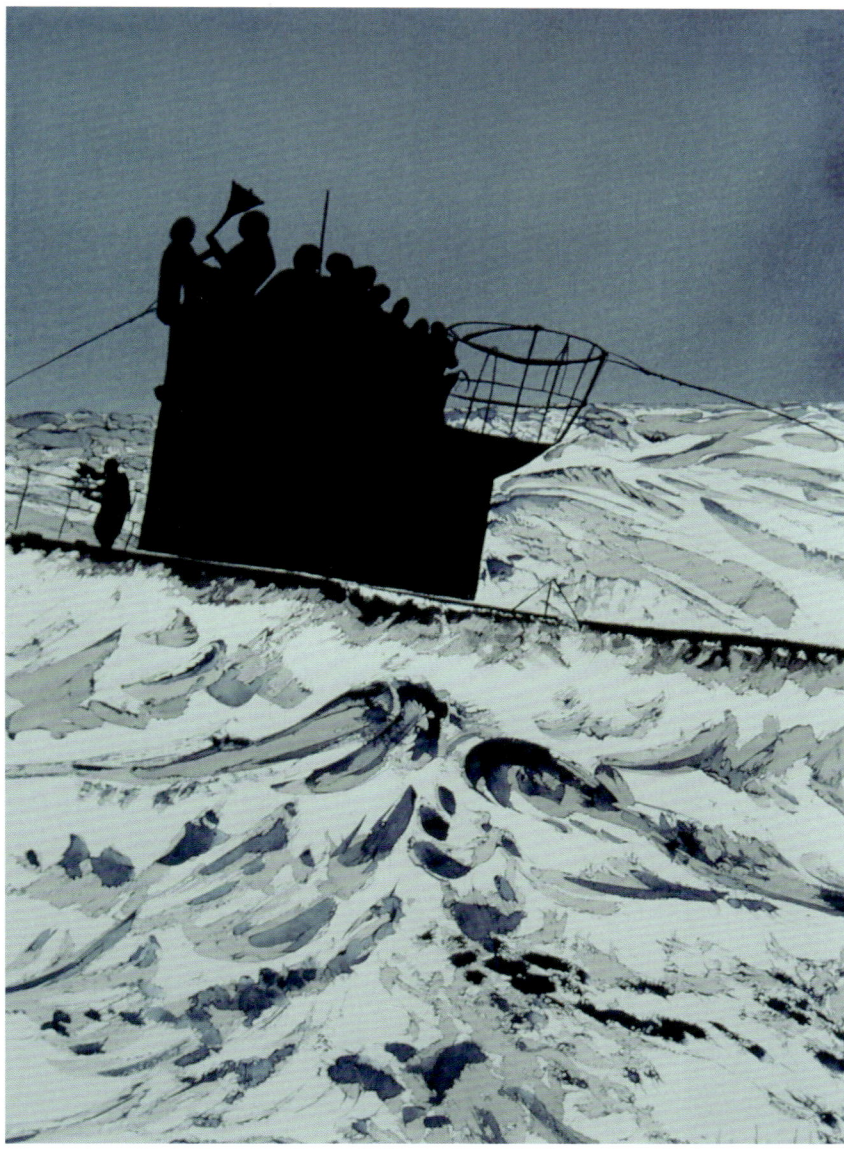

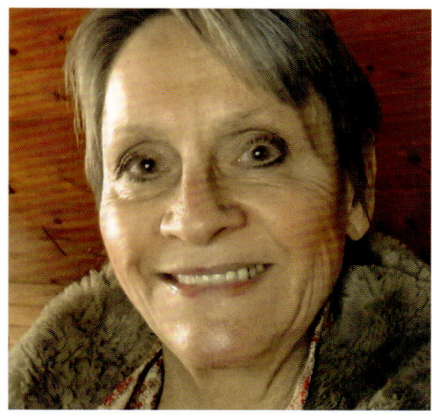

● **(facing page) Battered by the Sea**
Watercolor, 22 x 28 in., 1993

● **Street Lights**
Watercolor, 22 x 28 in., 2013

Helga Hohn-Heiberg studied theoretical and applied painting, graphics and sculpture in Germany as well as philosophy, psychology, pedagogy, art science and art history. She has had over 80 solo shows and has her private collections in 13 countries. She has done book illustrations and since 1969 has been constantly in newspapers and art journals. She has been a member of the selection Committee of the World Bank Art Society and has works at the Museum of Women in the Arts, Washington, DC, She has received numerous awards throughout her life.

Art is an idealization of experience and satisfaction of human being's hunger of truly experiencing experience. We see an ideal life in miniature, it invites us to view our own lives with the eyes of an artist, trying rounding it off or deepening experience, perfecting it and idealizing it. Art's purpose is not only to produce emotion or to give us experience, it gives something richer and deeper, it gives us understanding of experience. The esthetic attitude is definable in the simple and almost sentimental terms; the love of nature. Taking the time to see our natural world through symbolic eyes, we will find arrhythmic communications pressed into tiny shapes. There is no limitation of symbolism found in nature.

WWW.HELGAHOHNHEIBERG.ARTSPAN.COM

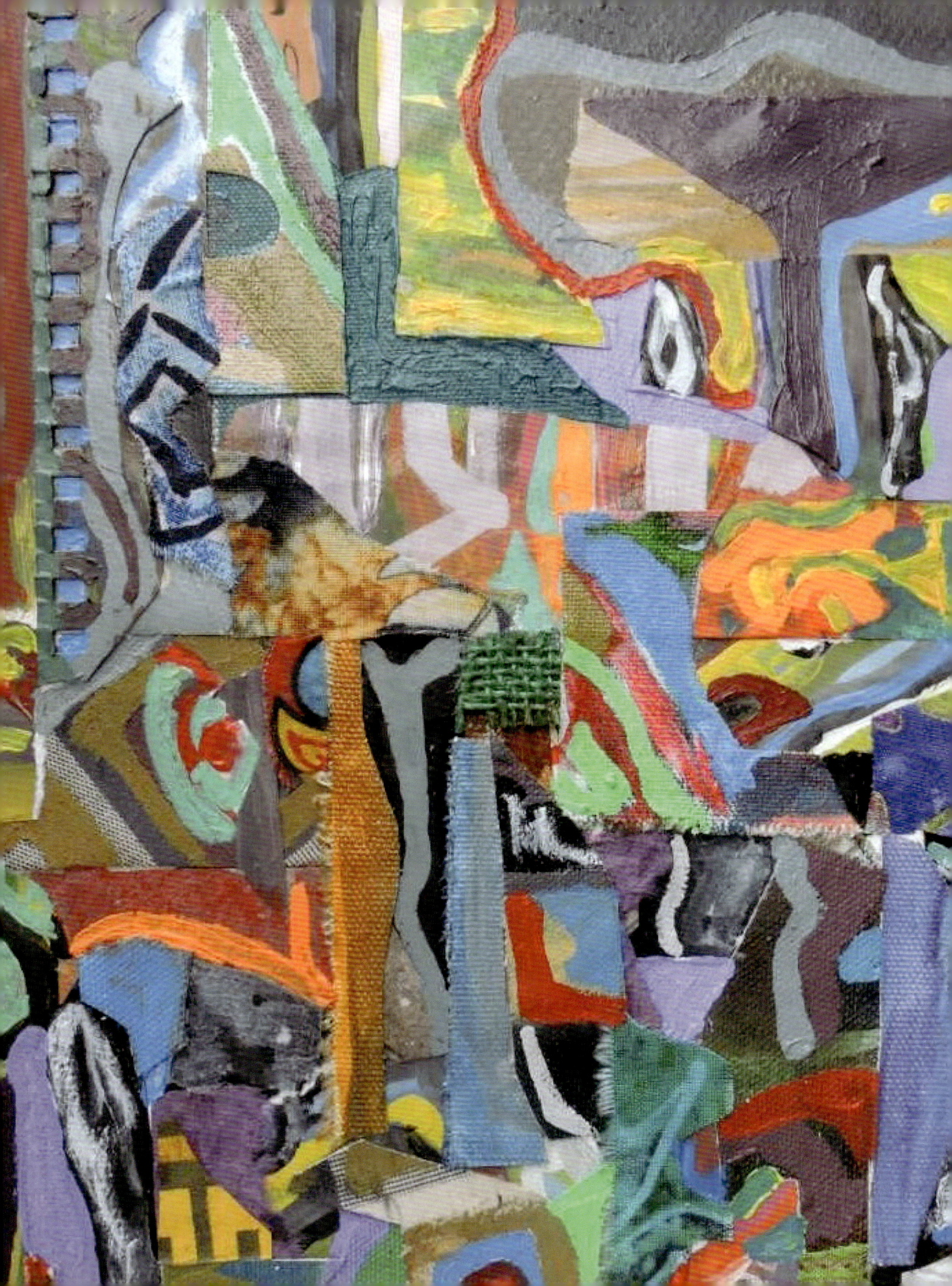

RANDELL HENRY

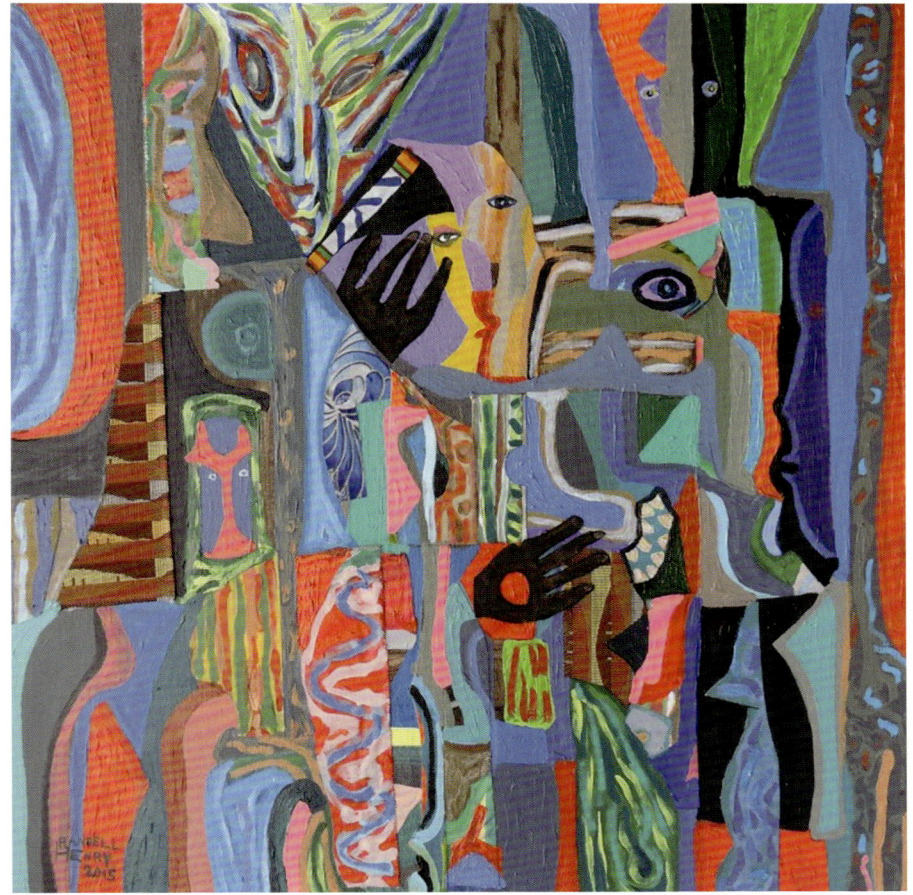

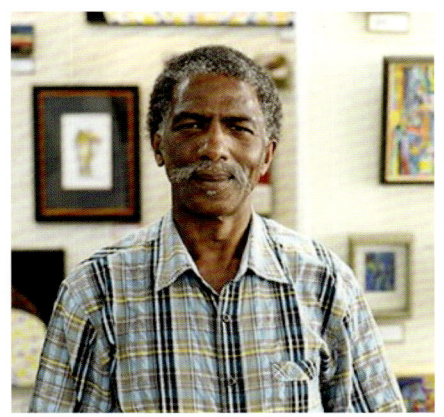

Randell Henry decided to pursue art and become a painter while in the sixth grade. He earned the B.A. in Fine Arts from Southern University (1976) and the MFA in Painting and Drawing from L.S.U. (1982) Today, Henry is Associate Professor of Art and Curator of the Southern University Visual Arts Gallery in Baton Rouge, Louisiana. Henry was recognized in November 2009 by Peter Falk, one of the country's leading experts on American Art after Falk discovered his collages at an art dealer in Connecticut where he acquired twelve of the works and showed them in an exhibition at Summer House Art Gallery in downtown, Madison. Works by Henry have been shown in exhibitions in Baton Rouge, New Orleans, Chicago, Houston, Miami, SCOPE in New York City, Dallas, Art Copenhagen in Denmark, The Makeshift Museum in Los Angeles, Ghana and Liberia. In May 2015 a large painting by Henry was included in the exhibition, "60 Americans" at Elga Wimmer Gallery on West 26 Street in New York City where lead New York Times Art Critic Roberta Smith chose it as her favorite work in the show. A collage by Henry was included in "Inspired," an exhibition held in 2016 at Stella Jones Gallery in New Orleans. This exhibition highlights well known artists across the U.S. who were inspired by famous masters of African American Art, with the works shown side by side in the gallery. He also made a collage for the 2018 Tricentennial Exhibition at the gallery in an exhibition that celebrated the 300th anniversary of the founding of New Orleans. The African American Museum of Dallas held a 30-year retrospective of works by Henry in a one-year exhibition that closed in March, 2018.

**WWW.BATONROUGEGALLERY.ORG/
RANDELL-HENRY**

SOL HILL

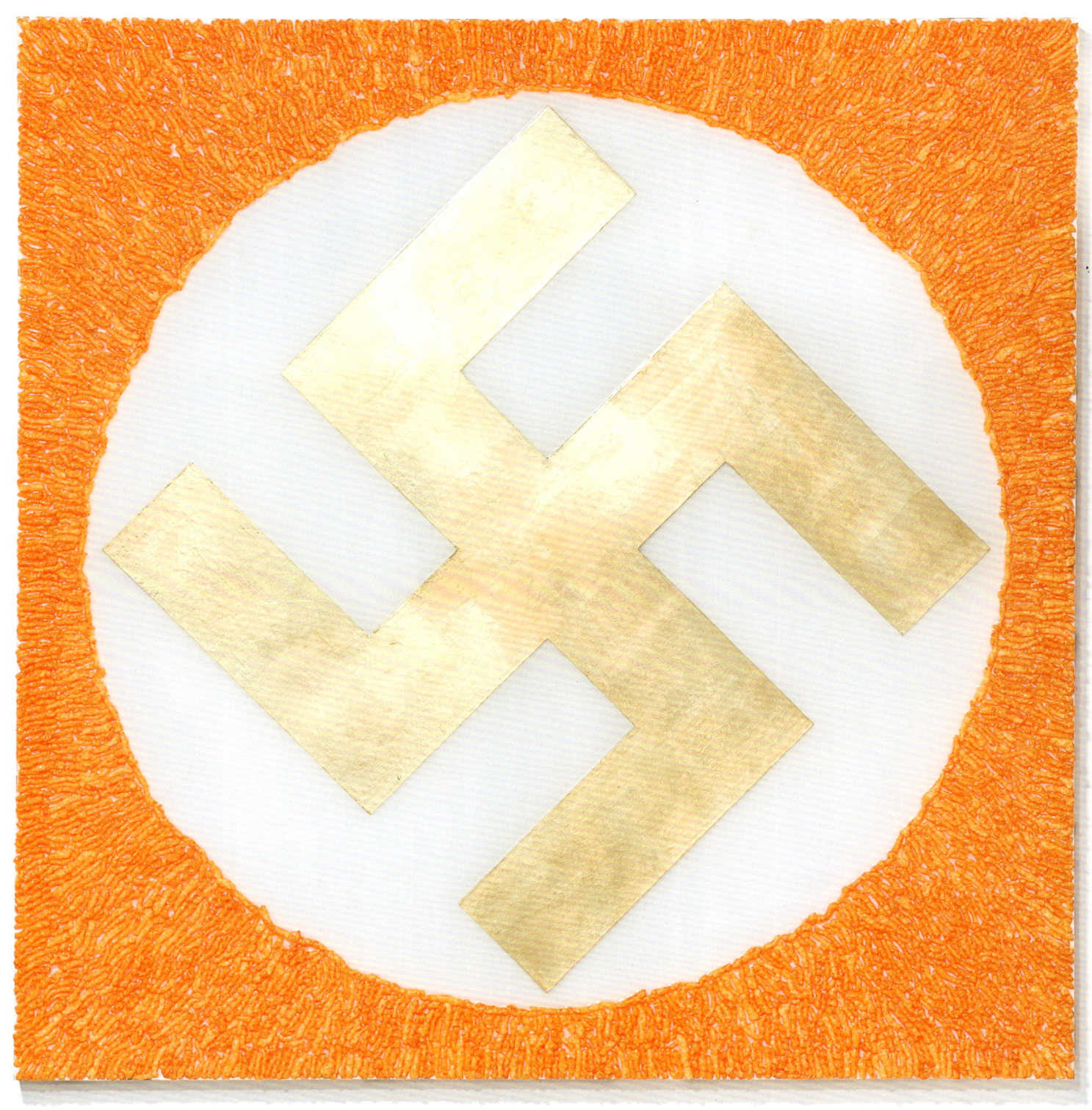

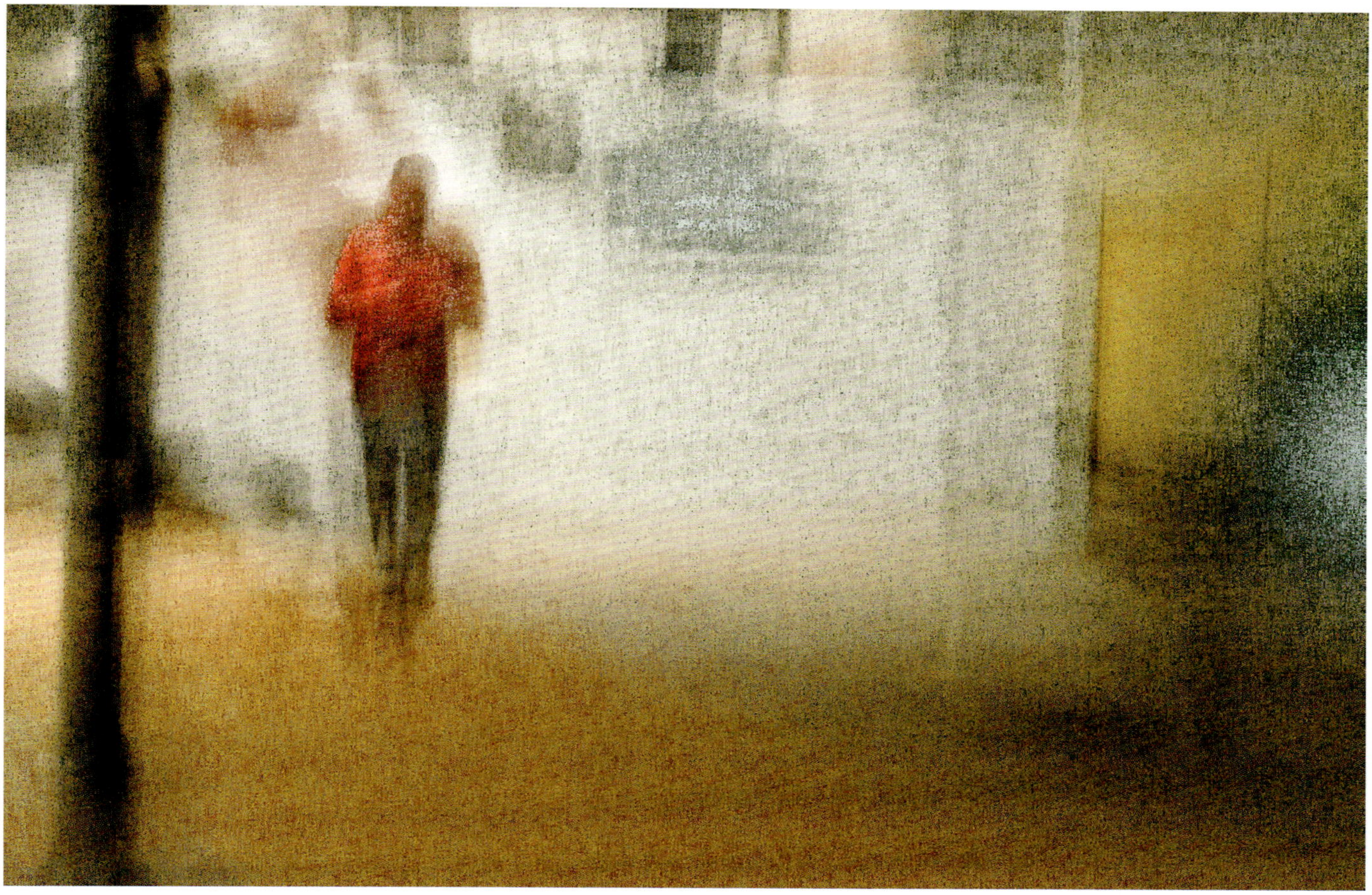

Sol Hill was surrounded by the arts his whole life. His parents were artists and opened the first contemporary art gallery in Santa Fe, NM. His early memories were of his parents in their studios and of Hill's Gallery. The mysterious objects that pervaded the gallery intrigued him. Looking at those artworks felt like observing some secret alchemical language that he yearned to understand.

In college Hill studied International Affairs and German Studies at Lewis & Clark trying to "do something practical" as his parents wished. Afterward he built earthen and straw bale homes before co-founding Zen Stone Lighting, a lighting design company, with his wife, a former paper artist from Brazil. After an intense medical crisis, Hill dedicated himself to pursuing art full time. He earned an MFA in Photographic Arts at Brooks Institute and has been working full time as an artist since 2010 still seeking to decipher that alchemical language, or at least to invent his own.

His artistic practice is divided between working with contemporary digital imaging technology to create what he calls Metagraphs, a mixed media hybrid blending the use of artifacts, generated by digital photographic technology's recording of energies other than light, with the aesthetic valuation of painting and by using art as a form of social activism through creating hard hitting social justice art projects and installations with strong presence.

WWW.SOLHILL.COM

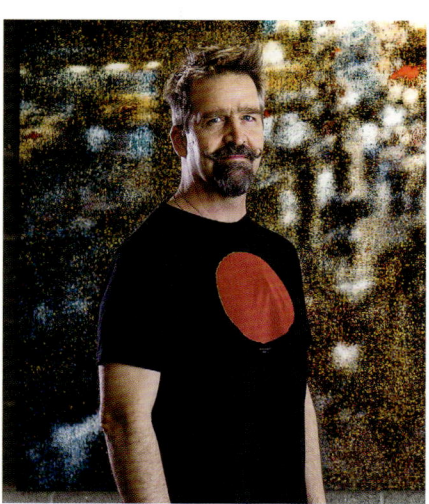

● **(facing page) Some Very Fine People!**
Cheetos, fake gold, acrylic, resin on board, 2017

● **Urban Figure # L1065273 - Red Shirt**
Mixed media Metagraph: photography, digital artifacts, rag paper, acrylic on board, 2011/2014

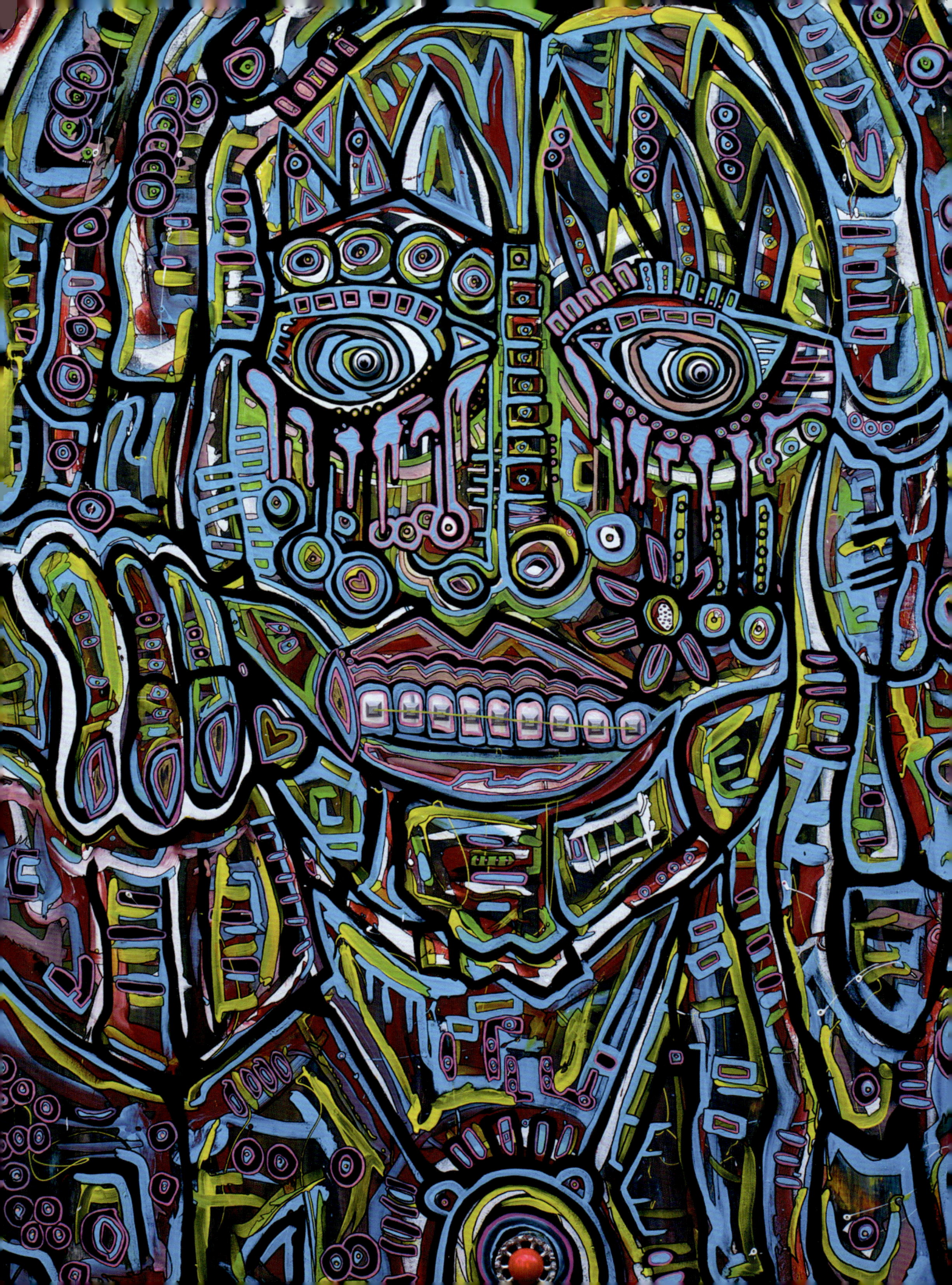

KEV VON HOLT

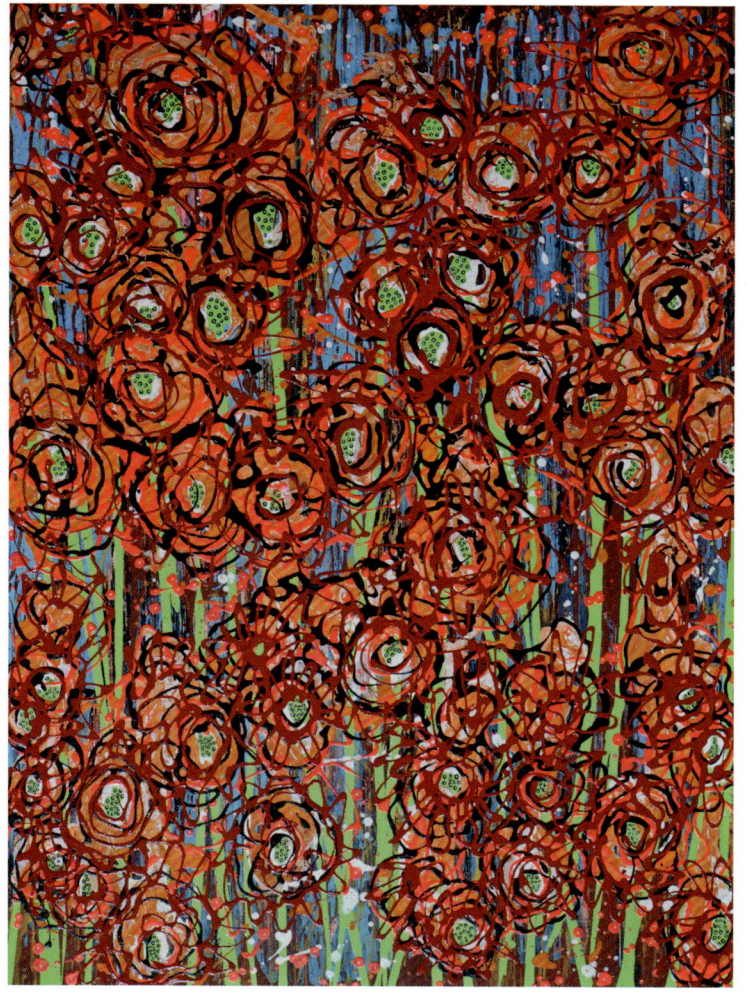

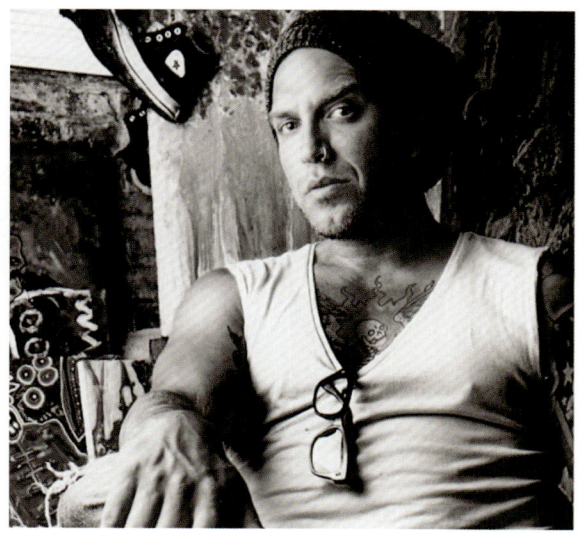

I paint in my studio under dull red light, in a trance of sorts, not seeing the full impact of a painting until I bring it into the light of day... thus revealing the true soul of the painting. Each piece is a true reflection of my ADHD.... sometimes I have 5 paintings going at once in 5 different styles.... I am easily bored! I almost never use paint brushes.... most of my work is done with my fingers .... palette knives.... strips of cardboard and squirt bottles. I work so fast and chaotic that I rarely even notice it all come together. There is really no rhyme or reason to what I do or how i approach it, it just happens.... when I paint I just wait for the spark and reach into my past and present emotions and enjoy every frantic moment of it. I use no references at all.... except for the feelings inside that guide me through the journey. I paint in a disarray of stacked paintings half done and tons of paint tubes lying around.... it is beautiful mess, but that's how I like it! I developed my art all by myself after I found a trash can full of paint that someone left out for the garbage man. I hauled it back to my then tiny studio apartment and locked myself away for a few years and experimented with the visions in my mind. I keep my inspiration to myself and keep it being about inner exploration.
Art is where the "outside" world never gets in when I am creating
I am free!

WWW.KEVVONHOLT.COM

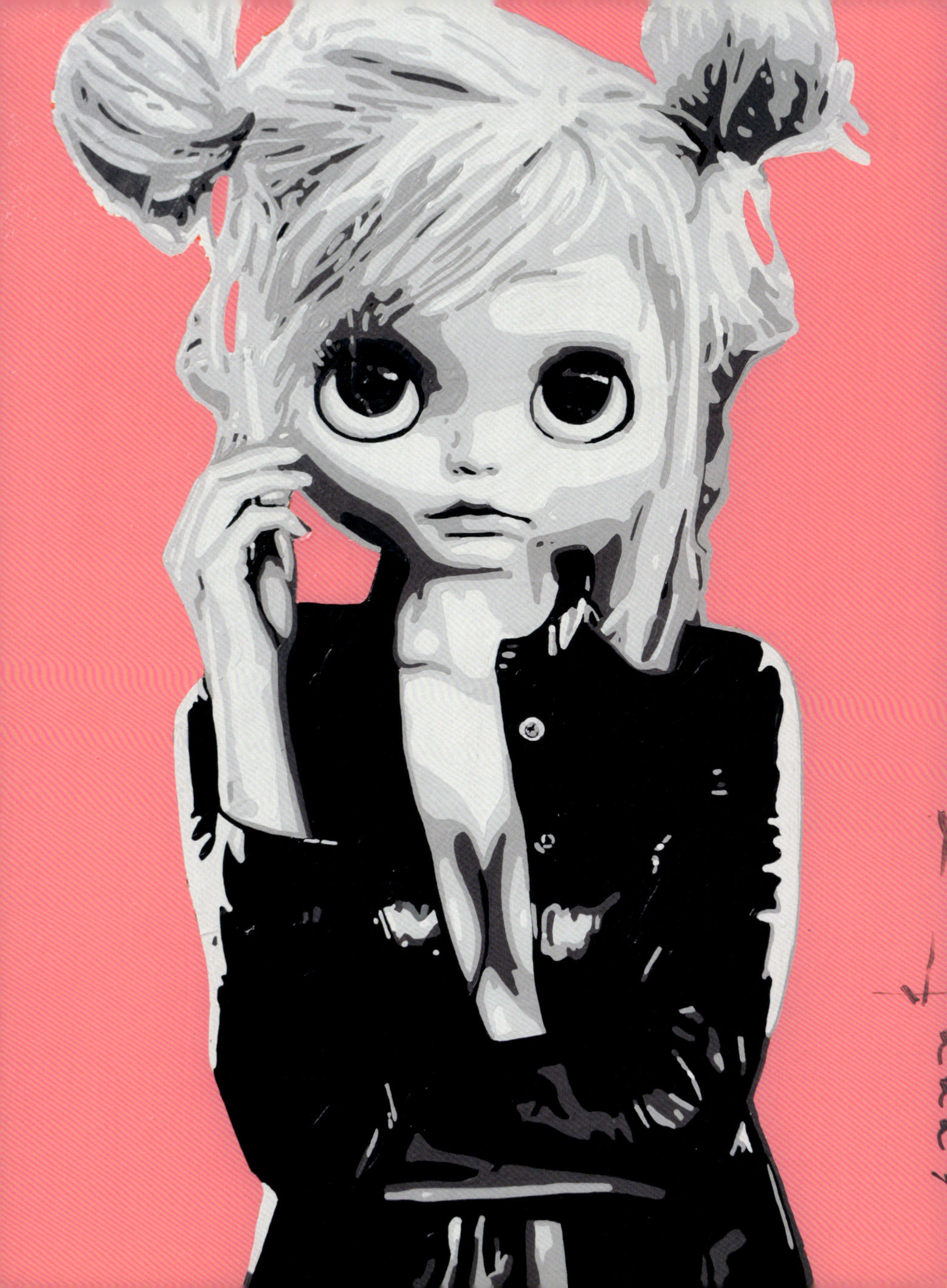

ANDRZEJ MICHAEL KARWACKI

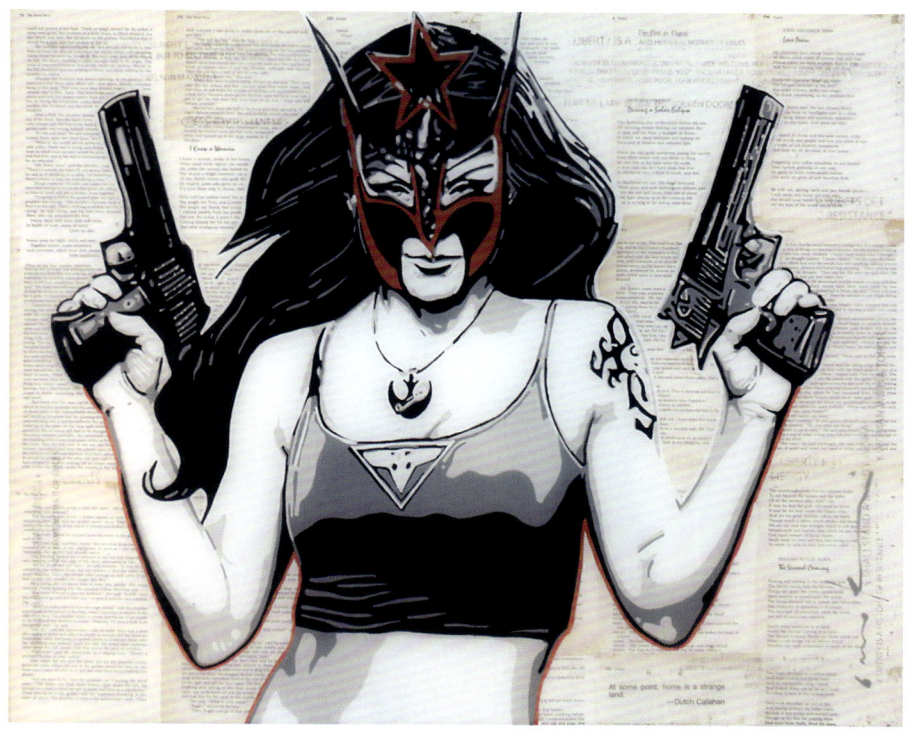

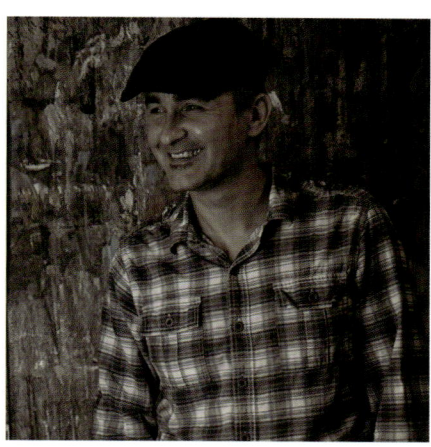

● **(facing page) American Beauty, Pretty in Pink**
18 x 24 in.

● **Her Beacon-Hand Glows World Wide**
24 x 30 in.

Born in Poland, Andrzej grew up during the years of political oppression and era of communist Poland. There he attended the School for the Arts and Literature. Unconsciously, these primary years were the platform for a deep attraction towards peace, poetry and art as a form of creative preservation. In 1984, Andrzej moved to New York, he consequently received BFA in painting and earned a Master's Degree in Urban Architecture from the University of Pennsylvania. After relocating to the San Francisco Bay Area in 1994, Andrzej's artistic direction began to take shape after integrating Eastern spirituality into his artwork. While Andrzej's current studio is based in Berkeley, his paintings are currently exhibited Los Angeles, the San Francisco Bay Area, Chicago, Dallas, New York, Boston, Paris, London and Hong Kong. His work is in private collections throughout the United States.

Relying on well-known images of man and women in the context of pop art, Andrzej have pulled together elements from mainstream aesthetics, both past and present, to address transpersonal relationships we have to select images. By juxtaposing the sense of identity with text from newspapers and textiles that speak of the social cultural of various decades and cultures, these paintings attempt to make sense of the world encompassing a wider aspect of humankind and the psyche. Andrzej's figure paintings explore ideas of fashion, feminism, human desire for love and beauty. It is Andrzej's goal to present women not within an objectified framework but women that constitute a dominant key symbol within a wider cultural context.

His figure painting works use variety of media. They are composed of written stories, which by use of newspapers, non-fiction book materials, posters and ads create background and content to an overall theme. They add a second dimension to the composition and to the personal life story of the model. All figures are free hand painted with few monotones thereby creating strong graphic composition. Andrzej often exposes parts of the figure to its background, fusing entire arrangement into a single story.

WWW.ANDRZEJMICHAEL.COM

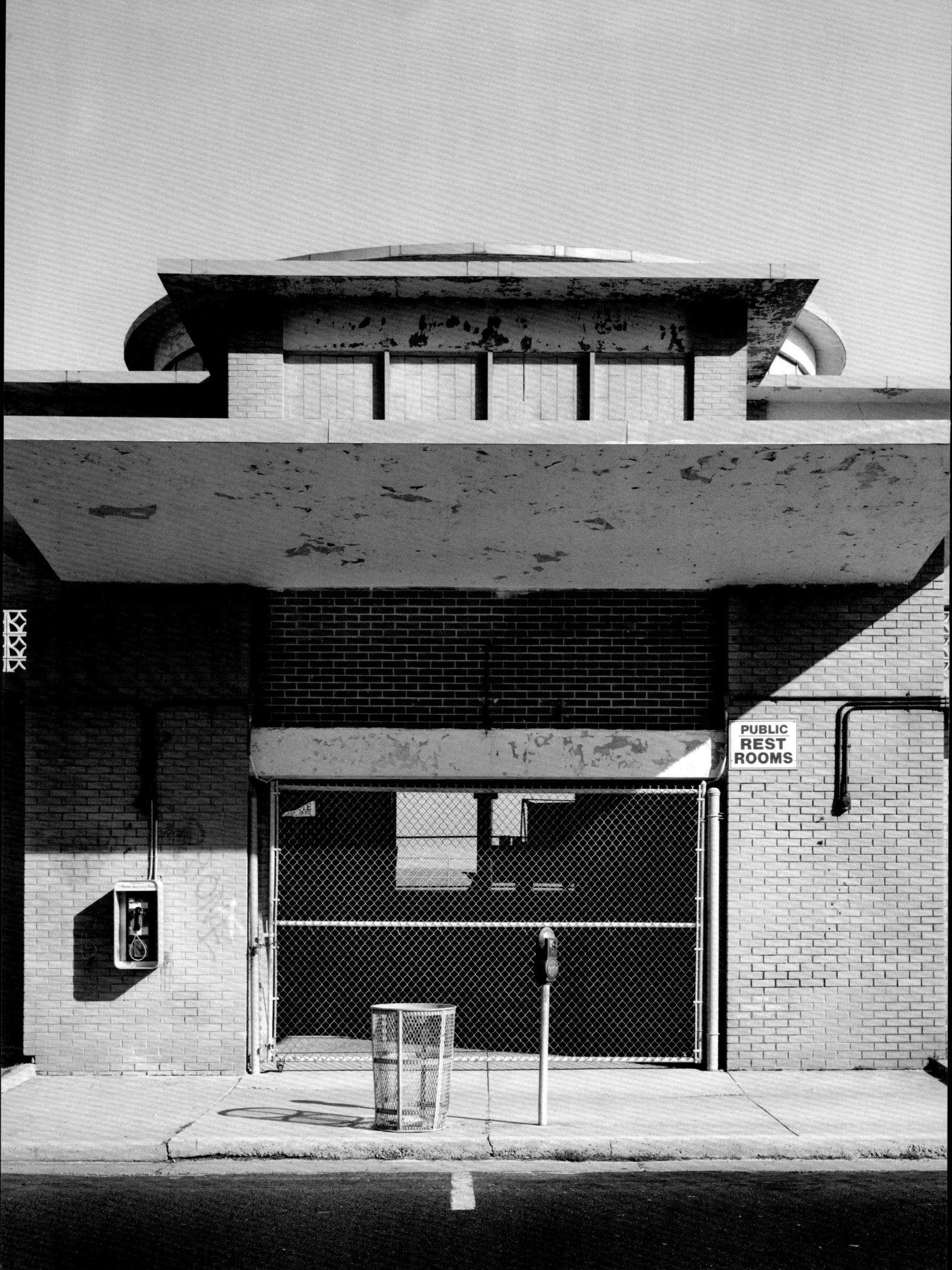

AUBREY J. KAUFFMAN

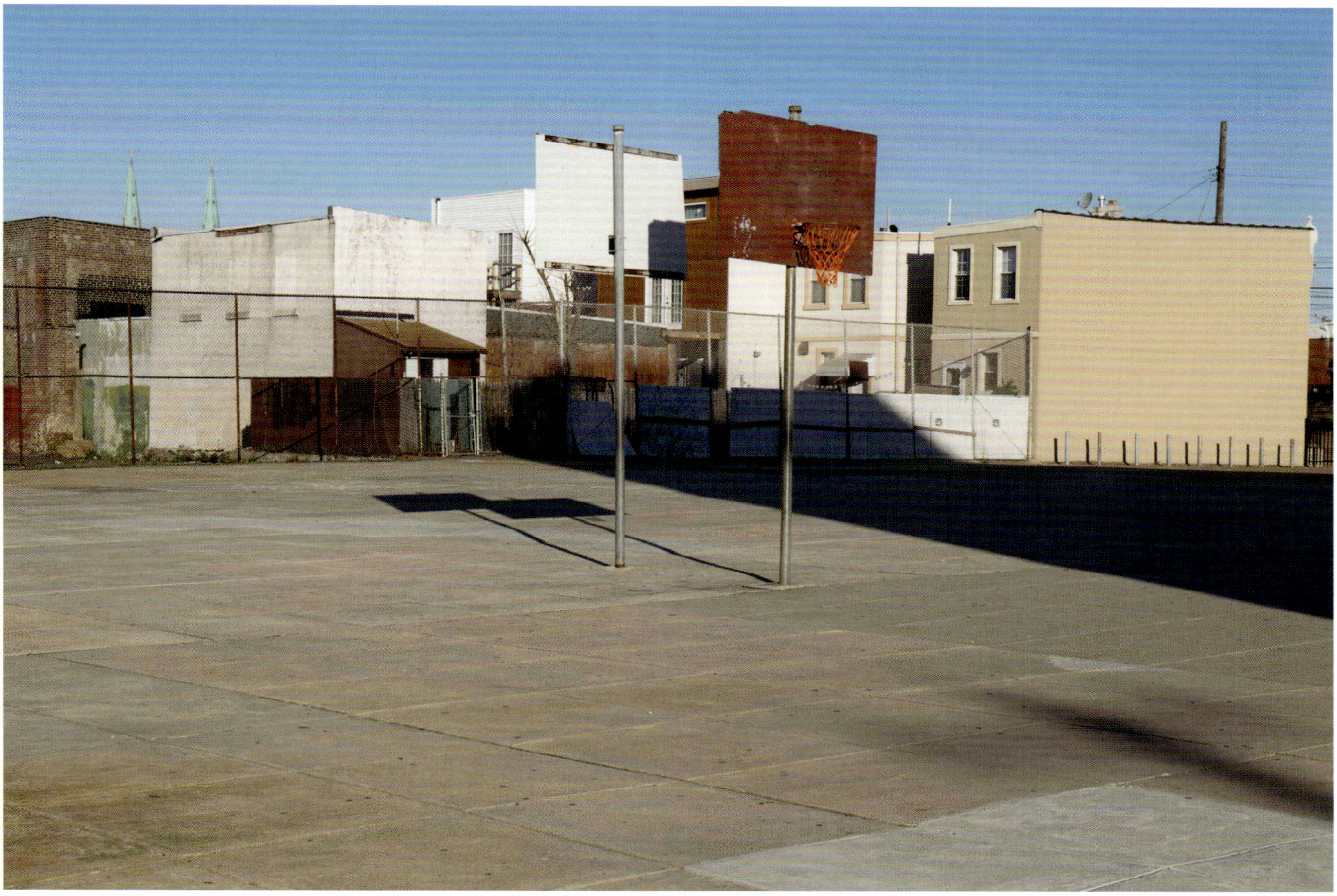

Aubrey J. Kauffman is a photographer living and working in New Jersey. He received his BA from New Jersey City University and his MFA in Visual Arts from Rutgers University's Mason Gross School of the Arts. He has taught photography at Mason Gross, Mercer County Community College and Middlesex County College.

His work can be found in the permanent collections of the New Jersey State Museum, Rider University and at Johnson and Johnson's Corporate Headquarters in New Brunswick, NJ.

WWW.AUBREYJKAUFFMAN.COM

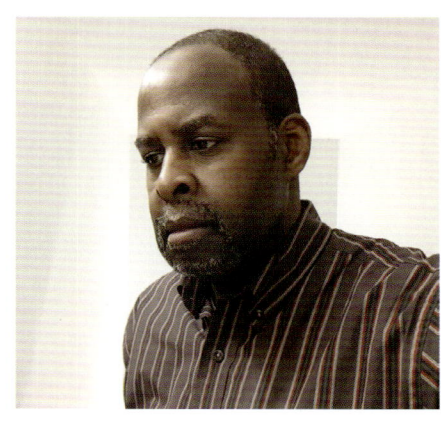

● **(facing page) Asbury Park, NJ**
Archival pigment print, 12 x 18 in., 1994

● **Schoolyard**
Archival pigment print, 17 x 26 in., 2014

JAKE KELLEY

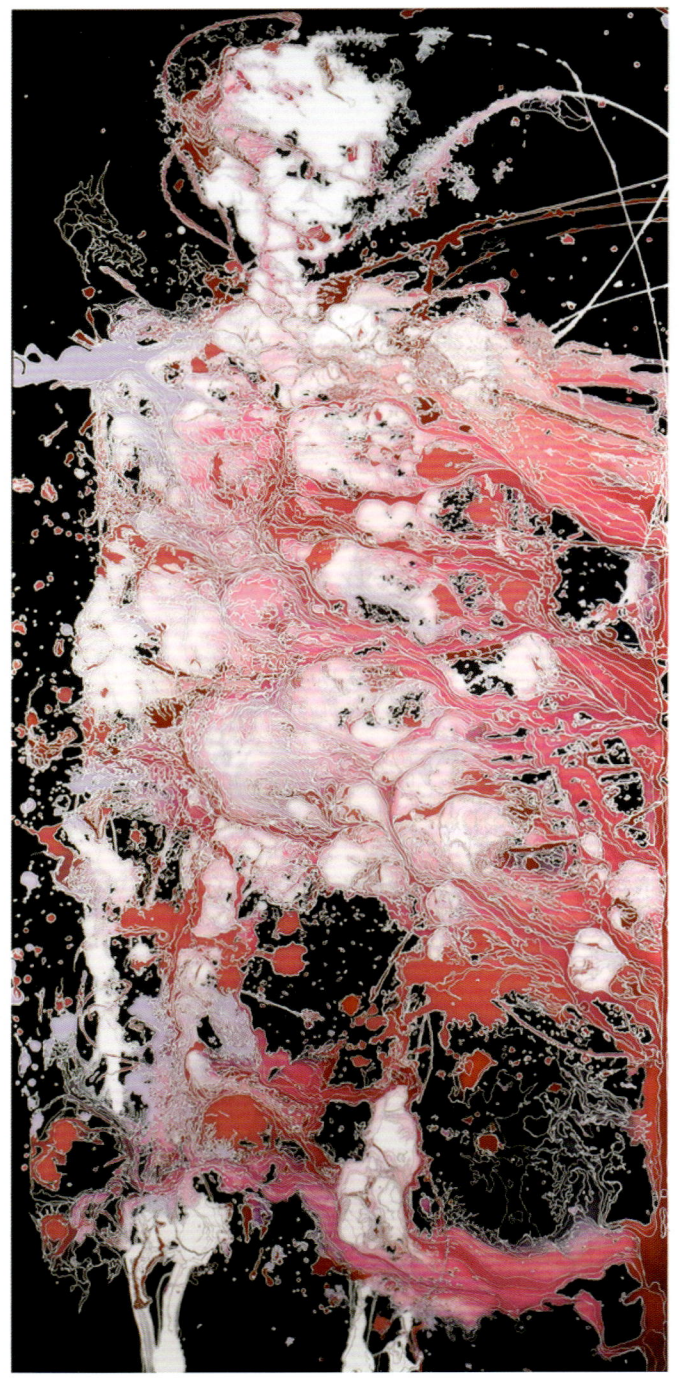 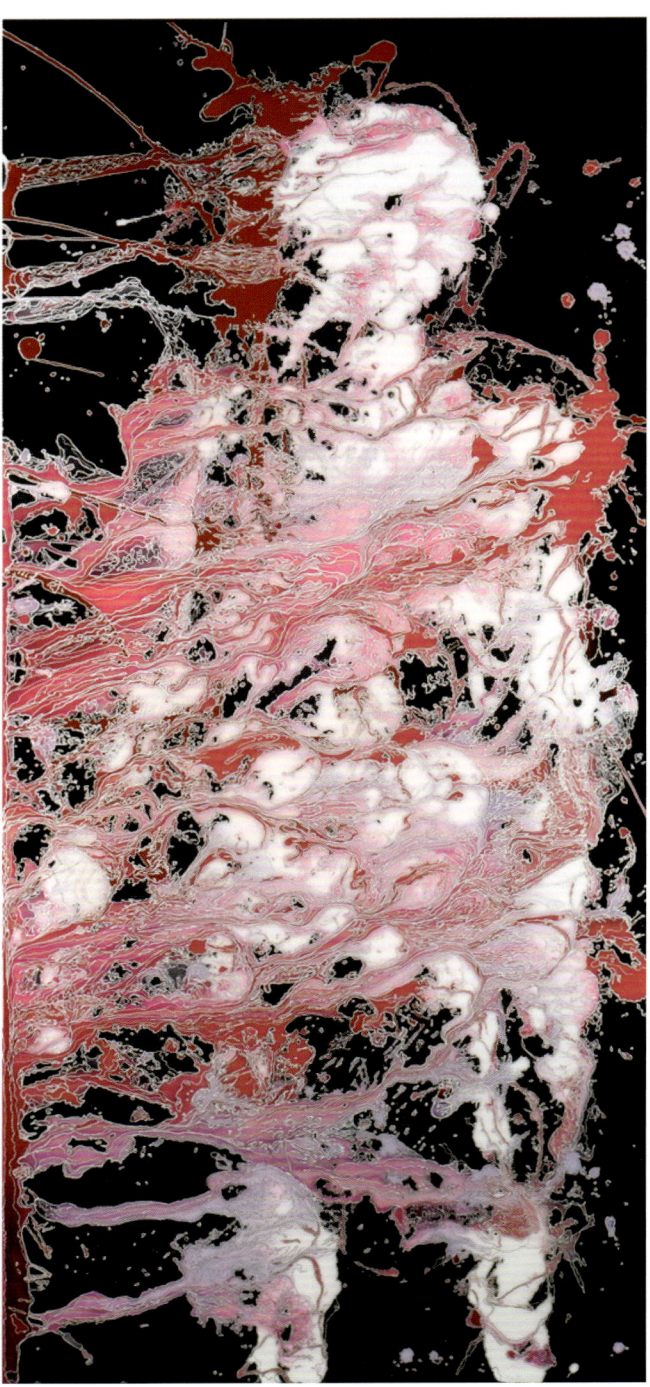

● **My River Runs to Thee**
Acrylic, latex, resin and ink on aluminum, 48 x 48 in., 2014

● **(Facing Page) Soul-Crusher**
Acrylic, latex, resin and ink on aluminum, 48 x 48 in., 2014

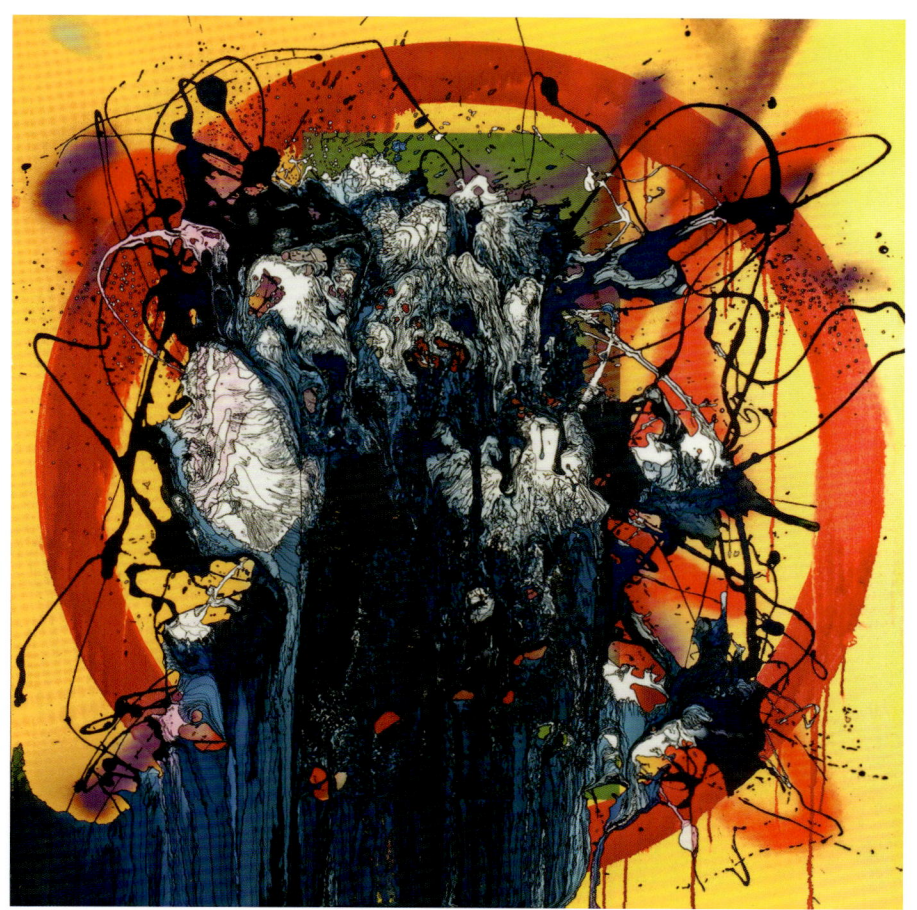

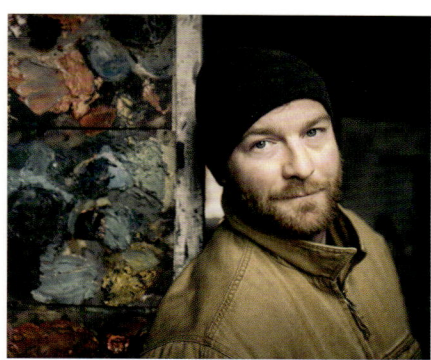

"My work is driven by a love of experimentation and mark making with the ultimate goal of creating meaningful yet challenging images that simultaneously pay homage to the historical narrative of abstract painting while pushing the dialogue in interesting and often complex new directions."

My work is primarily an exploration of materials in an effort to create images of lasting conceptual and emotional effect. I utilize a wide variety of mediums and techniques including, the use of water and oil based paints, latex, printer ink, wood stains, resin, and screen printing on hand cut aluminum panels, all of which have developed organically from hours of experimentation. My process, which involves the layering and removal of a variety of material and the simultaneous revealing and covering of visual information is informed by the collage techniques of early-mid Modernist painters such as Picasso, Motherwell, and Krasner.

My work is driven by a love of experimentation and mark making with the ultimate goal of creating meaningful yet challenging images that simultaneously pay homage to the historical narrative of abstract painting while pushing the dialogue in interesting and often complex new directions. I am also interested in mark-making as a method of exploring the inherent tension between opposites such as Euclidian/Platonic, organic/geometric, painting/drawing, etc. As an abstract painter, engaging in a cultural dialogue is also a concern. Therefore, the shared human experience, as well as perception itself are always primary subjects.

WWW.JAKEKELLEY.WORDPRESS.COM

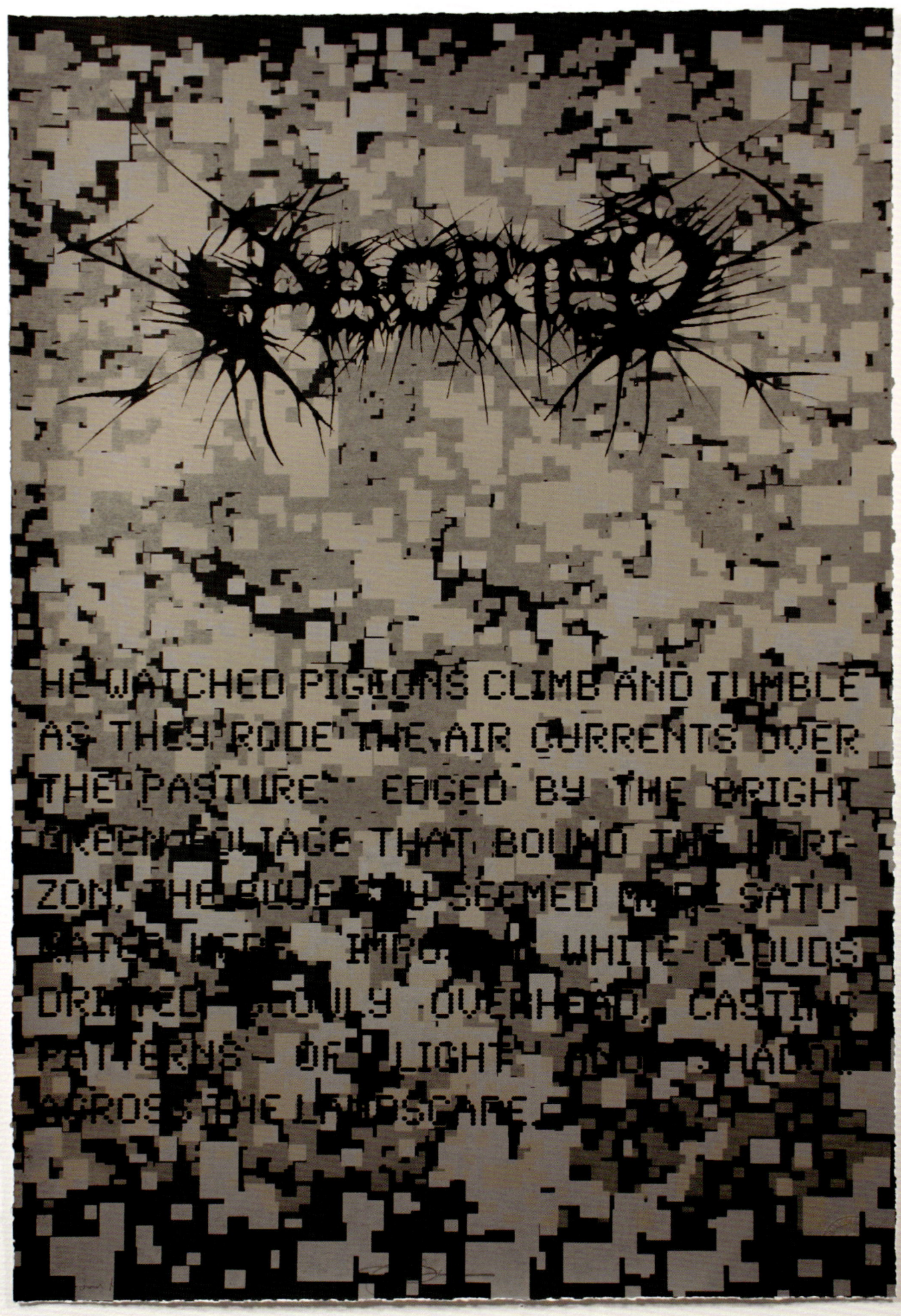

ABORTED

HE WATCHED PIGEONS CLIMB AND TUMBLE AS THEY RODE THE AIR CURRENTS OVER THE PASTURE. EDGED BY THE BRIGHT GREEN FOLIAGE THAT BOUND THE HORIZON, THE BLUE SKY SEEMED MORE SATURATED HERE. IMPOSSIBLY WHITE CLOUDS DRIFTED LAZILY OVERHEAD, CASTING PATTERNS OF LIGHT AND SHADOW ACROSS THE LANDSCAPE.

JASON LAHR

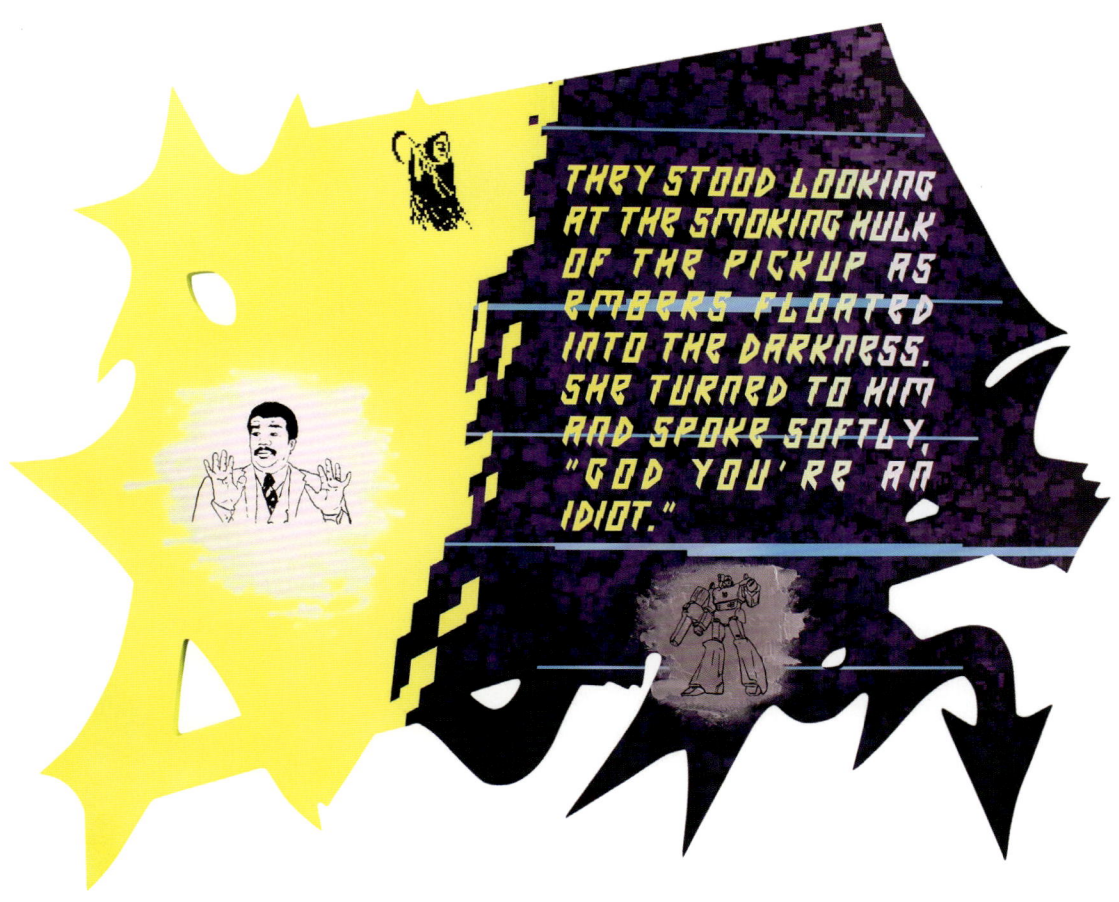

Jason Lahr was born and raised in rural Pennsylvania. He received his M.F.A. in drawing and painting from Penn State University and his B.F.A. in painting from Clarion University. His work is located in private and public collections across the U.S. and Europe. Since 2004, he has been represented by Aron Packer Projects in Chicago, IL.

Lahr's paintings combine darkly comic texts with appropriated images, creating shifting narratives of working class male identity. The work draws from feminism, narrative theory, contemporary and postmodern fiction, semiotics, and film theory to explore the formation and shaping of masculinity through mass culture. The images are pulled from a wide range of popular and sub-cultural ephemera while the texts are fragments that suggest their excision from a larger story and give the reader/viewer flashbulb glimpses at moments of narrative action. Centering on female characters that occupy positions of authority and male characters who are injured, inept, defeated, or perplexed by their dealings with women, the texts and images form narratives which question the wash of expectations and assumptions we experience and create through popular culture.

His work has been written about by Art F City, NewCity, Beautiful Decay, Nashville Scene, Chicago Magazine, and Bad At Sports among others. Lahr currently lives and works in South Bend, IN where he teaches painting at the University of Notre Dame.

WWW.JASONLAHR.NET

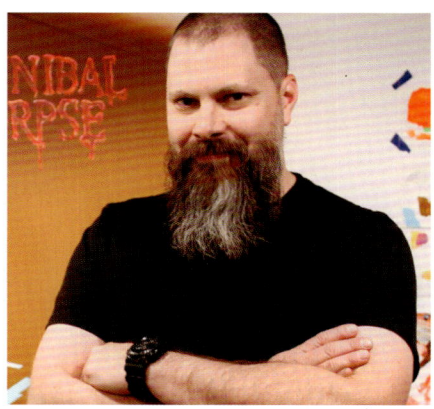

● **(facing page) Throw Hand Horizon**

● **Away With You**
2017

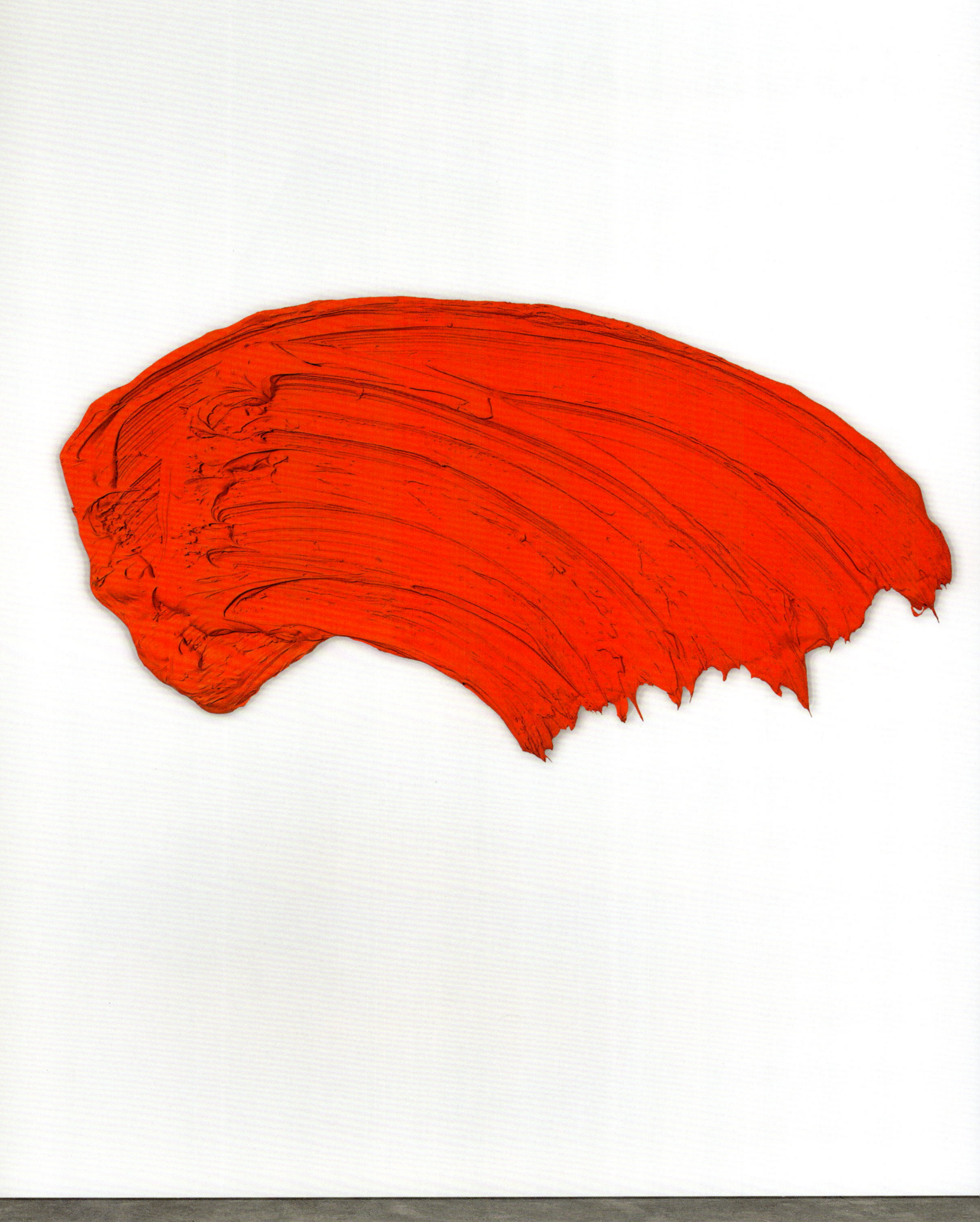

DONALD MARTINY

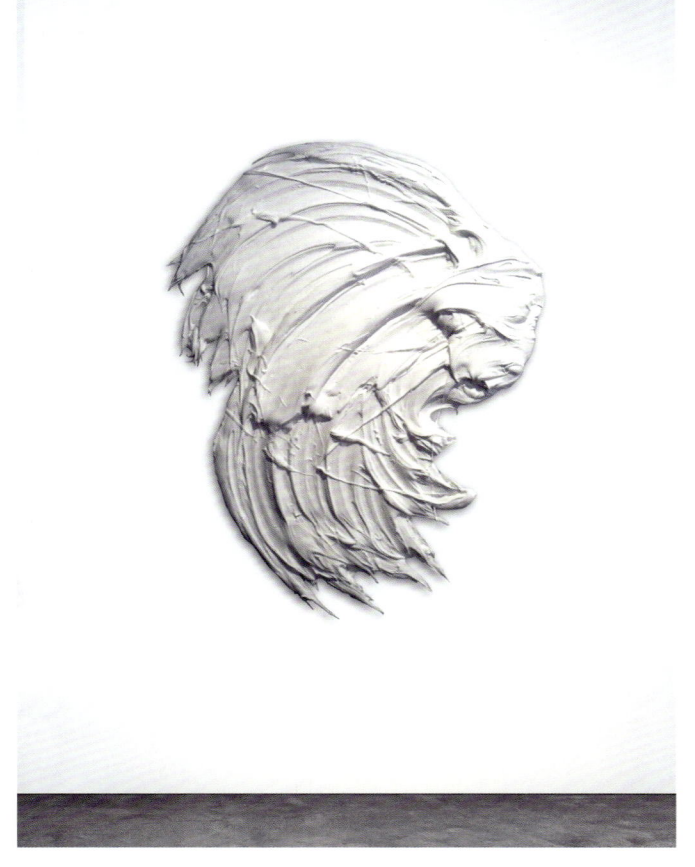

"Donald Martiny's work forces us to question the established definitions which form the backbone of our understanding of painting as both a pursuit and a product, and of paint as a medium. In challenging the viewer in these ways, it is not only visually exciting but intellectually invigorating."

- PROFESSOR DEBORAH SWALLOW MÄRIT RAUSING DIRECTOR THE COURTAULD INSTITUTE OF ART

Donald Martiny was born in Schenectady, New York in 1953. Martiny, who currently lives and works in Chapel Hill, North Carolina, studied at the School of the Visual Arts, The Art Students League in New York, New York University and the Pennsylvania Academy of Fine Arts. His work is in private collections in Amsterdam, London, Paris, Philadelphia, Washington DC, San Francisco and Los Angeles.

WWW.DONALDMARTINY.COM

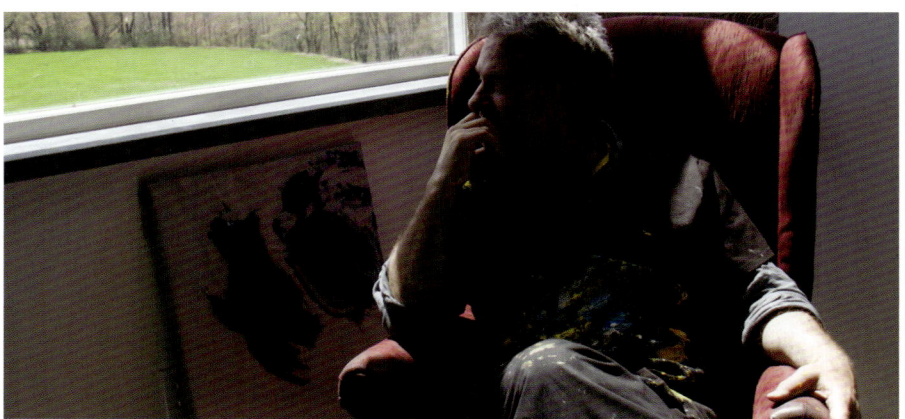

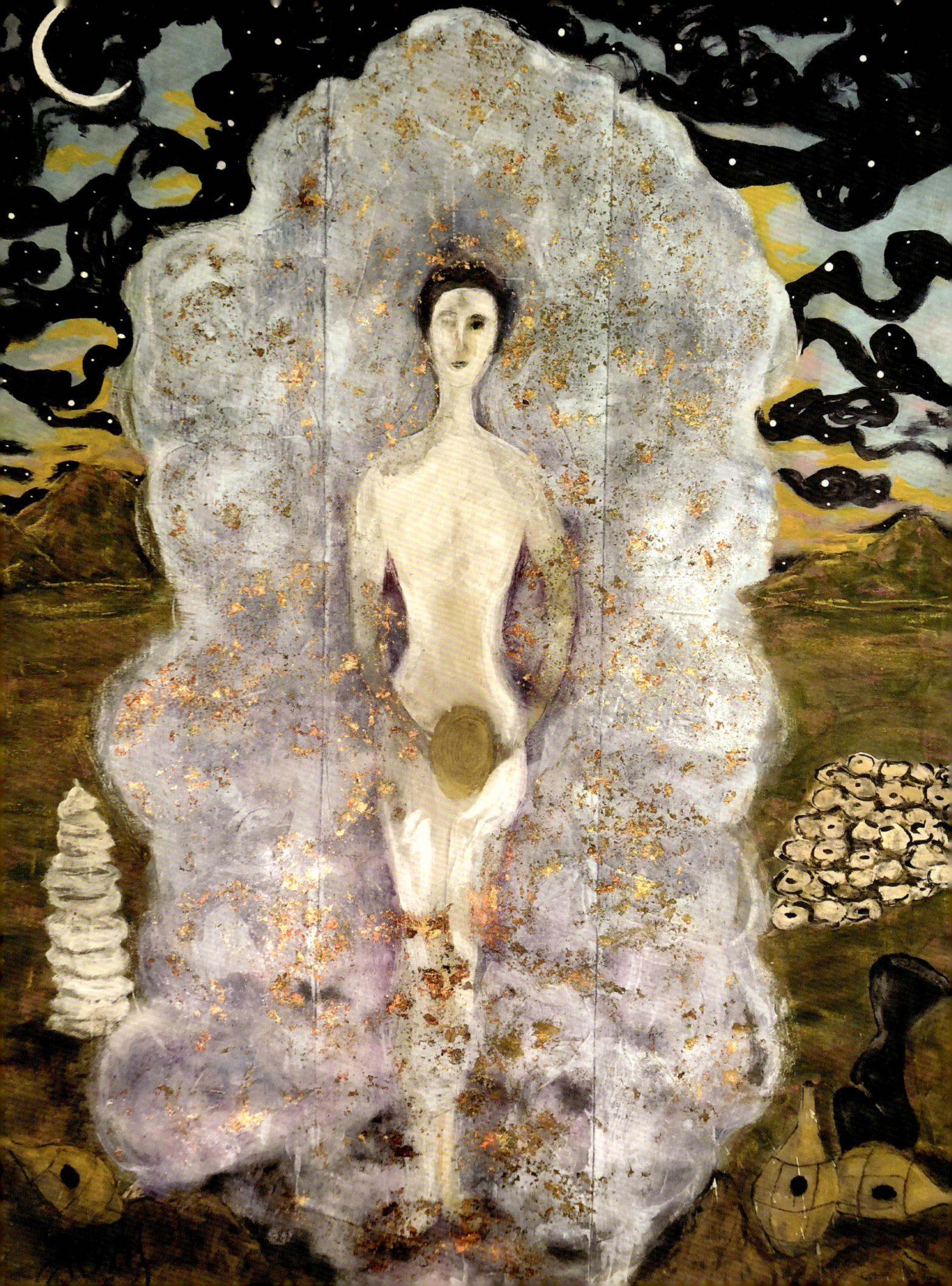

DAVID C. MENDOZA

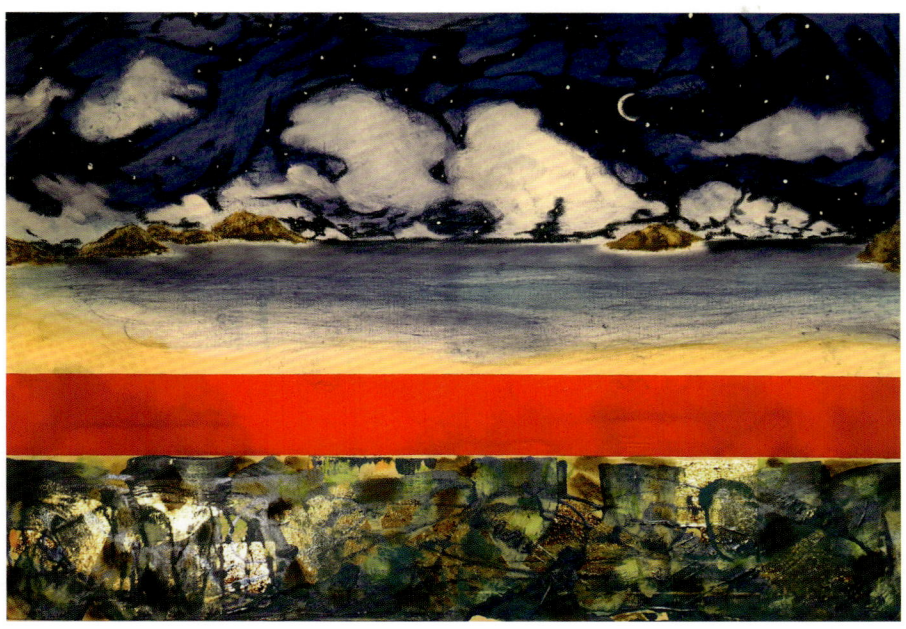

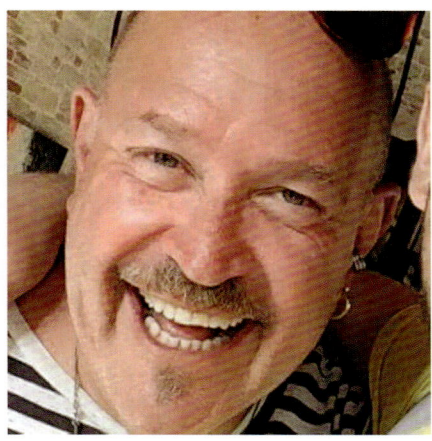

● (facing page) **OANA...WOMAN OF CLAY...GODDESS OF EARTH**
mixed media on paper, 60 x 48 in., 2018

● **DREAMS OF TURKEY**
mixed media on linen, 24 x 36 in., 2018

I am an aesthetic on the edge. Artist. Curator. Designer. Writer. Actor. An artist without an agenda but to create. Spontaneous in the execution of my creative inspiration I am motivated in a pure process. It is through humor, pathos, social commentary, nature, and beauty my vision and relevance take root. Like the caveman...I leave my mark!

It is through abstract and representational styles I integrate a fusion of my content and structure. "Gentle in form and inspired by nature, his paintings reveal a new reality created through a combination of delicate yet highly evocative lines, and equally disturbing spots. His is a daunting world that astonishes and evokes a sense of mystery instead of suggesting an explanation."
- *Anna Kroplewske, Curator, City Museum of Toruń, Toruń, Poland*

I was born on the sunny shores of Tampa Bay raised in a subculture of Spanish, Italian, Cuban, and Mexican heritage. Colorful. Festive. Loving. For four years I attended the University of South Florida majoring in Liberal Arts and Psychology which layed the foundation for my creative life.

Since 2014 my international travels and exhibitions have fund my works into museums and important collections in India, Tunisia, Poland, Turkey, South Korea, and the USA.

Through my art I find I am sentimental and unwavering in my dedication to the creative experience of an artistic life. I will create until I cannot.

"Let each man exercise the art that he [she] knows." Aristophanes

WWW.DCMENDOZAART.COM

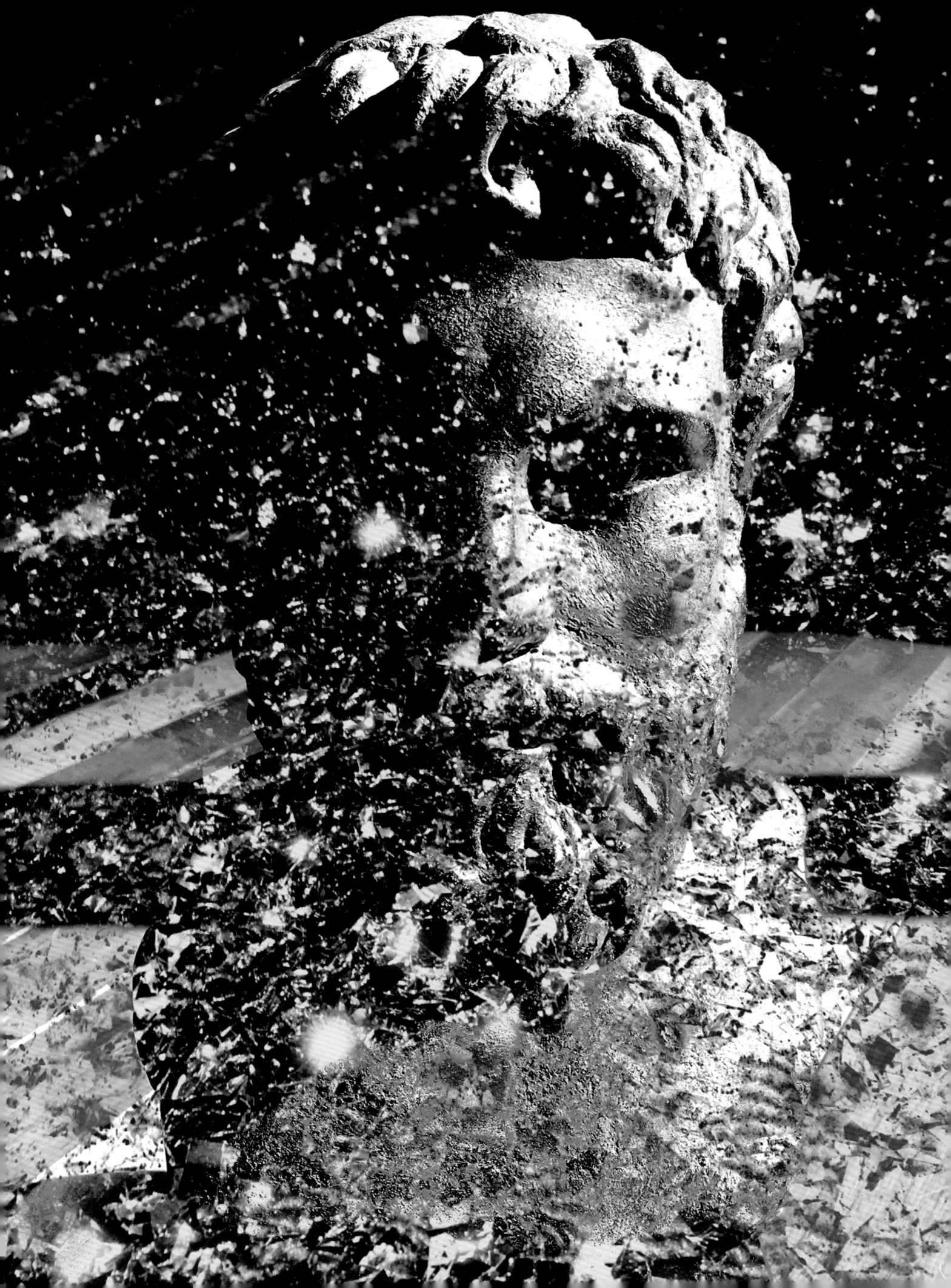

TREVOR MESSERSMITH

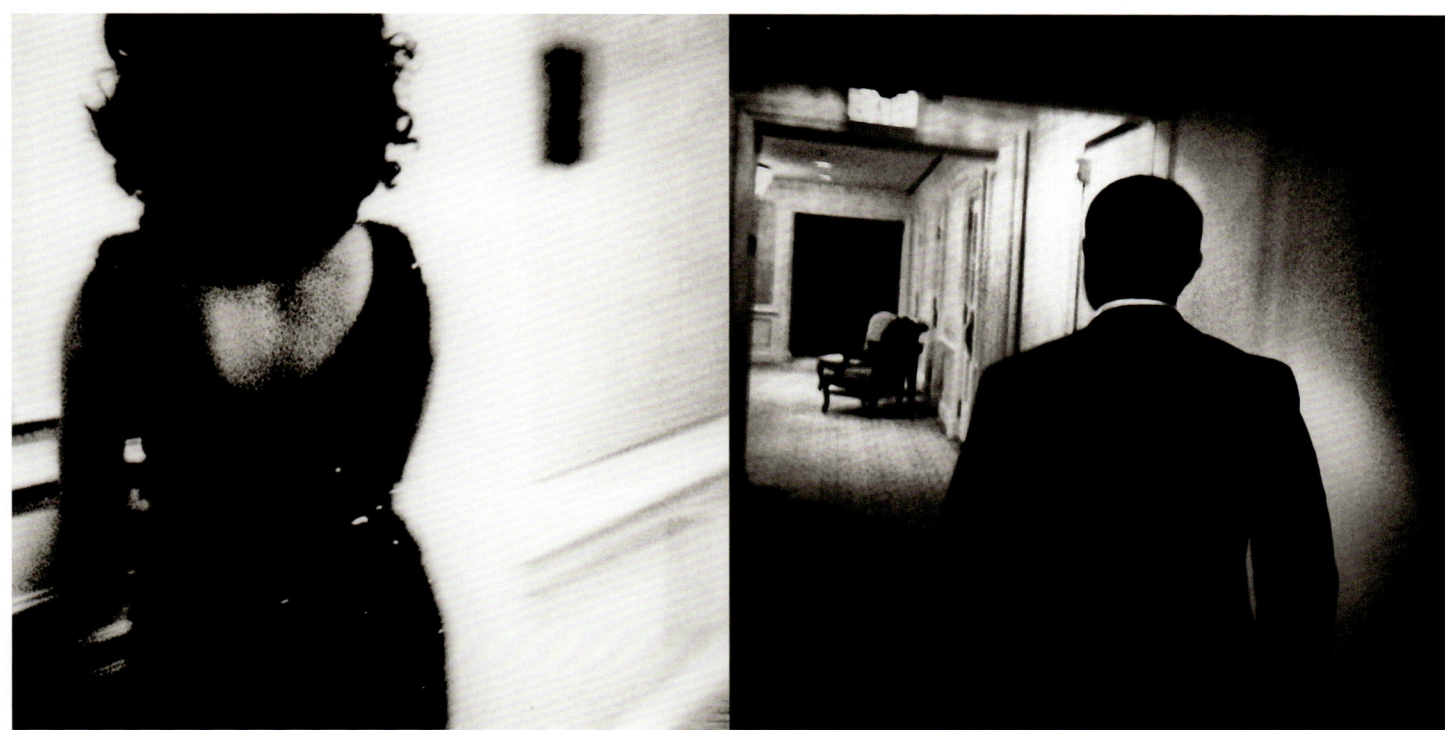

● (facing page) **Zeus Glitter**

● **Hotel**

Trevor Messersmith is an award-winning photographer and graphic designer based in New York's Hudson Valley. Trevor provides creative direction to a wide variety of online and print projects through **80east Design**, a studio he started in 2002.

Among other venues, Trevor's artwork has been exhibited at the California Museum of Photography, the Florida Museum of Photographic Arts, the Los Angeles Center for Digital Art, the Morean Arts Center, the Orange County Center for Contemporary Art, and the Center for Photographic Art. He has been featured in AIGA's **New York State of Design 2017**, Print Magazine's **2016 Typography and Lettering Awards**, the Mobile Photography Awards, the Pollux

Awards, Tumblr Radar, Print Magazine's 2017 **Regional Design Annual**, the 2017 International Design Awards, Creative Quarterly, and **Graphic Design USA**. Publications include the photography books *Fauxlaroids*, *Double Apollo*, *Blümen*, and *Objectives*. Trevor earned a B.A. from Bard College in Photography. He also studied graphic design at Rhode Island School of Design.

WWW.TREVORMESSERSMITH.COM

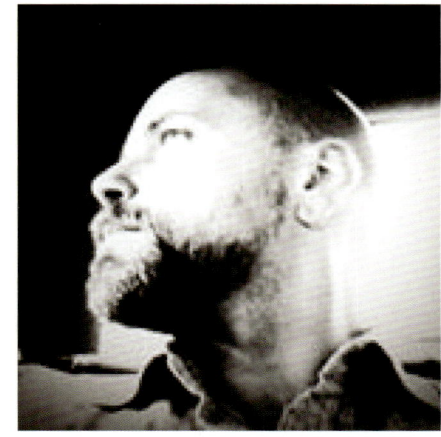

TIMOTHY NERO

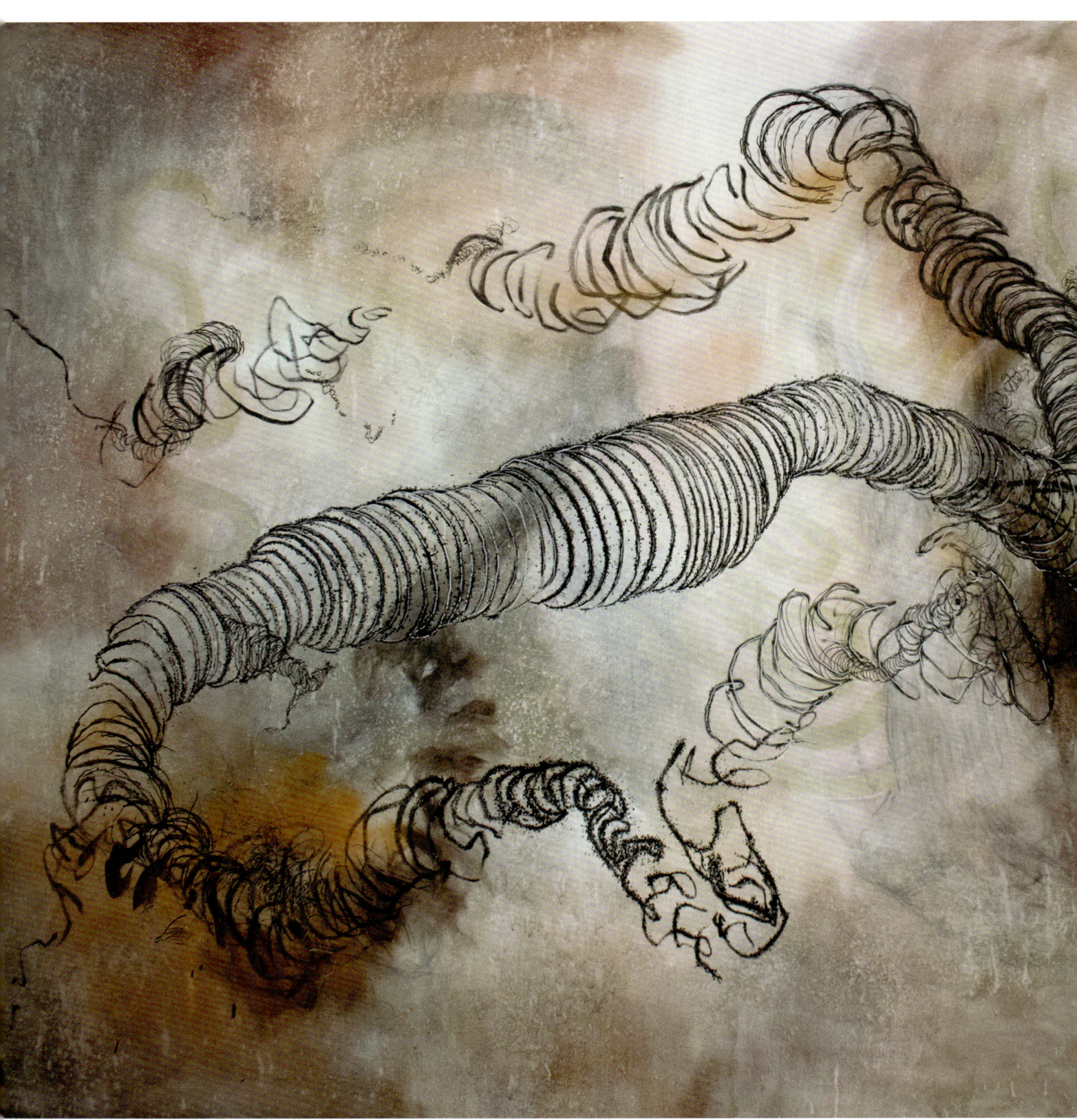

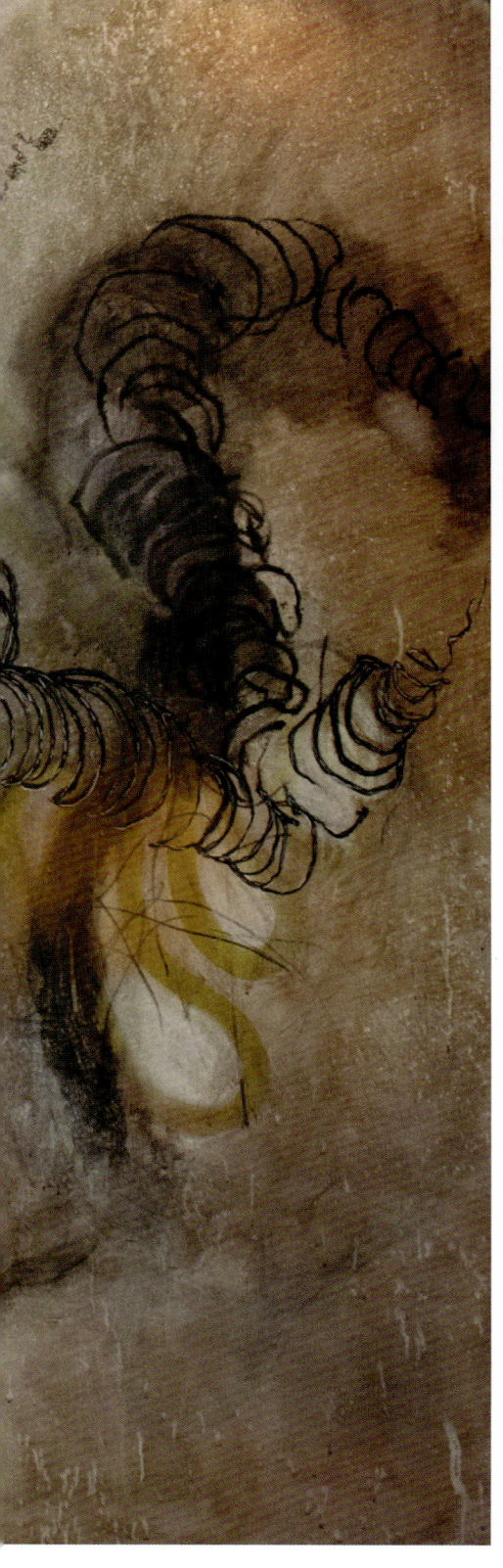

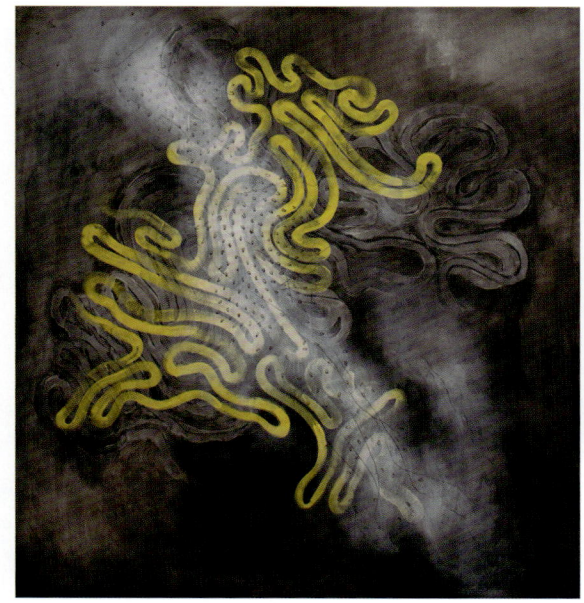

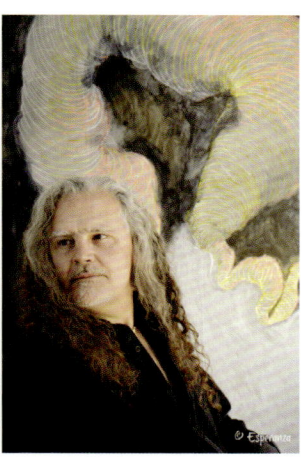

- (facing page) **Objects in Consciousness**
  acrylic/canvas, 68 x 96 in., 2018

- **Being or Desire**
  acrylic/canvas, 72 x 68 in., 2018

Timothy Nero is a multi-disciplinary visual artist living and working in Santa Fe, NM. He is currently painting in acrylic on canvas as well as making sculpture using wood, steel, marine vinyl, fabric and paint. The ideas that drive his work for more than two decades relate to the mind, conditioning, belief systems and stillness. He has taught drawing and painting at Florida State University, Tallahassee FL. Mount Union College, Alliance OH, The University of New Mexico at Santa Fe and Taos and Santa Fe Community College.

Nero has exhibited nationally and internationally since 1992 with solo shows at the Phyllis Kind Gallery, Chicago, "5." Gallery, Art Box, Ellsworth Gallery, Santa Fe NM. among others. Recent group exhibitions include Axle Contemporary, The Renga Project: Drawing Exhibition, Santa Fe, NM,

Ellsworth Gallery, Group Exhibition, Axle Contemporary, "The Gesture Rendered", Santa Fe, NM, 516 ARTS, "Flatlanders and Surface Dwellers", ABQ, NM, Harwood Museum of Art. "New Mexorado", Taos, NM, George Billis Gallery, "Rock and Elegance", Los Angeles, "Strange Weeds", Bridge Art Fair, Chicago, Il. 2008 Site Santa Fe Biennial, "Lucky Number Seven", as a member of mural team for Scott Lyall, Curated by Lance Fung. His exhibitions have been reviewed in ART LTD, 2014,THE Magazine, Dec 2015/ Jan 2016 and May 2014 among others. Nero holds a Master of Fine Arts degree from Florida State University summa cum laude, and a Bachelor of Arts Interior Design/ Architecture from Kent State University.

WWW.TIMOTHYNERO.COM

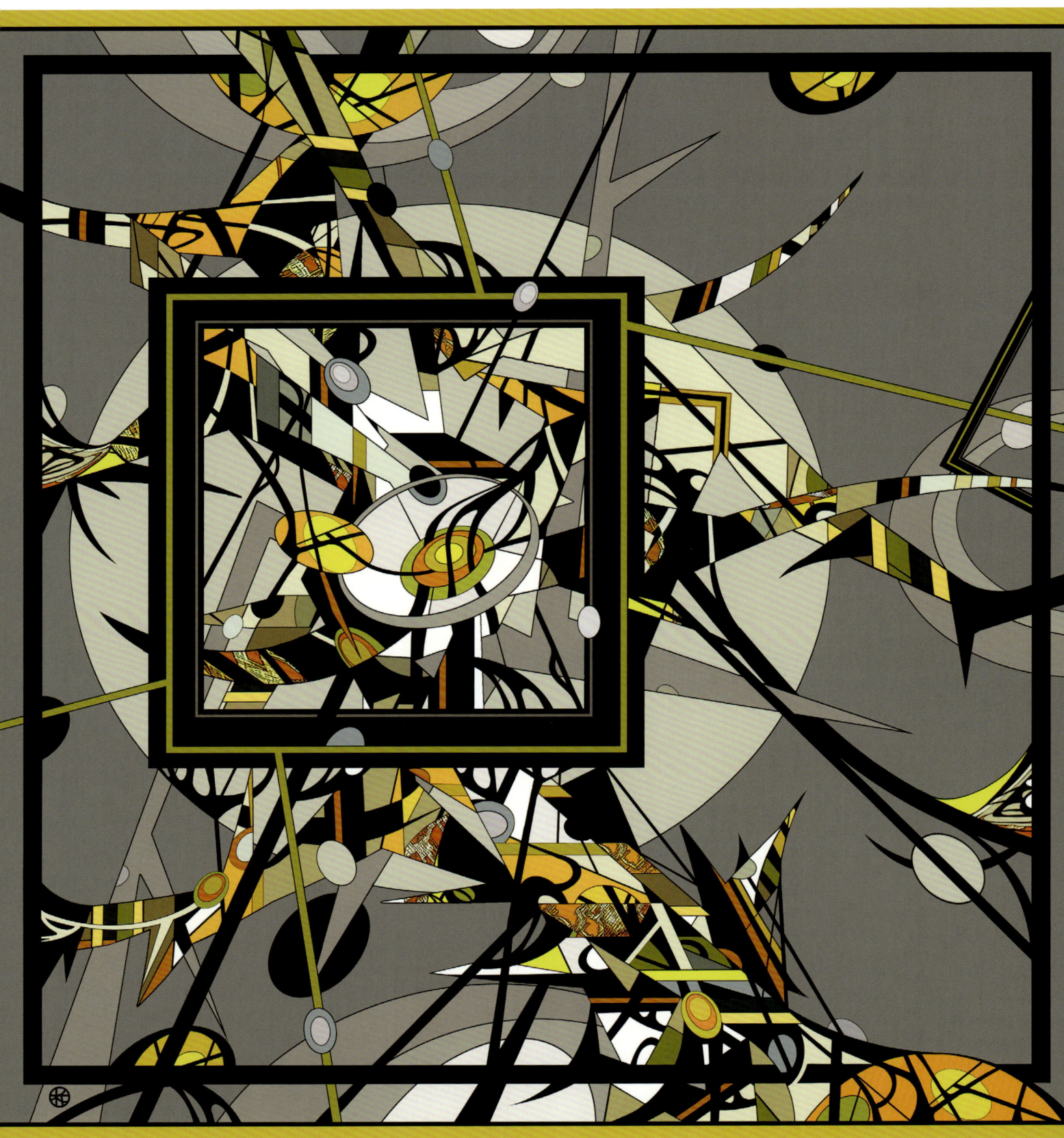

RONALD OWNBEY

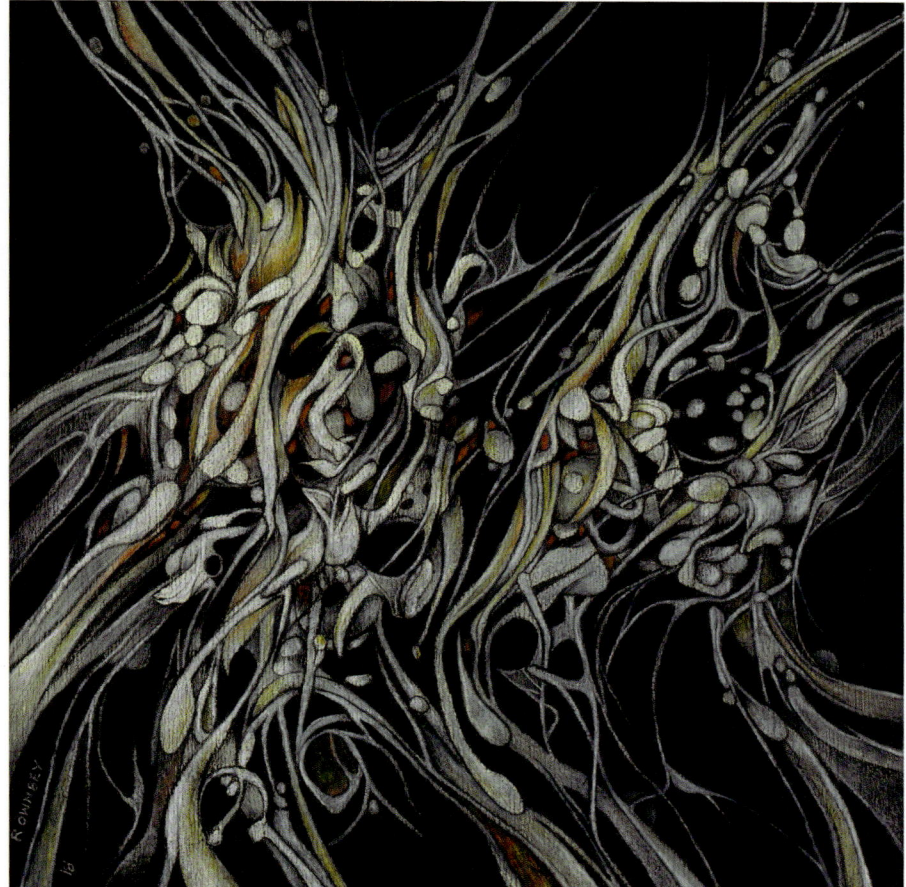

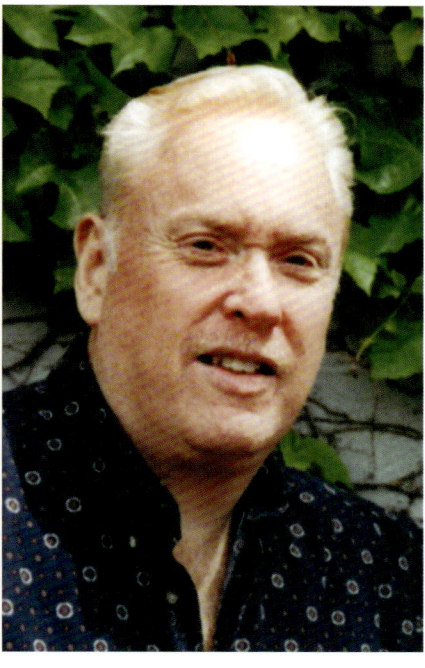

"The ideas formulated in my mind are filtered through my heart after much contemplation and travel through my hand onto the paper or canvas. The process is mysterious, frightening, exciting and introspective all at the same time during the struggle and the moment of creation."

The ideas for my work are very personal reflections and interpretations of my fantasies, emotions and reactions in response to my relationships, my family, and the history and state of the world and the moment in time in which I exist. The chaos, complexity, serenity and vastness of the universe and our world and the great variety of all living things at all visual levels that nature and God have created energize my creative spirit. The tearing apart, discovery and reinterpretation of systems, colors, shapes, space and lines mirror the constant changing thoughts and formations found in my inner soul and the universe.

My work is very biomorphic, plant like, of faces and the inner and outer appearance of the human body and animals, and the microscopic close-up of other living organisms. My work has a strong symbolic and surrealistic tone, monochromatic at times but usually with strong shapes, color and value contrasts. The ideas formulated in my mind are filtered through my heart after much contemplation and travel through my hand onto the paper or canvas. The process is mysterious, frightening, exciting and introspective all at the same time during the struggle and the moment of creation. The final birth of the work is but a small morsel of the inner spirit and the process that allows that to happen is the most important part of the experience.

WWW.RONOWNBEYARTIST.COM

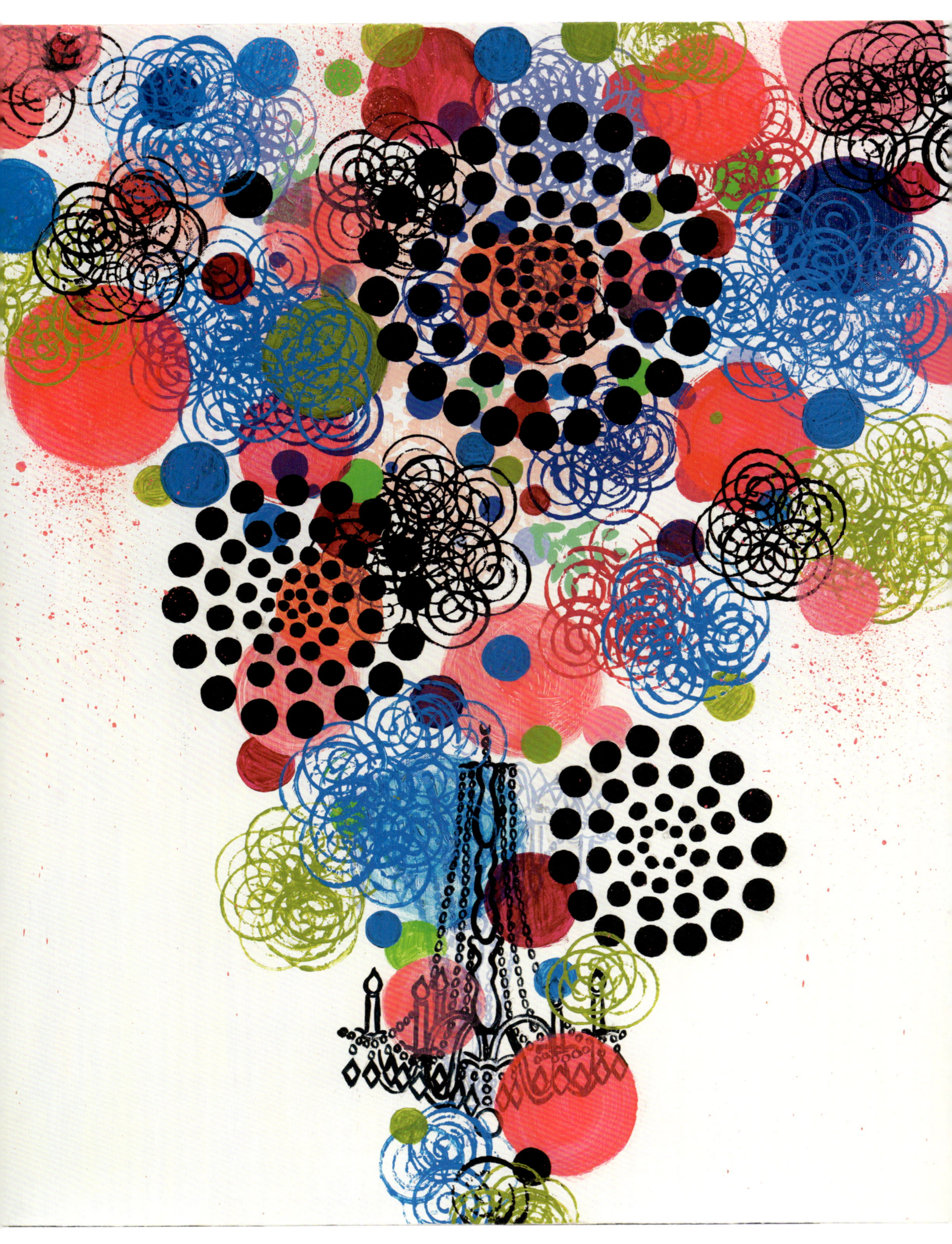

LORRAINE PELTZ

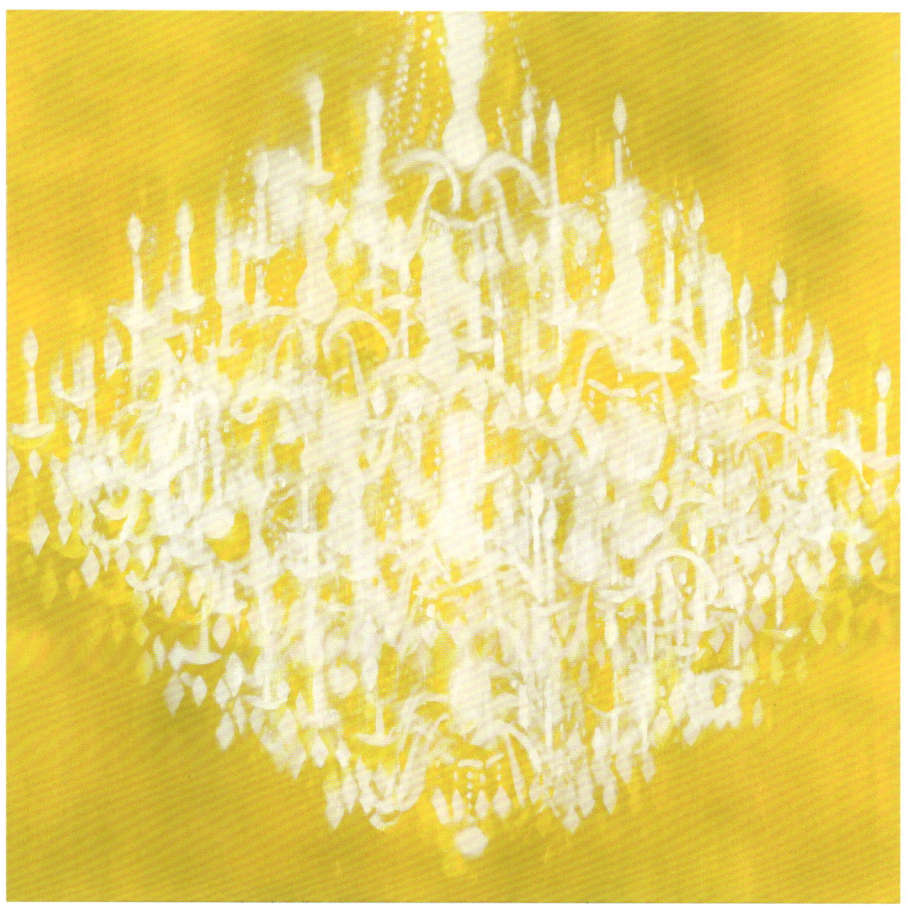

● **(facing page) Playdate**
Oil and acrylic on canvas, 36 x 30 in.

● **Chandelier Yellow**
Oil and acrylic on canvas, 40 x 40 in.

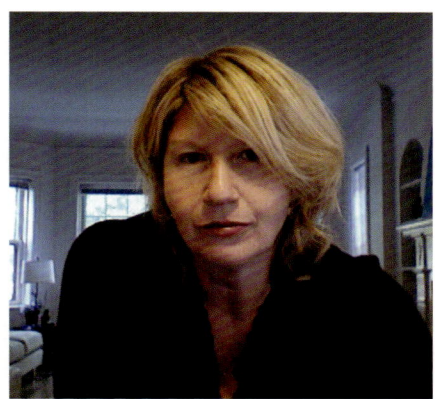

Lorraine Peltz paintings reflect her long held interest in place, identity, and memory. In each work she reimagines the real into images that coalesce into exuberant fields of color resonating with accumulated meanings and an expanse of visual pleasure. Using imagery culled from both personal history and the contemporary moment Peltz incorporates particular remembered images - often from the domestic arena and in this case the chandelier - with a range of provocative painterly events. Her paintings all share a delight in a painted surface rich with nuanced color that comes together to offer viewers an opportunity to situate themselves within the work, and then beyond it to reflect on ideas of home, celebration, and longing.

Peltz's work has been included in numerous solo and group exhibitions nationally and abroad including in Chicago, New York, Miami, Atlanta, Texas, San Francisco, Paris, and Verona, Italy. Her work has been exhibited in various museums, including the Rockford Art Museum, the Herbert Johnson Museum at Cornell University, the Renaissance Society, and the Elmhurst Art Museum. Peltz's work has been reviewed in Art in America, Art Ltd, the Chicago Tribune, the Chicago Sun Times, Flavorpill. com, ArtSlant.com, ArtMoco.com, and more and is included in many private and public collections. Born in Brooklyn, NY, Peltz received her MFA from the University of Chicago and her BFA from the State University of New York at New Paltz. Peltz lives and works in Chicago where she teaches at the School of the Art Institute of Chicago.

WWW.LORRAINEPELTZ.COM

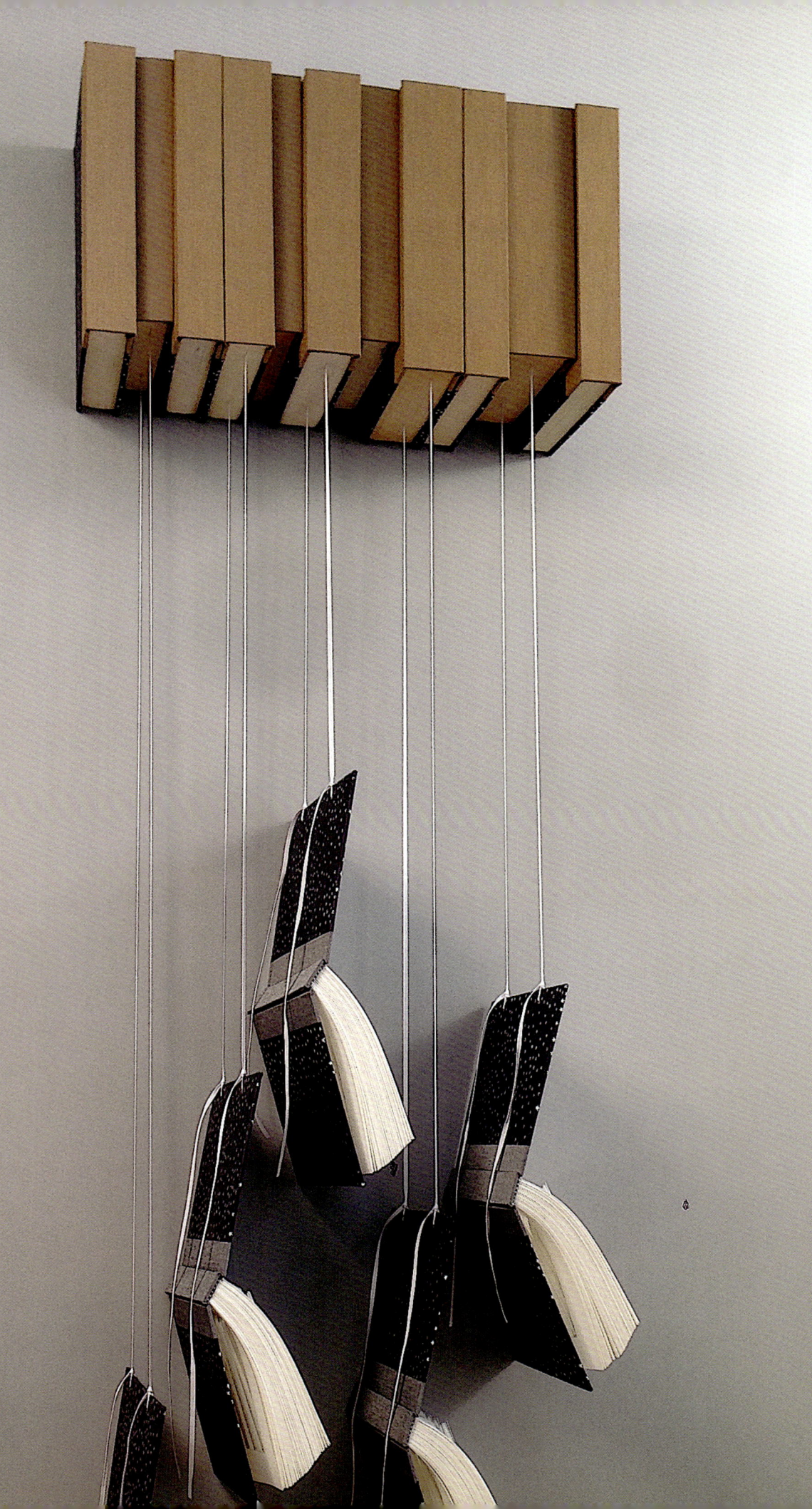

CHRIS PERRY

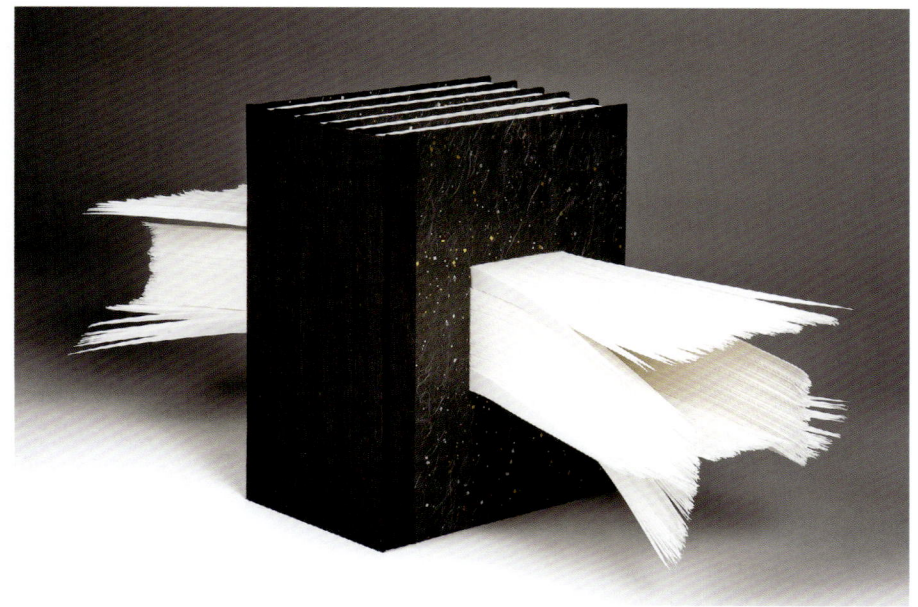

"Boundaries will be broached and rules will be broken. Don't tell me I cannot do something because you will only inspire me to try my hardest to do just that."

After graduating from Maryland Institute College of Art, Chris moved to New York to begin work at the Guggenheim Museum and later as an assistant for a sculptor. He, like many of his friends, entered the construction industry in order to secure a more steady income, eventually owning his own architectural woodworking business which he closed in 2007 to pursue makng art full-time again.

Chris taught himself book binding out of a need to present a completed work to a potential publisher as an example of exactly how he expected a finished project to work and look. The process of bookmaking soon took over the painting that he had been trained for and now all of his studio time is spent making increasingly large and complex sculptures composed of both his hand-made books and altered books he collects from the local libraries recycle bins.

He has work in the permanent collection at Yale University Gallery of Art as well as several other public collections, and continues to show around the country in paper and book art shows.

He currenty resides in Ridgefield, Ct.

WWW.CSPERRY.NET

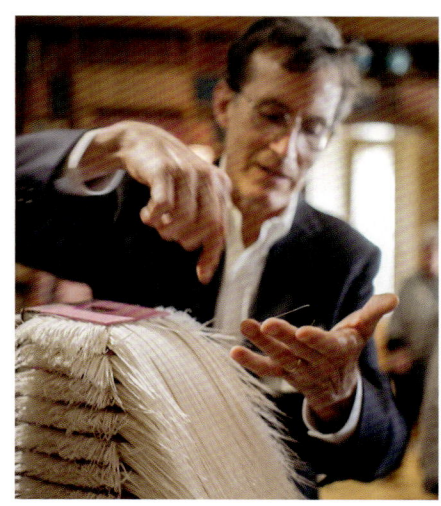

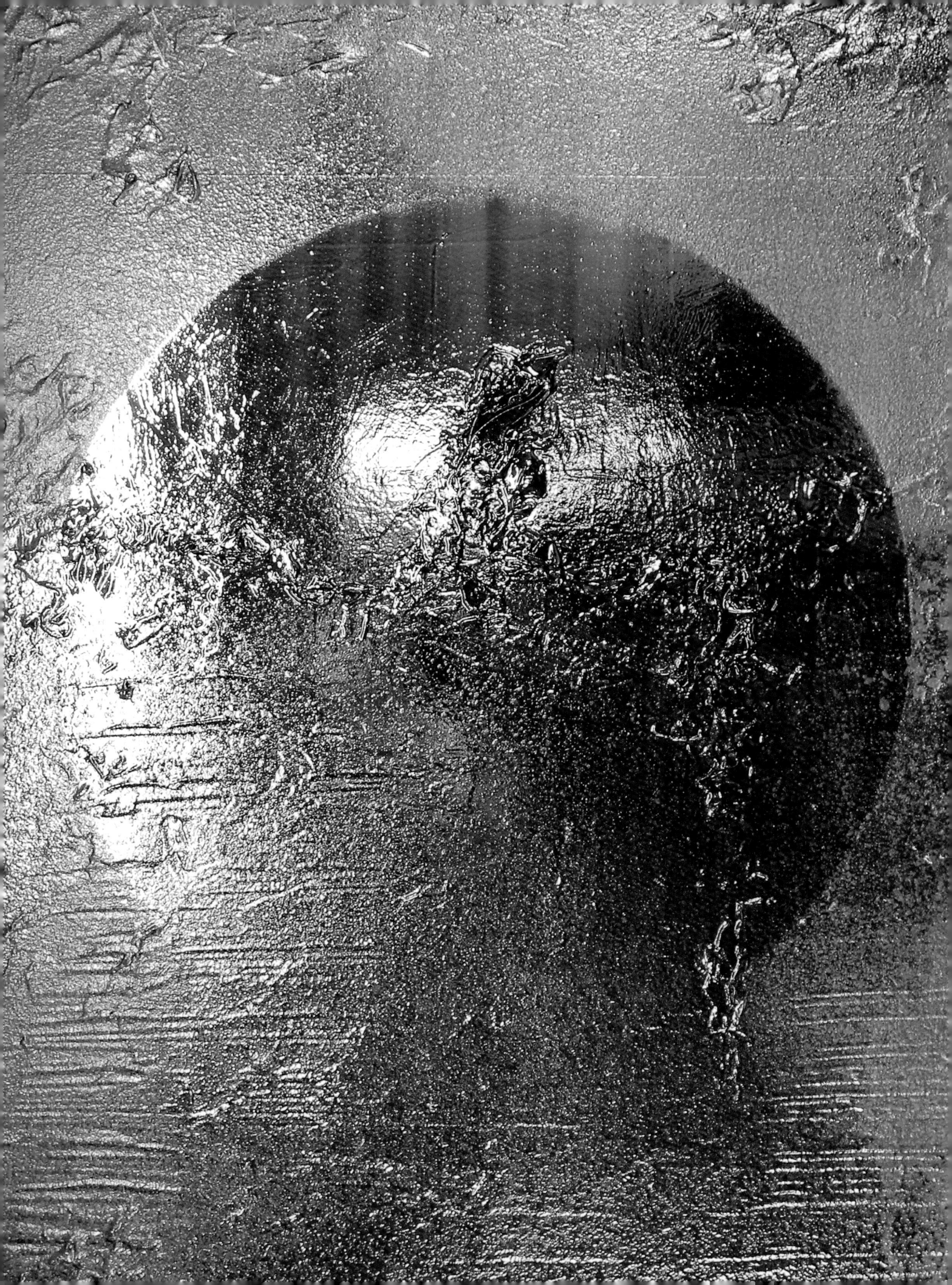

WALTER POOLE

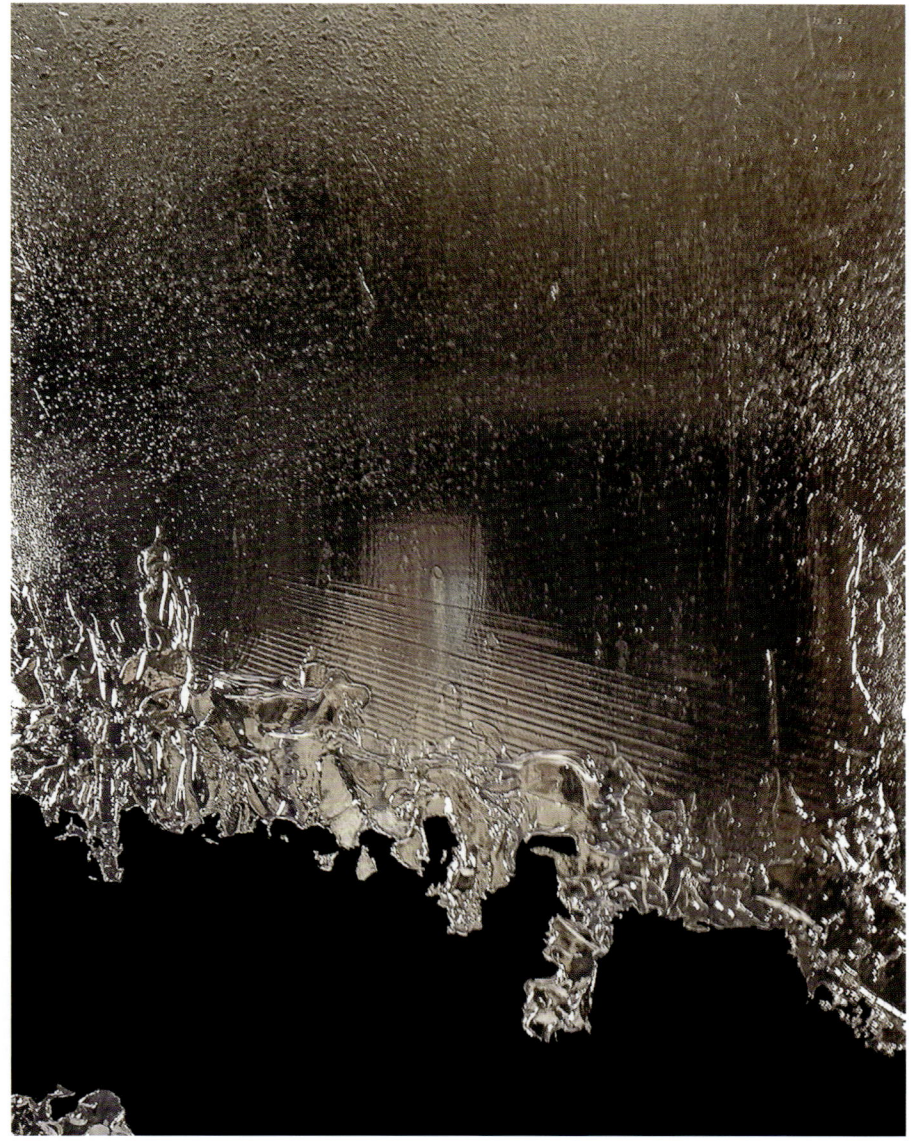

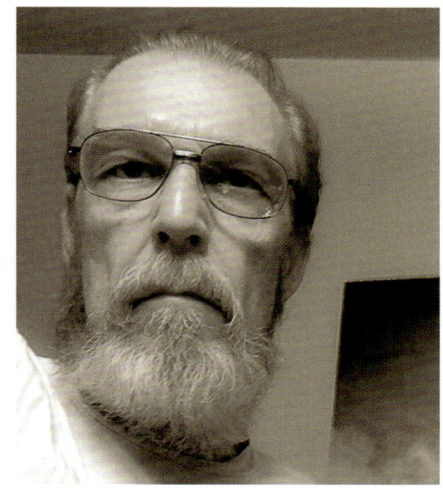

● **(facing page) Celestial 4**
  Silver deposit on panel, 30 x 40 in., 2017

● **Antamina**
  Silver deposit on panel, 30 x 40 in., 2017

Walter Poole is a disabled war veteran who earned an MFA while recovering from injuries that left him in a wheelchair for several years. He works in a unique medium: silver nitrate deposit with translucent polymer coatings on textured surfaces. The result is an iridescent, highly reflective environment that is constantly changing with manipulated light and thus interacting with the viewer. After witnessing the brutality of war, Walter needed change. He left California to live in the solitude of rural Alabama. He also abandoned his realism-based artistic style for non-representational abstraction. Now his only desire is to celebrate life with elegance and beauty as displayed by his latest series - *Celestial*. He spent a short time teaching while exhibiting in national venues. His works have received awards and been featured in publications. Walter has paintings in the permanent collection of the State of Alabama that are on display in the Capitol Building.

WWW.WALTERPOOLE.NET

LINDSEY PRICE

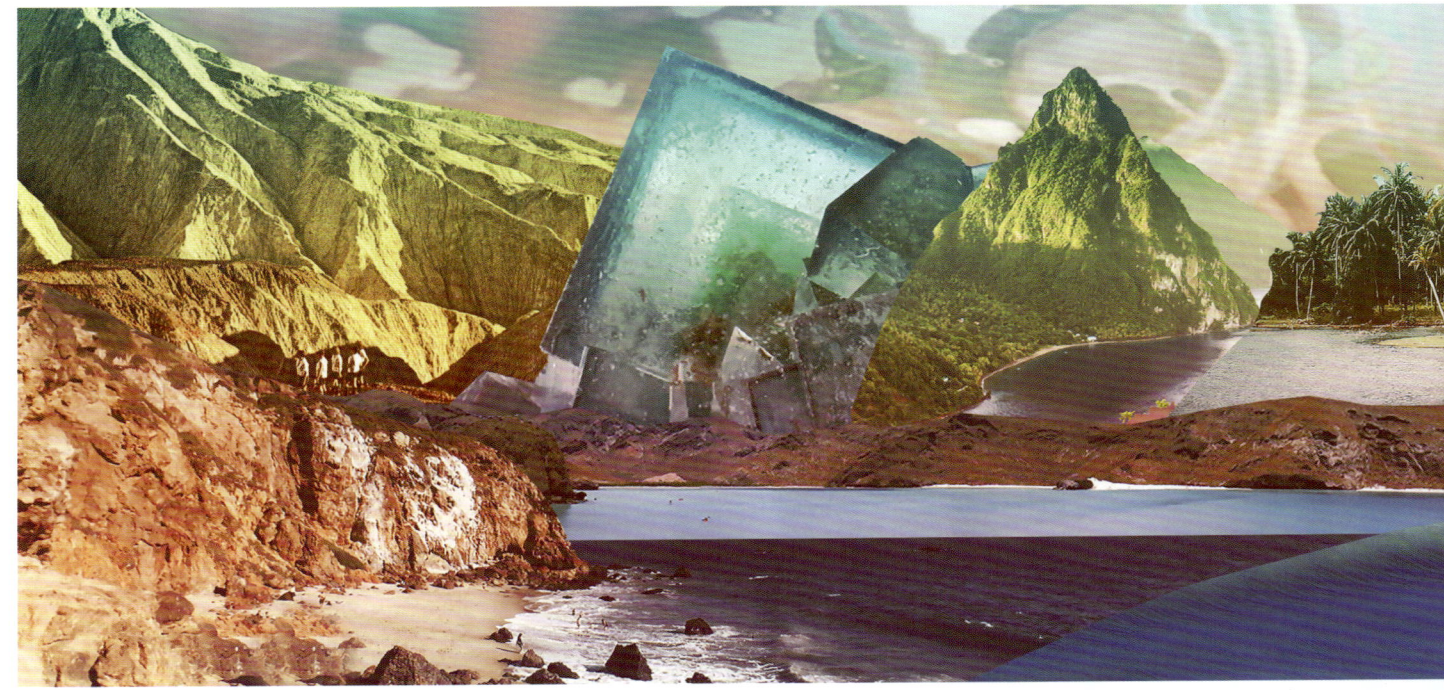

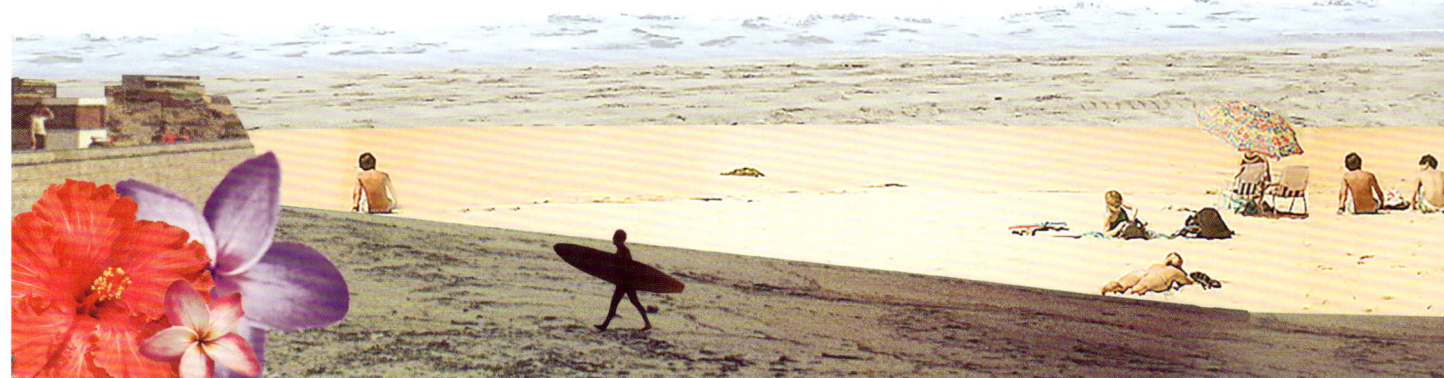

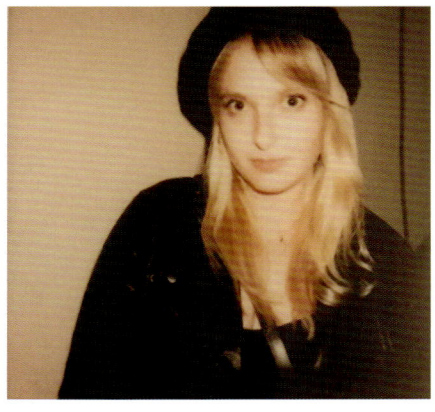

Lindsey Price is an artist, photographer, designer, and editor living and working in Los Angeles. She received her BFA in Photography and Digital Media from California Institute of the Arts. A freelance photographer, Price concentrates on collage, graphic design, and album covers. She has sold both nationally and internationally, is published in several issues of "Pacific Dissent" Magazine, as well as "Nailed" Magazine, and has been included in the several group exhibitions such as, "Where the Magic Happens", "Electron Salon", and "Beyond the Lines Art Show" in Los Angeles. Price is also a member of the Los Angeles Art Association.

WWW.LINDSEYPRICESTUDIO.COM

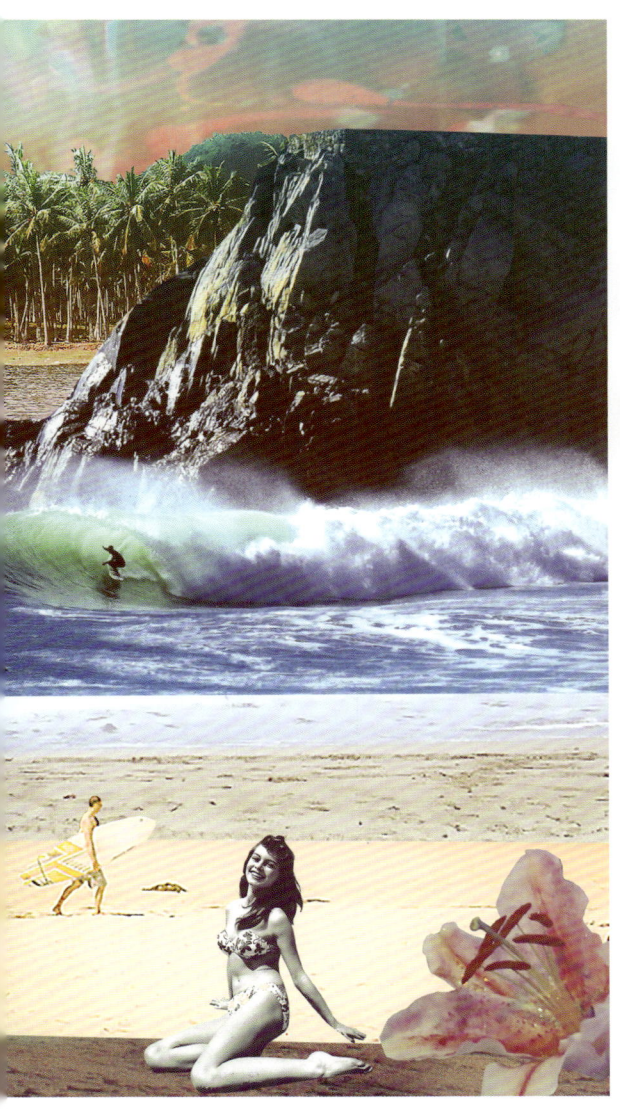

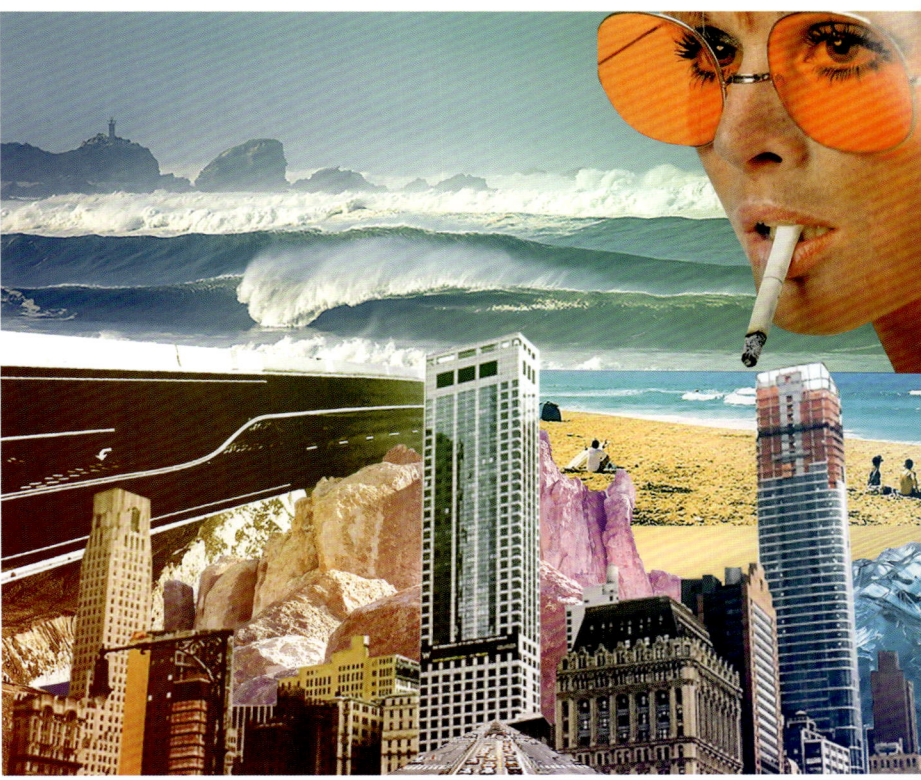

● **(left) New Beginnings**
Collage, 48 x 24 in., 2015

● **NY to LA**
Collage, 40 x 40 in., 2016

"I create psychedelic photomontages that represent a dream- like dimension of our universe... Each piece features different moods and energies that reflect my innermost desires, fantasies and dreams around the globe."

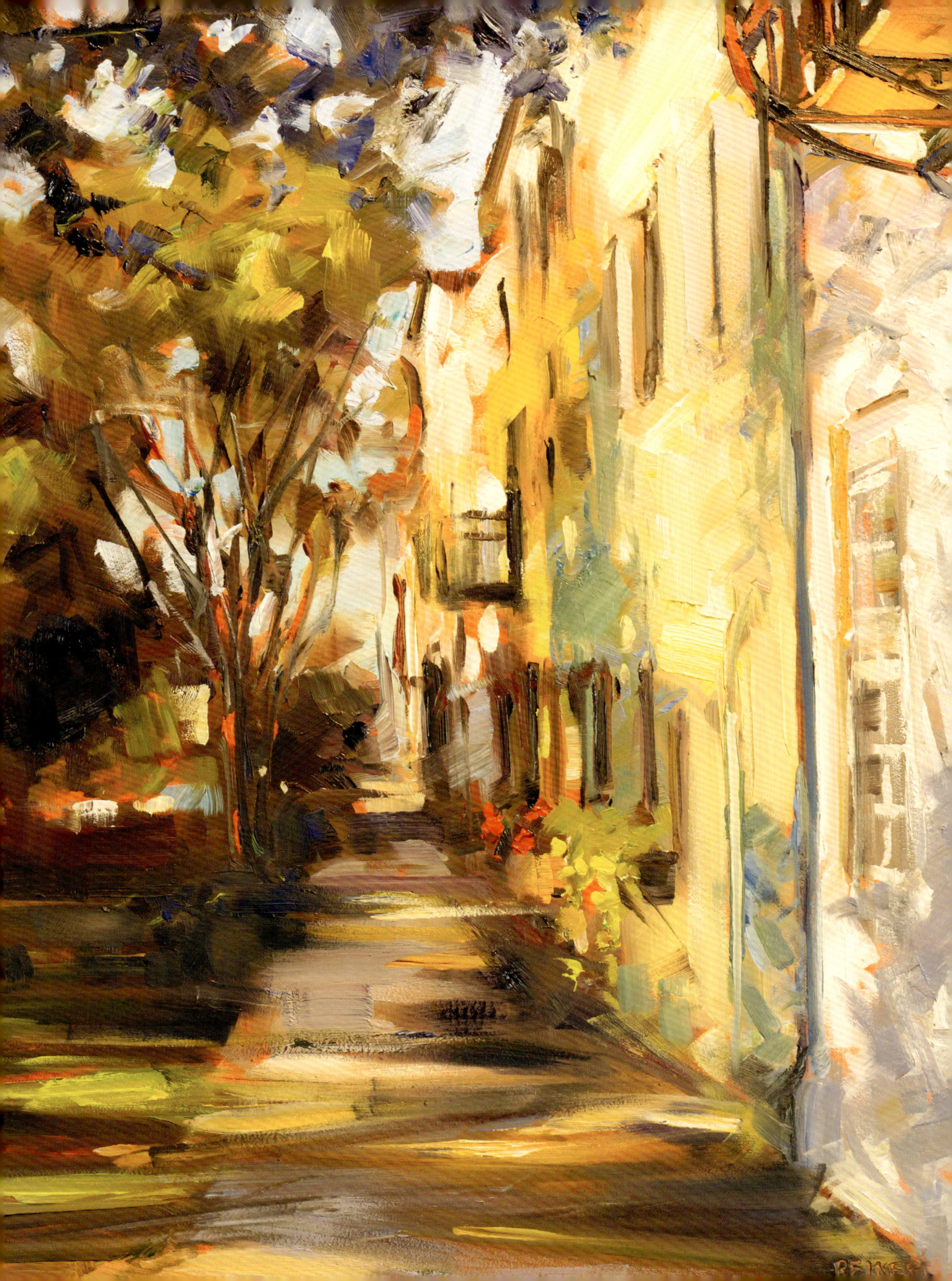

RICK REINERT

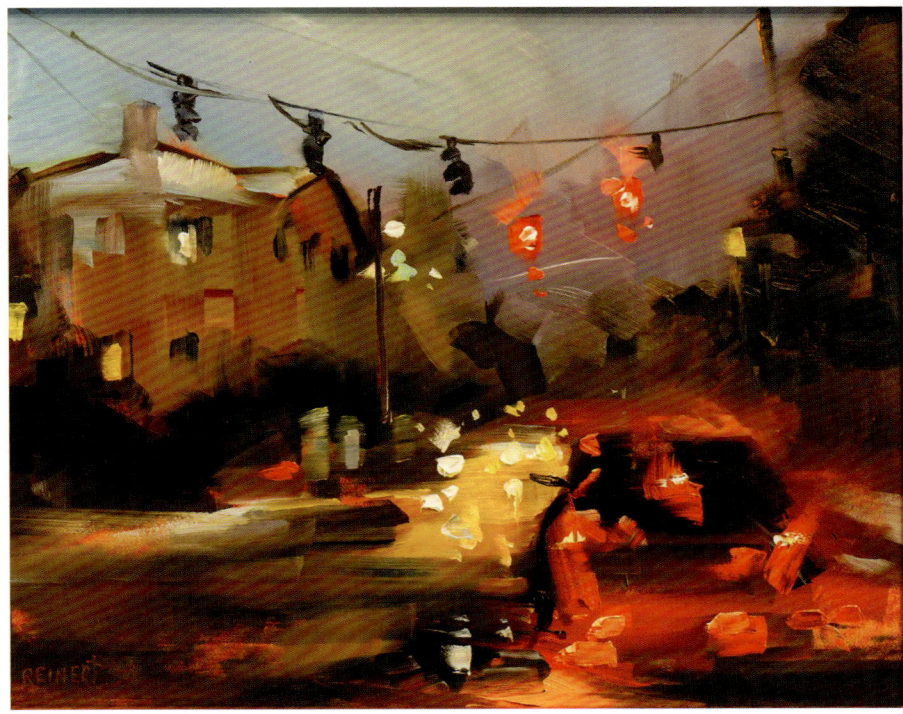

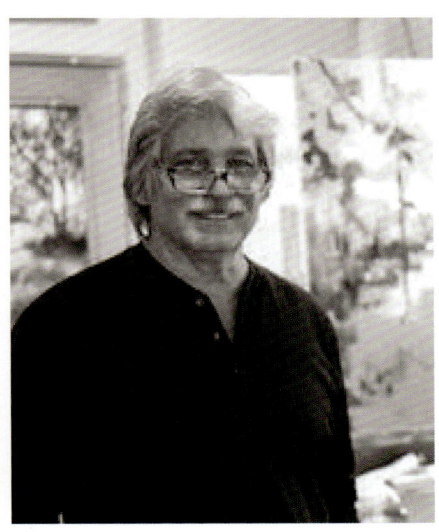

● **(facing page) Charleston Sunlight**
20 x 16 in., oil on panel

● **Downpour**
11 x 14 in., oil on panel

"Every effort is made push the boundaries with painting in color combination, technique and composition; his bold, dramatic style has become recognizable as his own and retains a common denominator of passion."

Painting has become much more than a passion but a compulsion and consumes most of each day. Every effort is made push the boundaries with painting in color combination, technique and composition; his bold, dramatic style has become recognizable as his own and retains a common denominator of passion.

His formal art education was in the 70's at Western Kentucky University and continued in the Army in Europe leading to one-man shows in both Europe and Canada. Her has won numerous awards during his career and has exhibited with fine galleries throughout the United States.

Reinert's private collectors' number in the thousands and his work hangs in the United States, Canada, Europe and the Middle East in both private, corporate and museum collections. His work has appeared in numerous art publications throughout the years and he continues to gain notoriety on a daily basis.

Reinert Fine Art with 2 locations in Charleston, SC and 1 in Blowing Rock, NC was founded a number of years ago with his wife Ann and represents not only Reinert's work, but the work of sixty of the finest painters and twelve superb sculptors working today. The galleries are well known for the quality and depth of work represented. The main location at 179 King Street in Charleston exhibits work on 2 floors and a magical sculpture garden where paintings are displayed daily in an outdoor setting.

WWW.RICKREINERT.COM

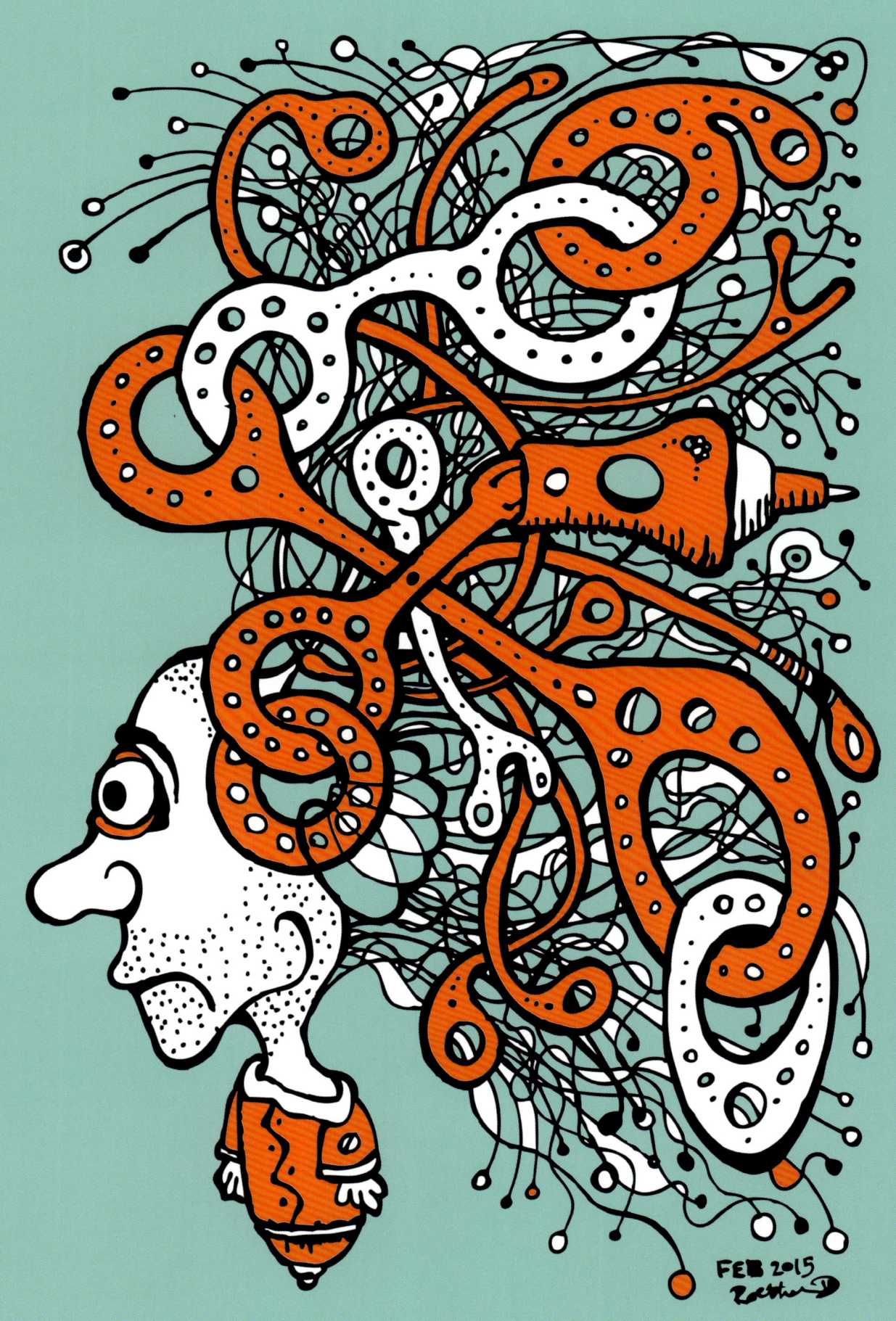

FEB 2015

RALPH ROETHER

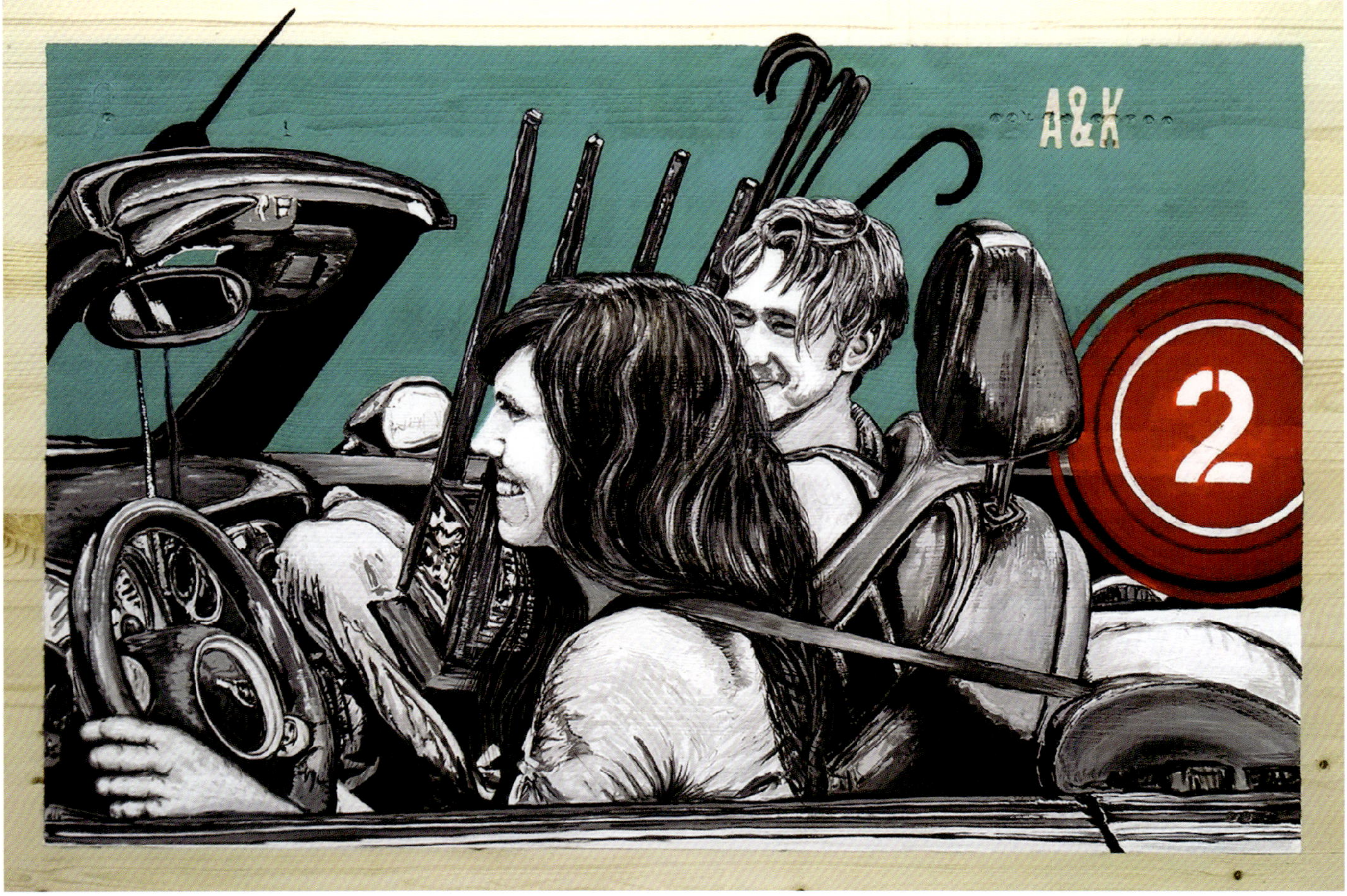

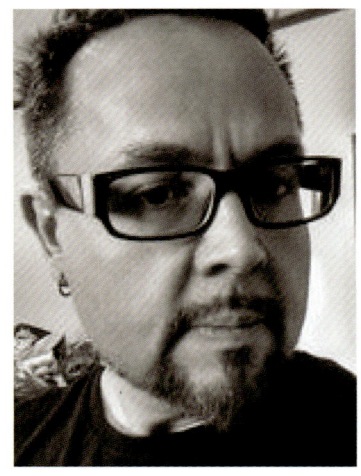

● (facing page) **Big Brains**
digital print (original drawing in ink), 16 x 20 in., 2018

● **Al and Kayla**
acrylic on wood (commissioned piece), 36 x 24 in., 2015

As a professional graphic designer for twenty-four years, I often infuse my graphic design sensibilities into my artwork and illustrations. I prefer painting on various types of wood instead of the traditional canvas. My style ranges from semi-realistic portraits with typography to cartoon, doodle, graffiti-esque creations. I often resort to creating stream-of-conscience doodle drawings on any piece of paper or bar napkin I can find. I then scan these doodles into my computer, colorize them, and make prints on paper, canvas, or shirts. I was invited to paint murals at a local skate park and participated in various art shows; including Dirty Show/ Dirty Detroit, a Solo Show at Indigo Art Gallery, and Boneyard Arts Festival in Champaign, IL. My artwork has been published in Studio Visit Magazine, Art Voices Magazine, and the Artist book 101 Artist curated by Terrence Sanders. One of my pieces was used in a living room scene for the feature film X-Men: Days of Future Past. I doodle, draw, paint,and create work that turns me on. It's the only way to go.

WWW.RALPHROETHER.COM

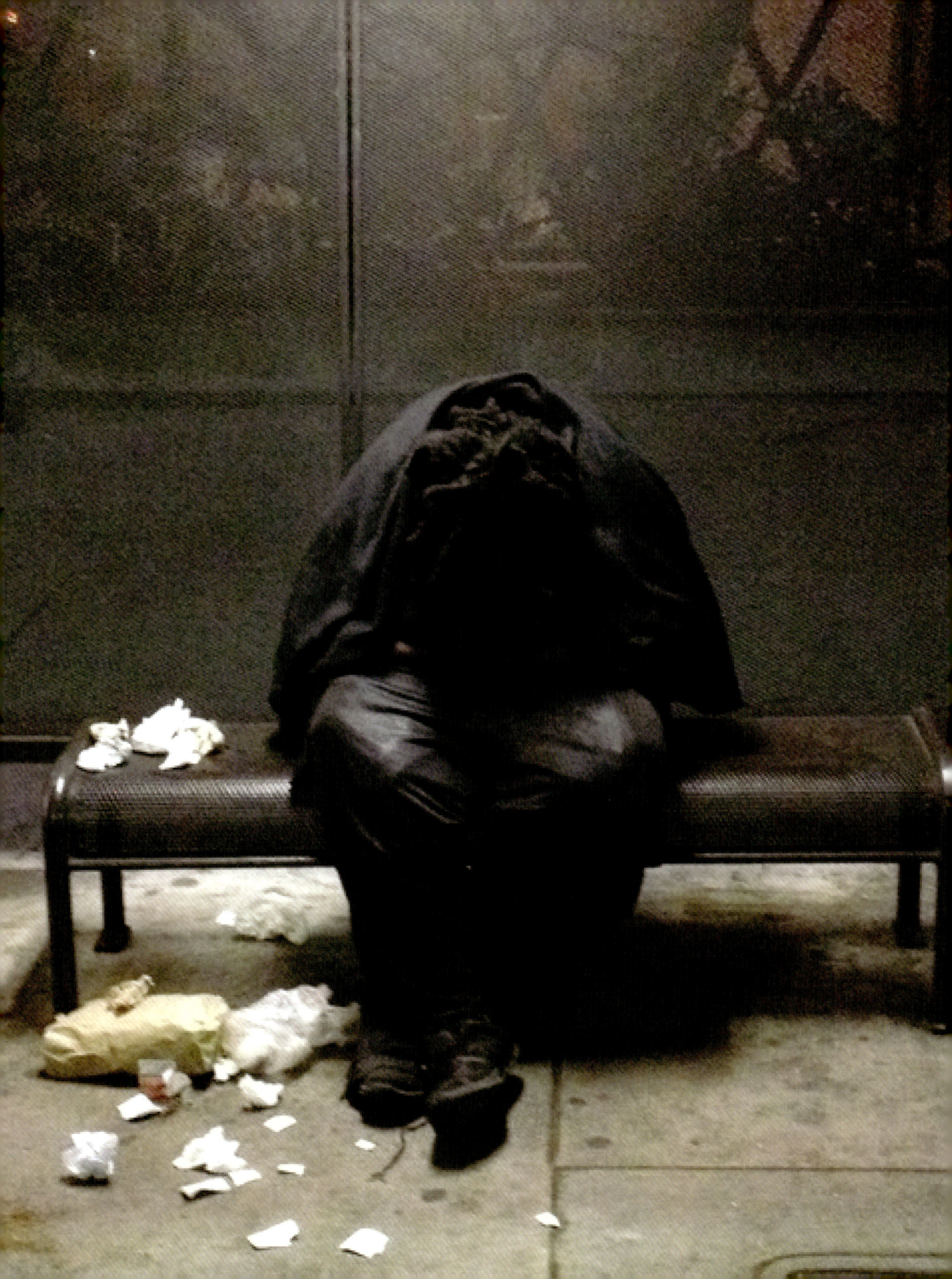

TERRENCE SANDERS

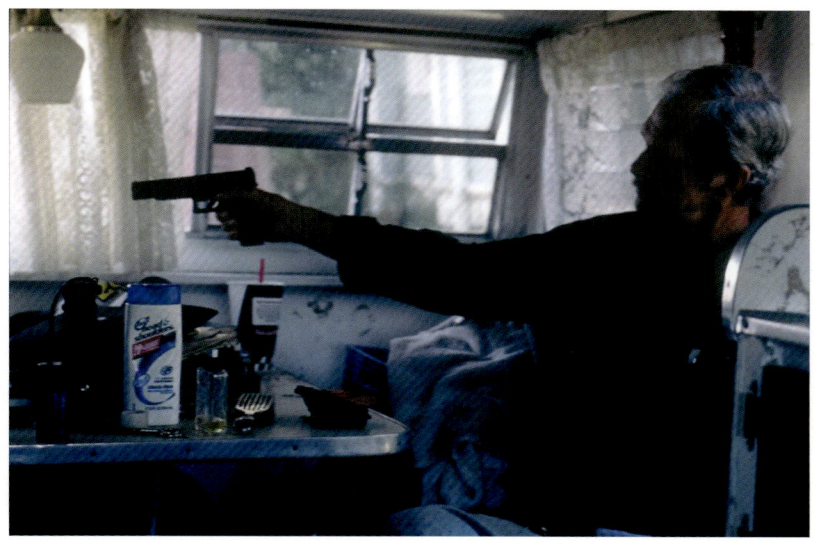

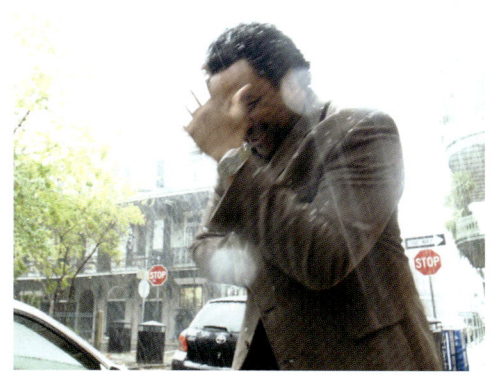

My mother told me when I was three months old, my biological father attempted to suffocate me while she was out shopping. She left him and relocated to NYC, where she re-married a Marine who had just completed a tour of duty in Vietnam. I was raised in tenements and housing projects on Manhattan's Lower East Side. I was exposed to asbestos and lead poisoning. I was categorized as a "have not," I attended Head Start, I hated school, I was sent to schools that taught me just enough. My neighbors were Chinese, Jews, Italians, Hispanics; I was physically abused by my step-father until I was 16 years old, when I ran away from home. I slept in 24-hour movie theaters on 42nd street, park benches on the FDR drive, rooftops of housing projects, and trains. I was exposed to petty criminal elements during my informative years. I was lost, I had no skills to survive in a capitalist regime; my role models were actors, athletes and Jesus. I was called a nigger; I watched MTV 24 hours a day. My stepfather kept pornography and sex tools in the house, I witnessed my stepfather physically and mentally abuse my mother. I wanted to kill him; I didn't love myself. I played basketball but I knew I wasn't going pro, so I sold drugs. I started gaining weight. I went to church on Sundays but I lost my faith in God daily; my step father smoked crack, my biological father never attempted to contact me, my parents didn't tell me about my biological father until I was 18. I wanted to be a priest, I wanted to be rich and famous, I lived to want. I dropped out of high school in the 10th grade. I went to jail for a week for larceny.

I served celebrities at nightclubs, and I met Jean Michel Basquiat when I was 16. I joined the Army at 18 because drug dealers were attempting to kill me; I started smoking marijuana, drinking alcohol and snorting cocaine—but I became best friends with Alexander Venet, the son of Conceptual Artist Benar Venet, when I was 21. I was exposed to the blueprint and philosophy of contemporary art. I was a lead singer of Kingstone a 90's East Village band. I slept with one eye open. I got married and had a son. I stole my ex-mother-in-law's camera and began documenting my surroundings; I sat in on classes at Parsons School of Design in Los Angeles. I was becoming my stepfather so I got a divorce. I had made so many mistakes but I wanted to change my life because it seemed I was running in circles.

I forgave my mother for not leaving my stepfather; I wanted my son to respect me. I raised money for homeless families, I went to the public library everyday from opening to closing and read every art book they had on the shelves and what I couldn't find I found on the Internet. I traveled and visited galleries and museums all over the world. I began to express myself through photography, painting, mixed media, poetry, film and stage plays. (I'm a quick learner—as a teenager I taught myself to play chess by watching the men in Washington Square Park.)

In retrospect, I never gave up on myself, I didn't want to be a slave or live in fear any longer. I didn't want to walk amongst the walking dead. I am an Artist and my son Lucien Smith attended The Cooper Union and now is known Worldwide as noted artist. Art and Art alone saved my life; it completes me. It is my therapy, my weapon of choice; it helps me to cope with the day-to-day struggles of being a human being. My contribution to humanity will be my art, my voice, and in this is the reason I am alive.

WWW.TERRENCESANDERS.COM

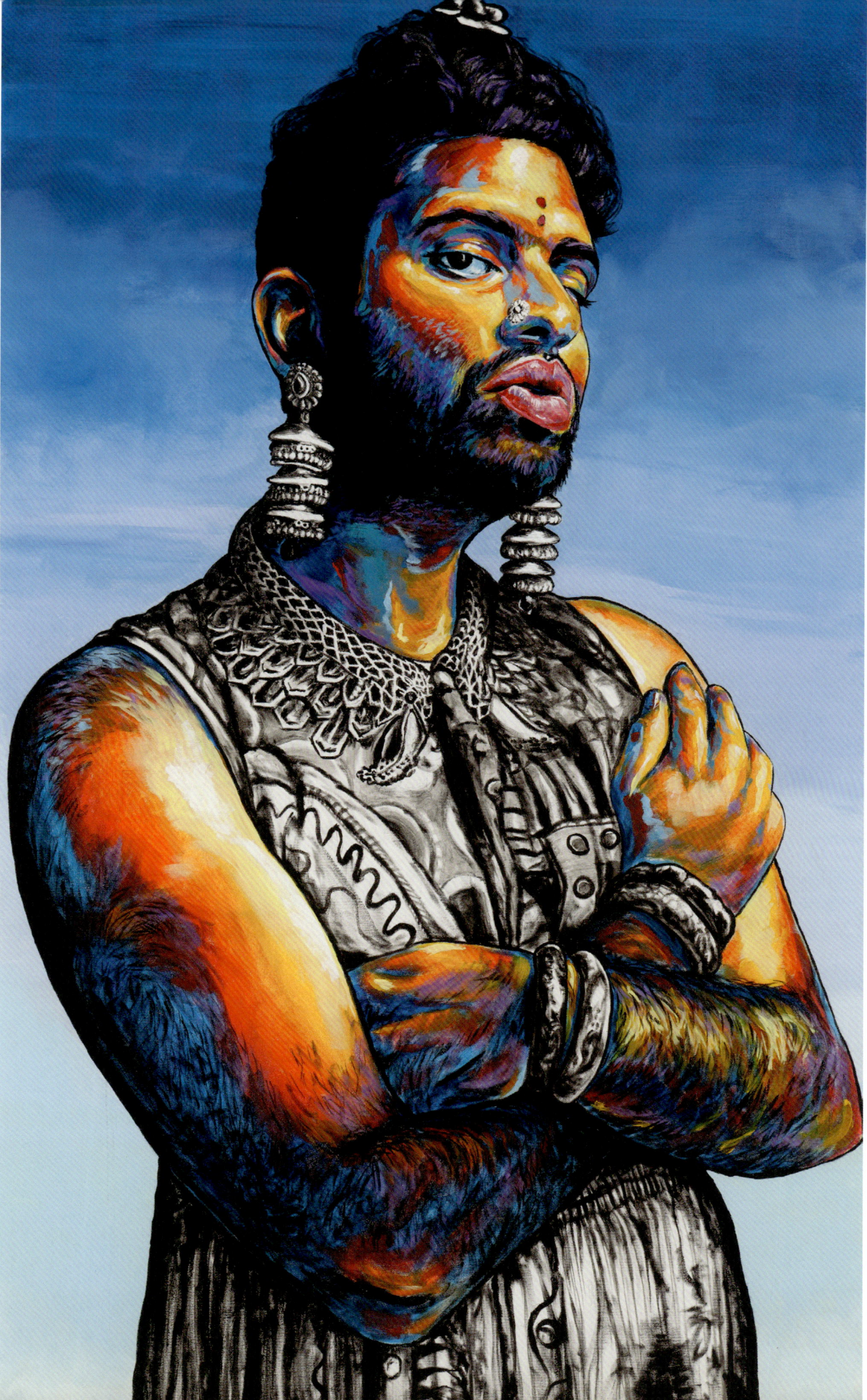

RAE SENARIGHI

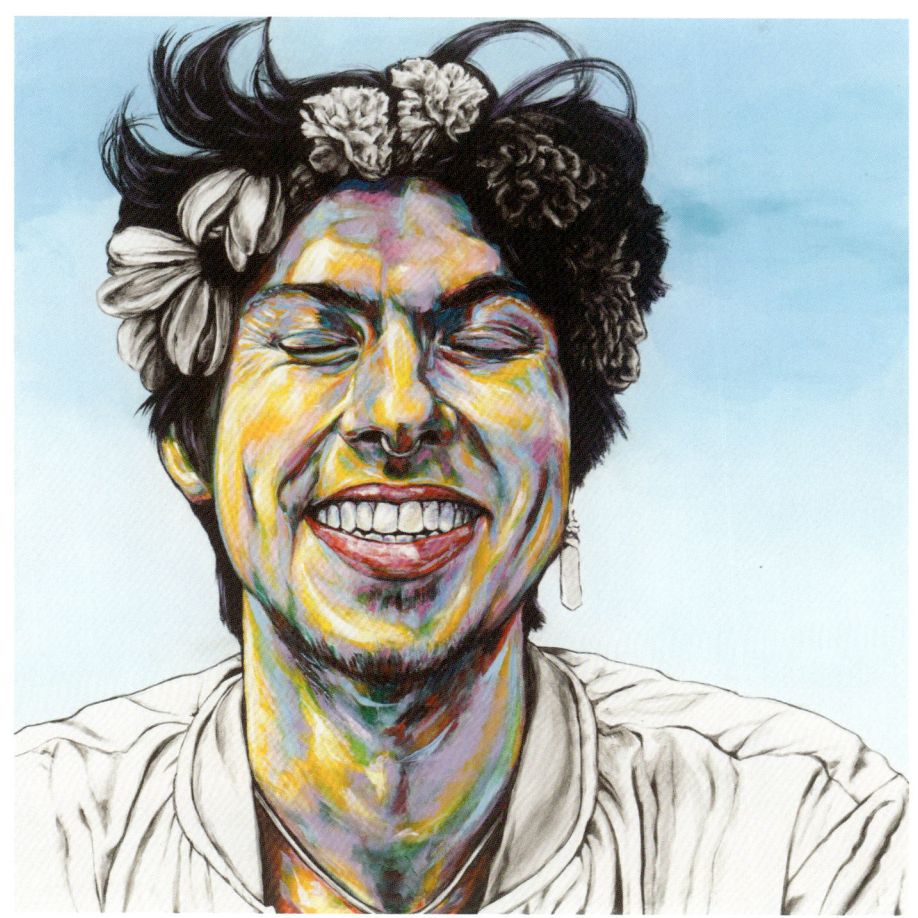

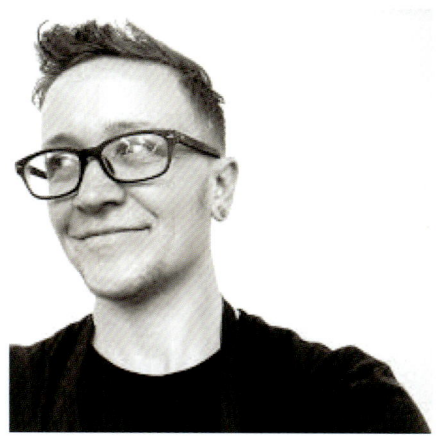

Transgender is not just about one experience, not linear and not simple. Each transgender person is unique with incredibly diverse experiences yet we are united in a common struggle. Portraits in this series depict individuals throughout the world, living their lives out in the open, choosing integrity over safety. The artist deliberately uses only vibrant rainbow colors deliberately chosen to take pride in our intersectional identities uniting us in celebration and paints all clothing in gray-scale using simple black paint on white canvas. Choosing gray-scale (especially in the cases of many fashion trailblazers) helps to not distract from their vibrant humanity while carefully respecting their style. This series is a direct response to the oppression experienced by transgender people as they reclaim space, both literally in larger than life portraits and figuratively under a vast blue sky. May joy, power, and blue skies be a reality for transgender and gender non-conforming community everywhere.

Rae Senarighi (b. 1979) is best known for vivid colorful abstracts, intricate typography, and bold transfixing portraits of modern icons. After studying fine art at the University of Montana (2000,2004), Rae finished his BFA degree at the Art Institute of Seattle in 2009. Rae's detailed, thoughtful works are influenced by nearly a decade of scientific illustration, studying the natural world in micro and macro. After facing cancer in 2015, Rae refocused energy into creating fine art. Rae is a transgender non-binary artist currently living and working in Portland, Oregon.

WWW.TRANSPAINTER.COM

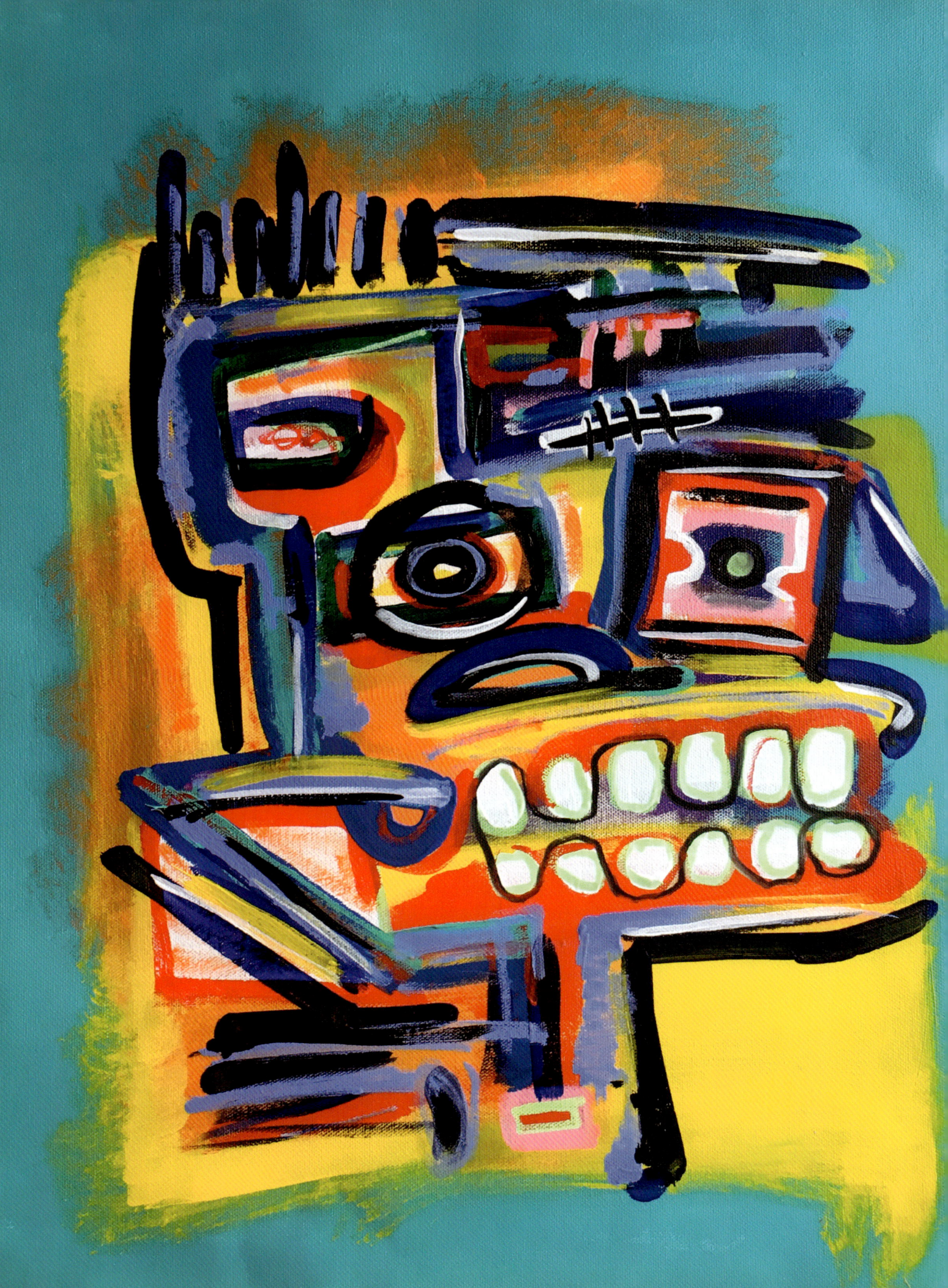

TODD SERLIN

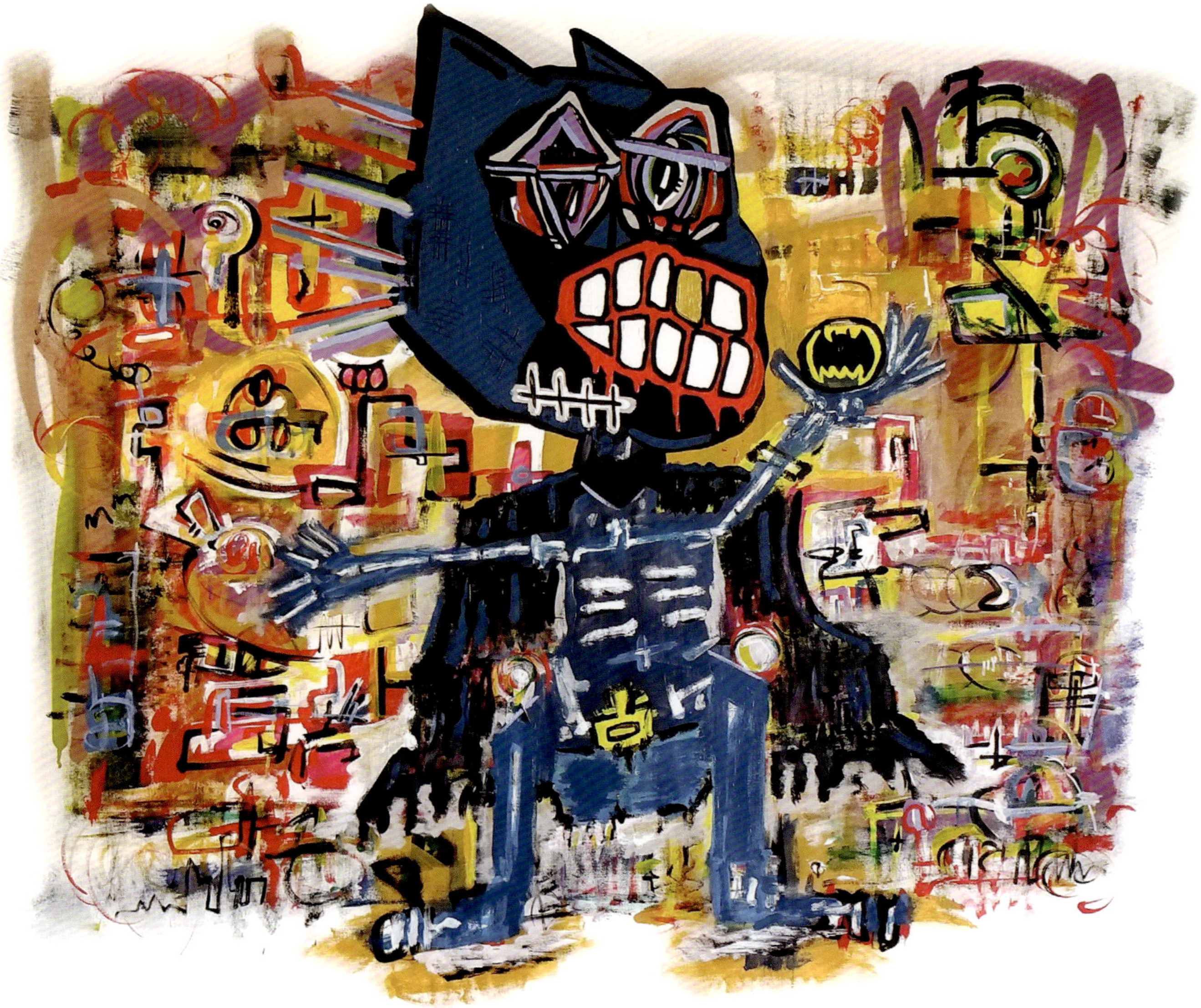

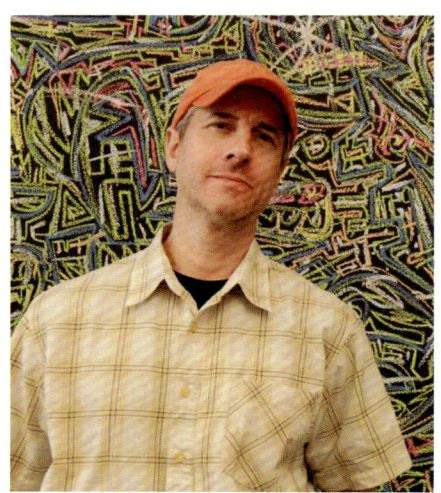

A childhood fascination with monsters and myths evolved into the body of enigmatic faces and primitive subjects featured in Todd Serlin's current work. Often presented alongside elements of danger and turmoil, his toothy characters exhibit unique personalities, underlying tension, and colorful boldness. Serlin's art often projects a false sense of youthful simplicity that, upon closer look, reveals facets of self-perception and a critical worldview. Whether in the more recent series of close-ups or his full figurative characters, Serlin's paintings and drawings suggest that our experiences can be distilled into a momentary figment, bound by real consequence.

Todd Serlin is a contemporary artist who lives and works in Los Angeles and Palm Springs.

WWW.SERLINART.COM

● **(facing page) Untitled Acrylic Head**
Spraypaint, charcoal and acrylic on canvas, 20 x 16 in, 2017

● **Crime Fighter**
Spray paint, graphite, charcoal and acrylic on canvas, 48in x 60in, 2017

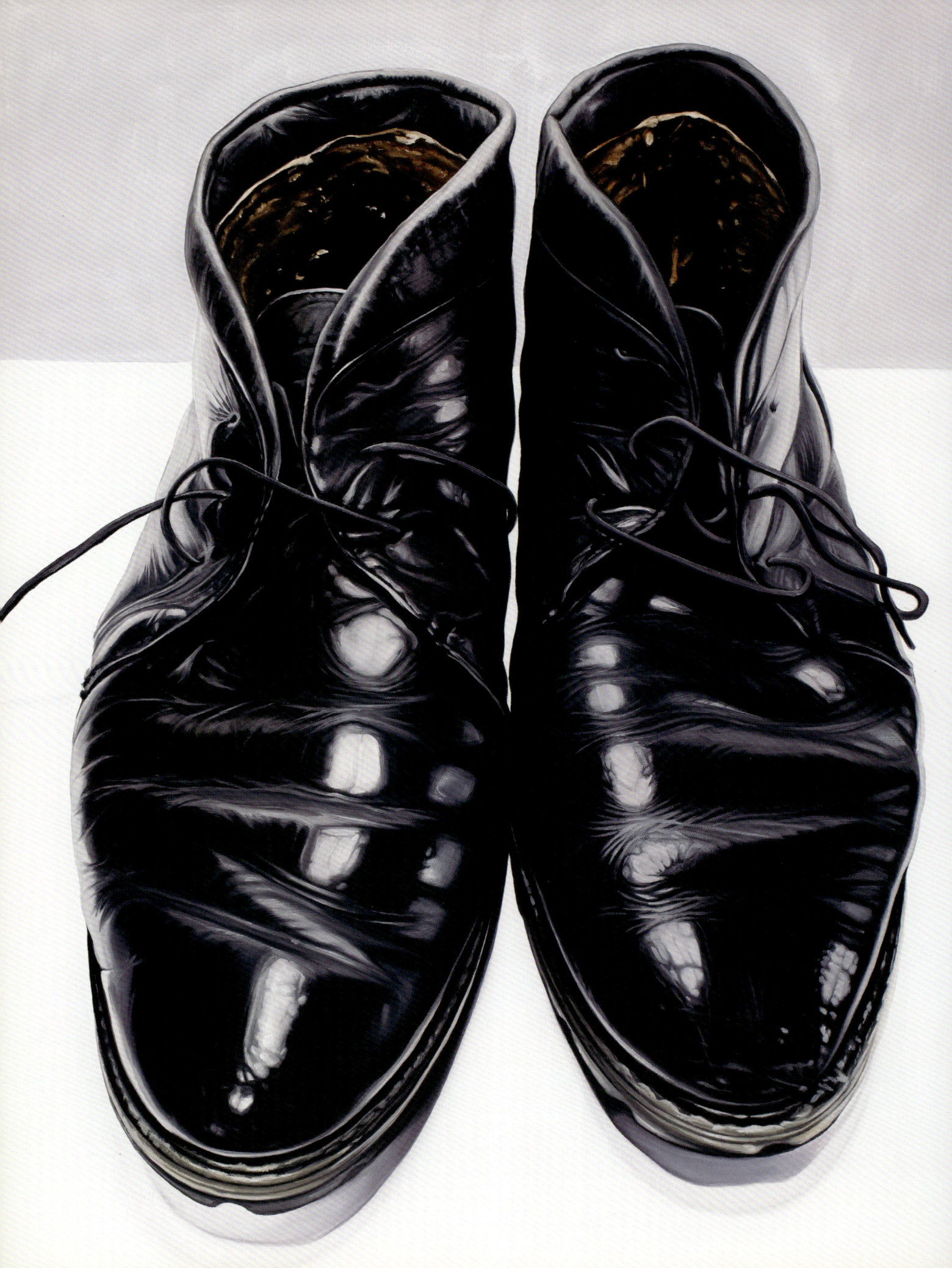

KELLY JO SHOWS

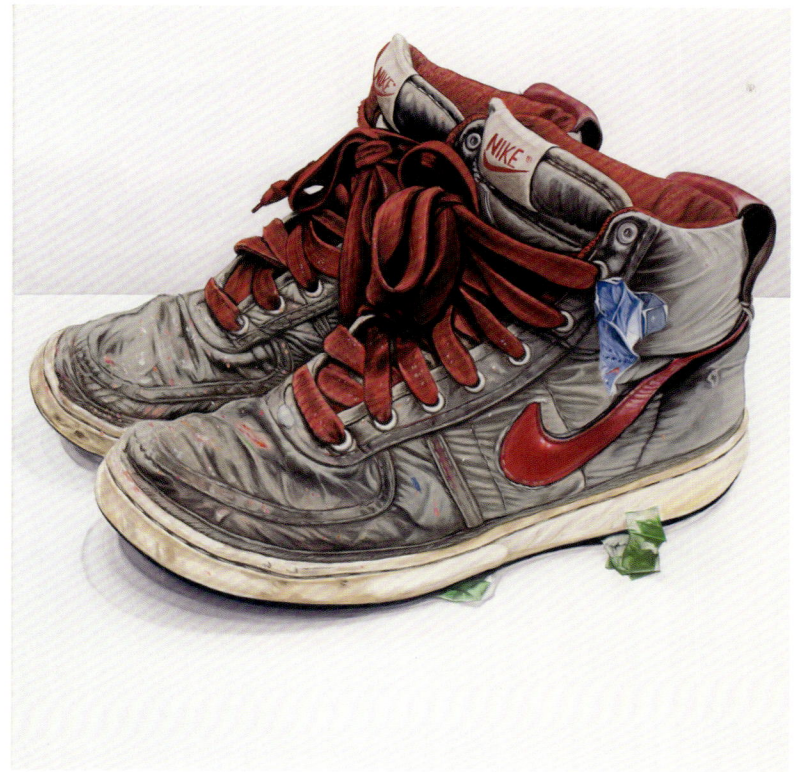

● **(facing page) Ed Ruscha**
Oil on museum canvas, 30 x 40 x 1.5 in., 2014

● **The Sucklord**
Oil on mseum canvas, 24 x 24 x 1.5 in., 2014

"I have worked on this series for over 6 years. Shoes speak volumes about who we are. After time they develop a character all their own."

This series is about paying homage to a variety of contemporary artists worldwide and being able to connect with them personally. Creating art is my greatest purpose, yet it can become isolating. This series gives me the opportunity to connect with other artists all over the world. To date I have painted over 100 shoe portraits of both world renowned and obscure artists, including: Jamie Wyeth, John Baldessari, Ed Ruscha, Jenny Holzer and the list keeps growing.

I personally contacted artists and asked them to send the pair of shoes that best represents them. The number of positive responses that I've received so far pleasantly surprises me. Most of the shoes

are sent back to the artist but many of them have allowed me to keep them. I now have a wire in my studio with over 50 pairs of shoes strung above my easel. The growing number of correspondence, ephemera and photos that I've collected has become an additional point of interest. Every day I look forward to going to the mailbox to see who has responded. I plan on putting together a book chronicling the portraits, correspondence and contributing artists as a way for people to discover these great artists on their own. I plan on developing this series the rest of my life.

WWW.FEARNOART.NET

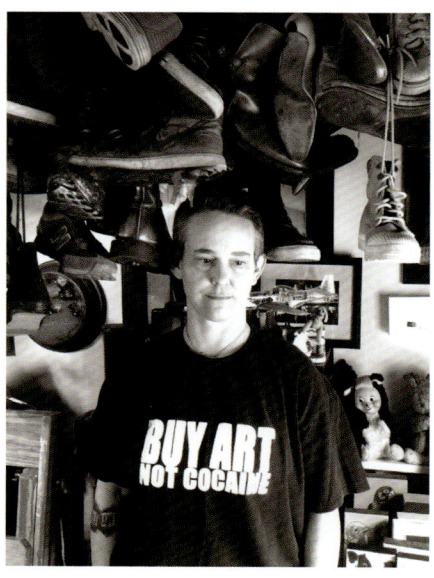

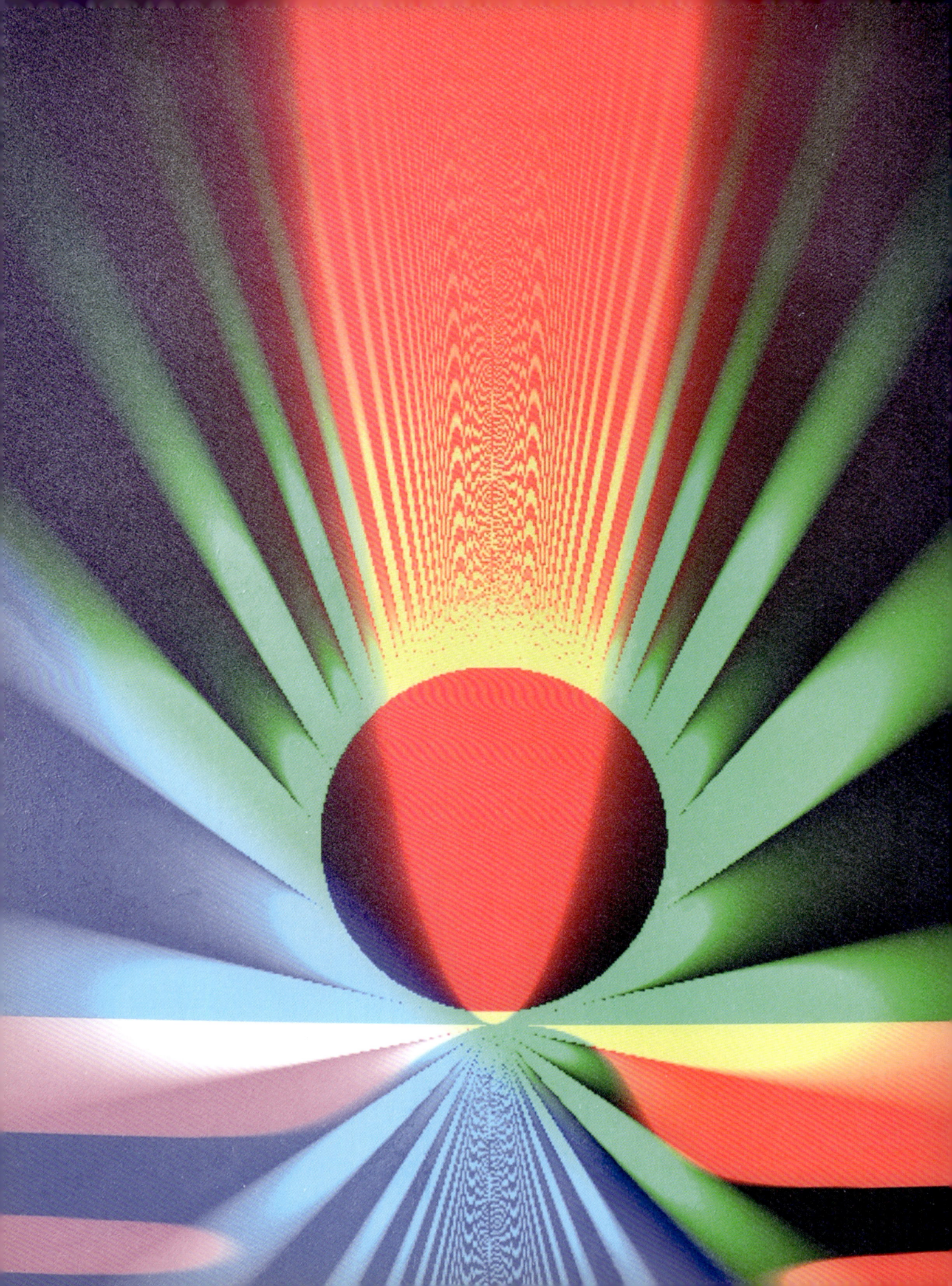

ALAN SINGER

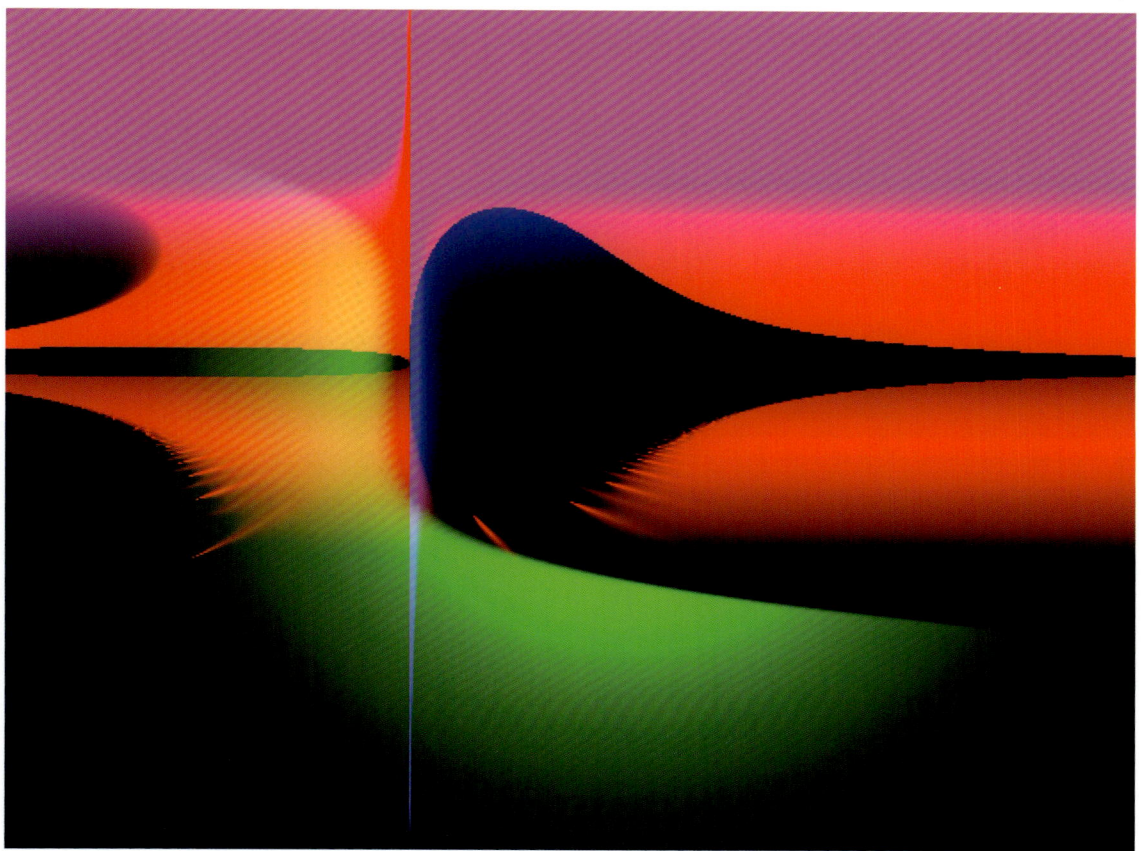

Alan Singer was born into a family of artists and designers in New York City. As a young student, he spent Saturdays at The Art Students League in Manhattan, drawing the figure. Later, he went on to The Cooper Union to earn a BFA. His MFA is from Cornell University where his major interest was in painting. During that time he developed his illustration skills working for publishers. Singer received scholarships to study at Yale University in Norfolk, CT, Boston University at Tanglewood, MA, and at The Skowhegan School of Painting & Sculpture in Skowhegan, Maine.

Singer went on to post-graduate work in graphic design and was employed by The National Geographic, Random House, Dutton, and the U.S. Postal Service among others. Today, Alan Singer is a Professor in the School of Art at Rochester Institute of Technology in Rochester, New York, where he puts his life experience to good use in his classes.

Singer's interests in science and nature frequently influence his artwork. His recent paintings and prints blend measurement and mathematics with color and composition. His artwork has been shown for many years in galleries and museums including The Smithsonian in Washington, D.C. and the Everson Museum of Art in Syracuse, New York.

The images you see here have come about through a study of geometry that is ongoing in his artwork. At present, he is deeply engaged using digital imagery to create these compositions.

Alan Singer has written about visual art for publications and continues on his blog: *"The Visual Artworker"*.

WWW.SINGERARTS.COM

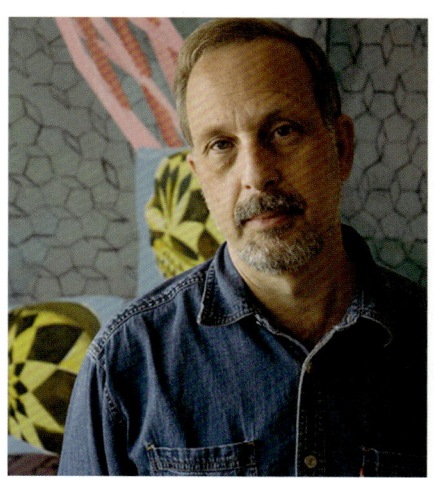

● **(facing page) Action Central**
details?

● **Distant Shore**
details?

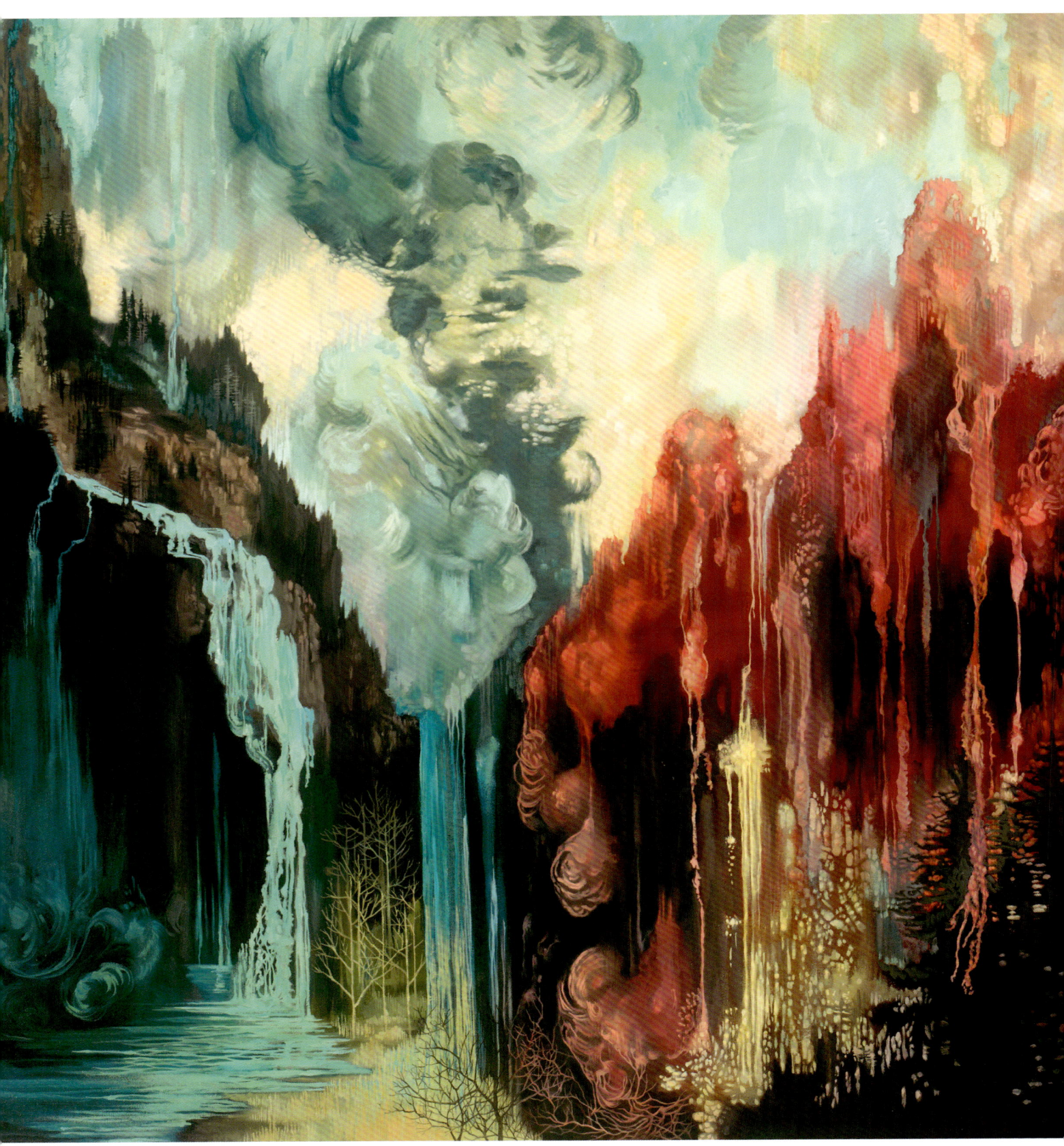

KATHRYN ST. CLAIR

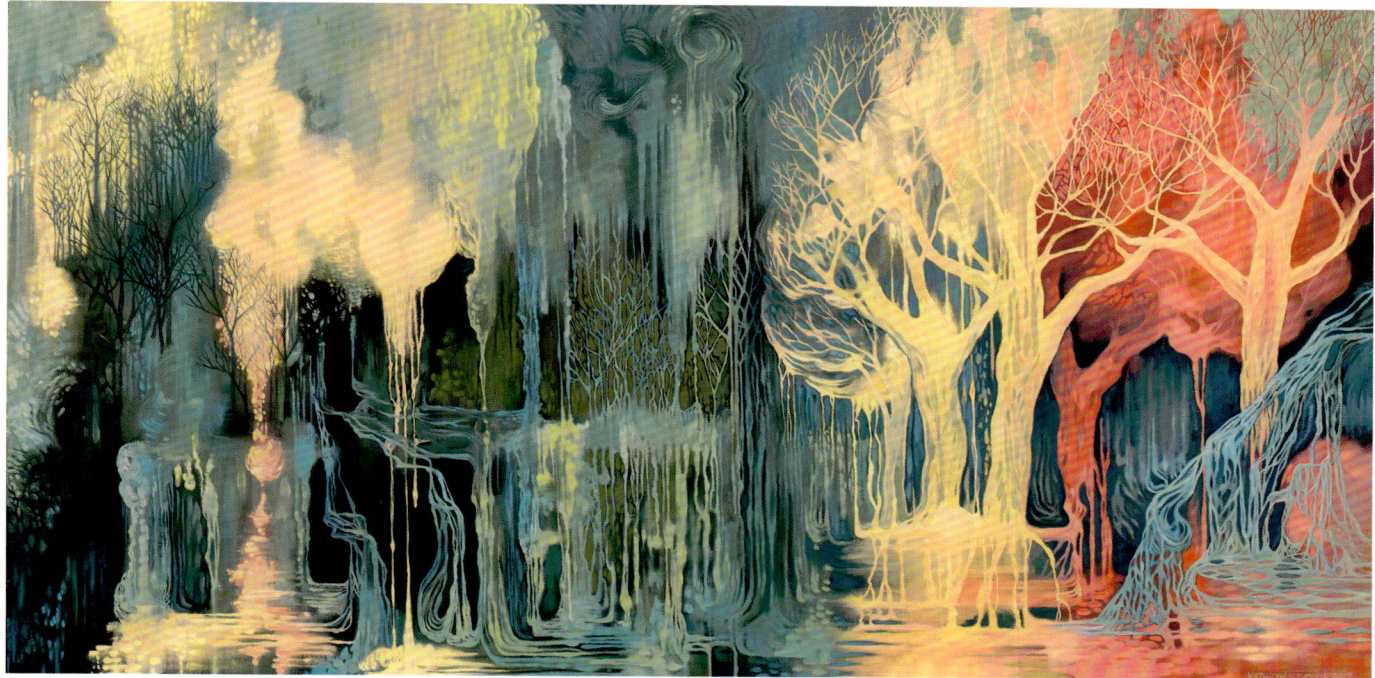

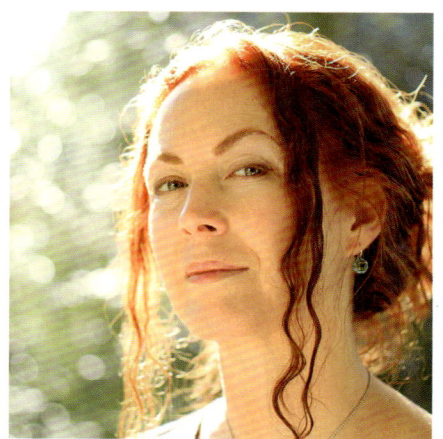

I paint landscape-inspired work in an age of volatile weather conditions and fragile, vanishing ecosystems. My work is driven by the state of flux in our world. The ecological processes of 'disturbance' and 'succession,' as well as the delicate interconnectedness of living things, are concepts that move me.

In this shifting, unpredictable, often chaotic world, my process has become a romantic exploration of drifting, pulling apart, converging, ascending, and descending. I appropriate situations in landscapes and allow deviations and disruptions to occur with the paint; I then find myself reacting to these random changes in the composition. My process becomes a metaphor for the shifting earth and environment.

We currently deal with a myriad of threats to our environment and future - extreme weather due to global warming, radioactivity, genetically modified organisms, and drug-resistant pathogens are a few examples of these man-made disturbances. I feel compelled to create work that expresses a sense of urgency to change course and react in new ways, while also celebrating the wonder found in the attributes of the natural elements.

I am drawn to how light shifts our perception of what surrounds us, creating halos of soft diffusion or pockets of ambiguity. I am intrigued by patterns and distortions in landscapes- where images of what is 'real' and what is 'reflected' are set adrift or submerged in a nebulous space. I marvel at the mystery that exists in the shadows and the emergence of light from darkness.

WWW.KATHRYNSTCLAIR.COM

SAM STILL

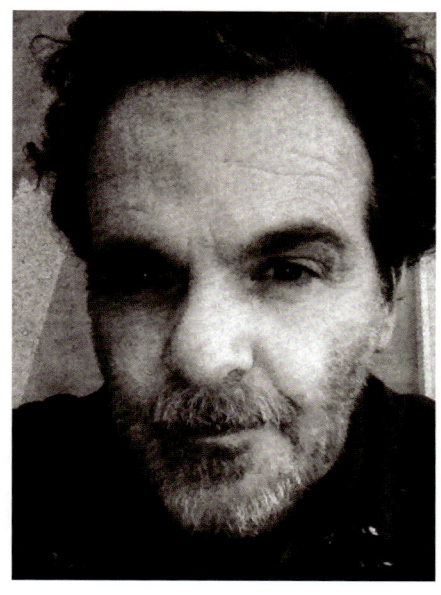

● **(left) 16.081**
Higgen's India ink, still ash, Arches 300 lb hot press watercolor paper, 22 x 28 in.

● **Name?**
Details?

"I arrange with a conversation in mind. Best thriving when arranging intimate thoughts brought together in conversation. Conversations with an individual work or a series, are fluid. There is a beginning, an awakening, a fresh conversation with subsequent encounters. There is knowledge encountered and discarded. This constant rearrangement, for all investred, suggests unending perspectives for consideration."

WWW.SAMSTILL.COM

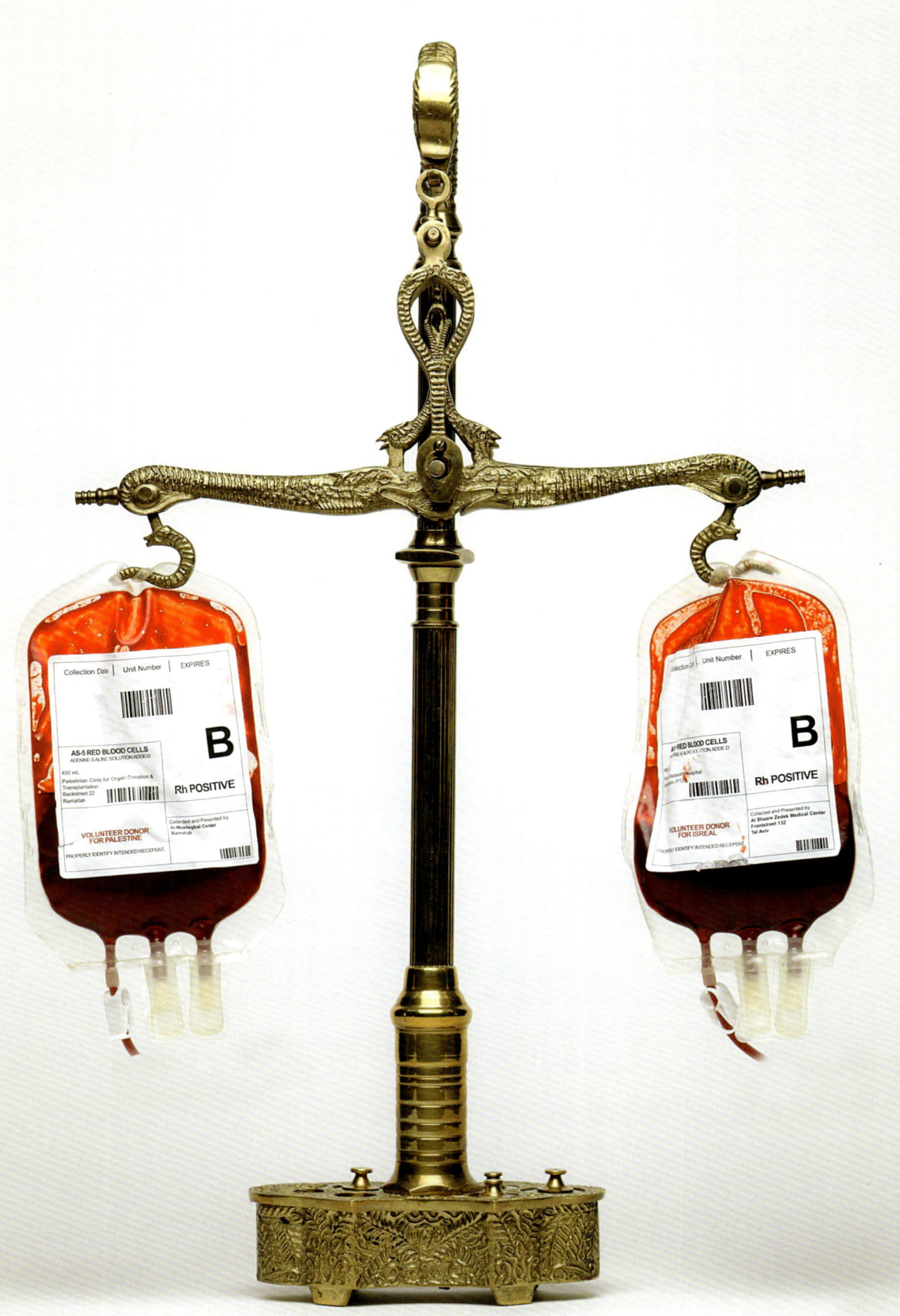

JOHN TRASHKOWSKY

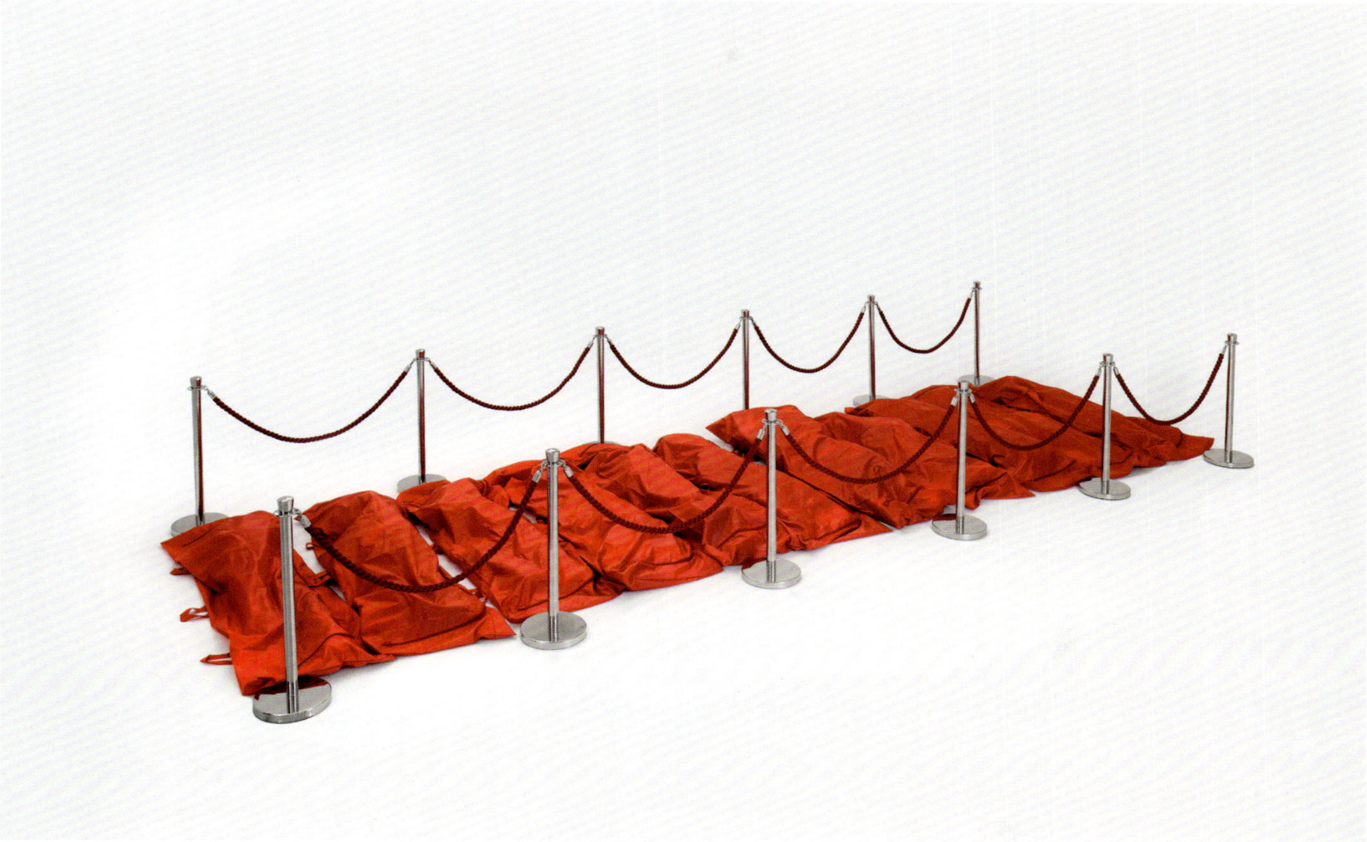

John Trashkowsky is contemporary art for the big questions of our time. The issue is one of purity, I suppose. Mining a seam that comes at us every day of the week from all sides. The mission is to surprise us out of our anti-psychotic, coffee-swilling, anxiety-ridden pill-popping paranoia with products that make us want to jump out of our skin, with joy or irritation. The choice of ingredient is thrilling anyway.

WWW.JOHNTRACHOWSKY.COM

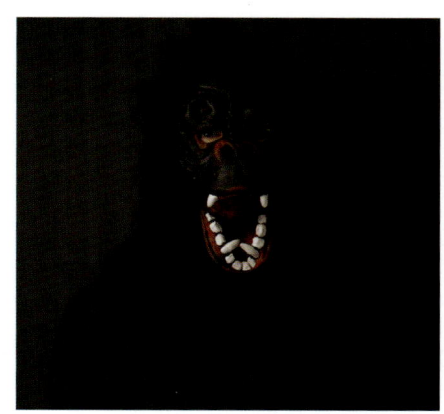

● **(facing page) No Blood is Better**
Pharmacist scale, Palestinian & Israeli blood donor, 2015

● **Red Carpet**
Installation, red body bags, cord stands, 2013

FERN SHAFFER

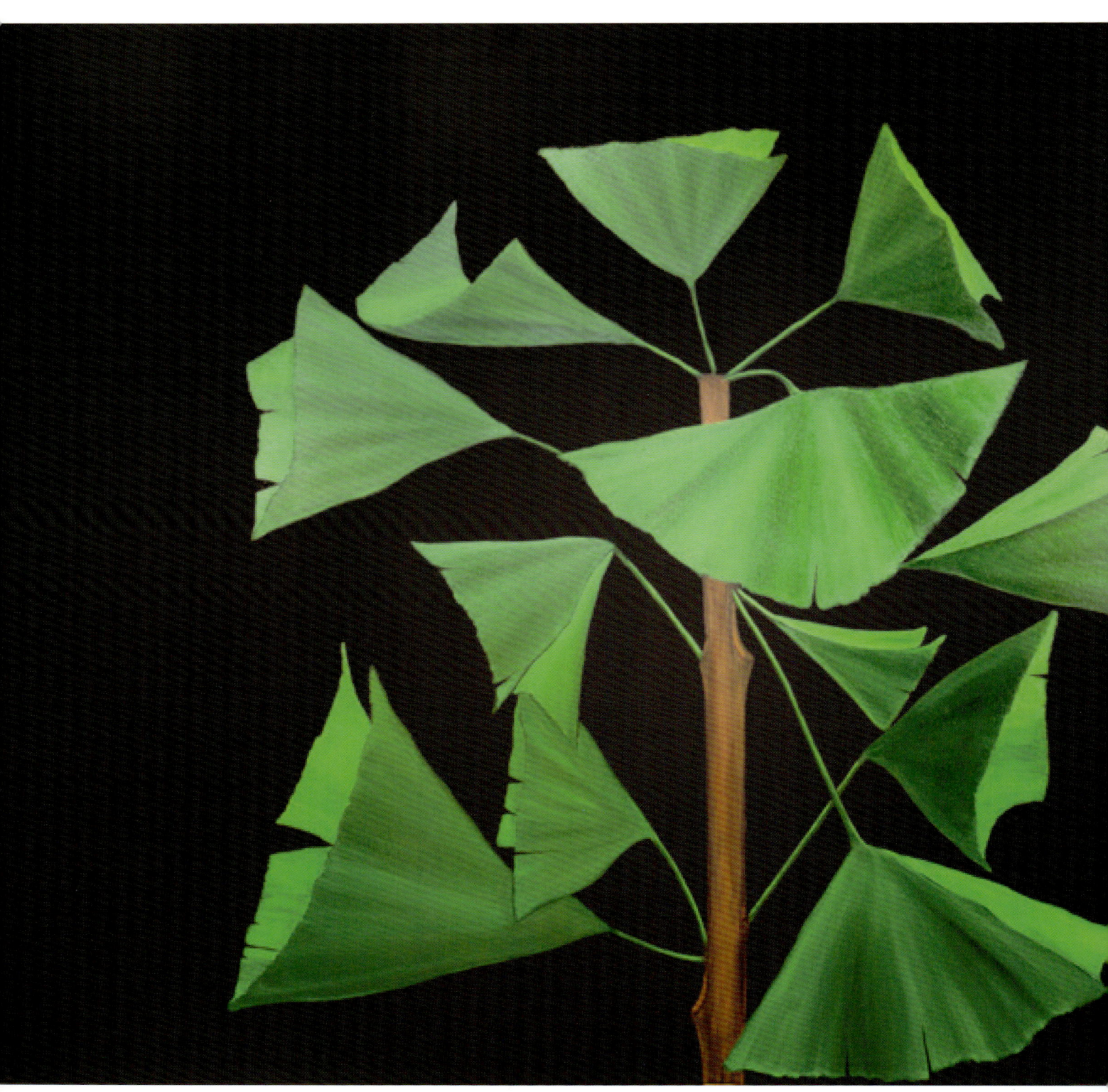

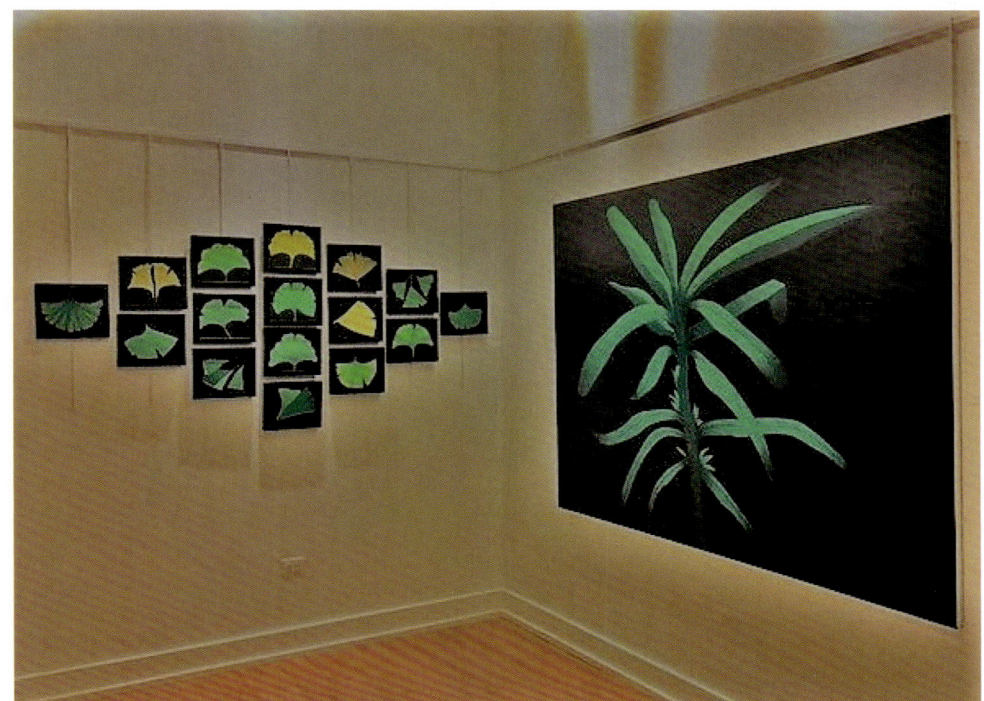

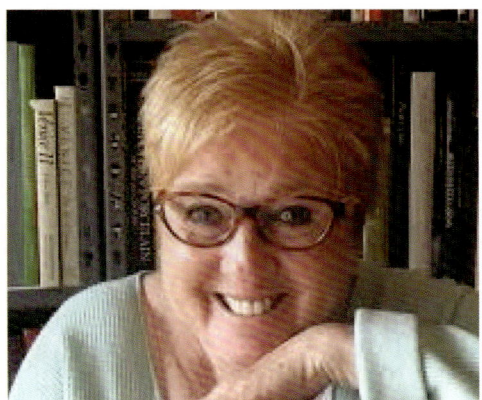

My interest is in plants, science, history, spirituality, and the environment. By recognizing how everything is interconnected, we can avoid mistakes by observing what is enhancing our world and what is destroying our world. It makes no sense to poison the water when we will ultimately be the ones to consume it. The pattern is repeated over and over again revealing the crisis of our culture's desire for immediate gratification. Living in an increasingly dangerous, toxic, and stagnant environment, for both animal and plant life, led me to change my subject matter for both my paintings and rituals.

I was born and live in Chicago, IL.
I received my BA from the University of Illinois and MA from Columbia College. Lectured all over the world and have been published in Magazines, Books and local Newspapers. As the president of Artemisia Gallery in Chicago for over 10 years, I juried many exhibitions in the US and South America. My work has been exhibited nationally and internationally, in solo and group shows. I have been collected by national and international museums. On the cover of Suzi Gablik's book The Reenchantment of Art, I am seen in one of my rituals for healing the earth. My paintings for the past 30 years reflect my interests in Healing Plants, and now, the survival of plants over long periods of time.

WWW.FERNSHAFFER.COM

CHINA FAITH STAR

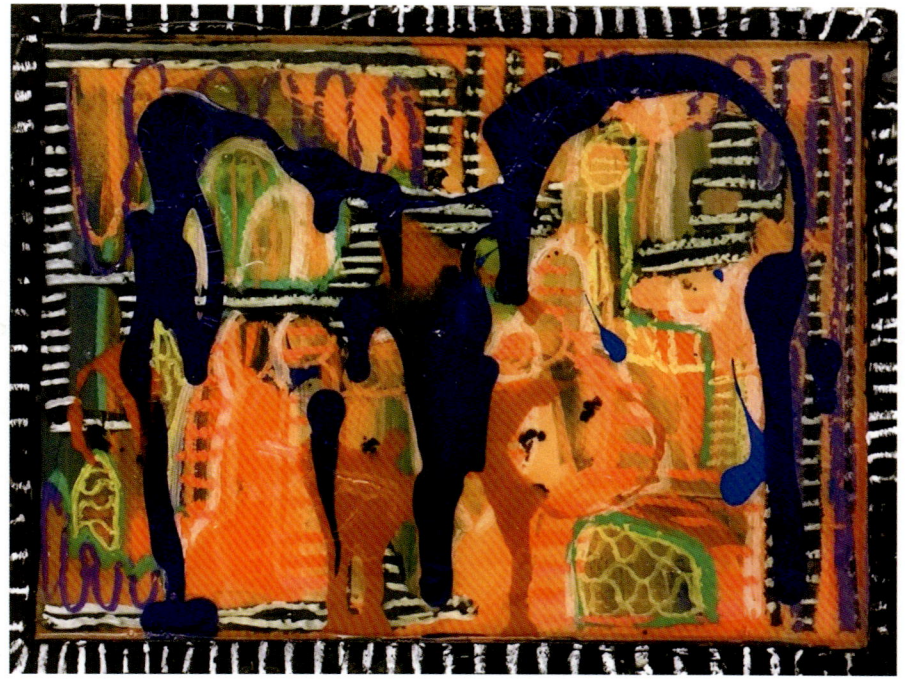

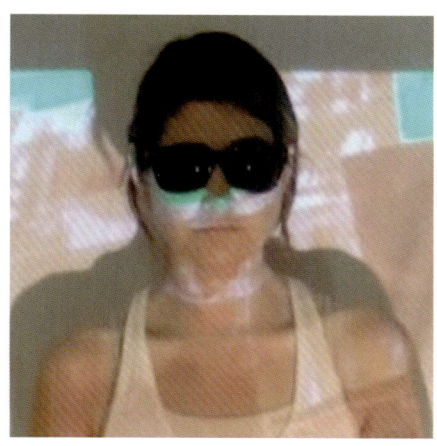

- **(facing page) Things We Cannot Shake or Change**
  32 x 23.5 x 1.5 in., 2018

- **A Magical Gathering**
  15.5 x 12 in., 2017

"I've painted since I could hold a brush, listening to the whispers and beats laid by elders, retreating to moss land forests to pray to the ancients from which we come. I make art to escape the mortality of monotony"

Enter from/through/into the precipice of the underground, raised from the streets of colors, to star-lined "death s(c)ells", oil fields, ocean horizon, heritage patterned horse trails upon orange groves. the double entendre of acid hitting skin is real. I've painted since I could hold a brush, listening to the whispers and beats laid by elders, retreating to moss land forests to pray to the ancients from which we come. I make art to escape the mortality of monotony. Art outlives the living, inspires futures and pasts. Baby Crone, entering a trance, channelling through wells of spirit and emotion ablaze: release mediums {let go}. Painting pictures now, after heritage exploration, every medium a thought to solution, a crazy potion saving the world. I am artist, other, lost soul trying to survive. Fuck it. I paint because friends died. Who cares. We all die. I die to do this: survive. Helping you live another day. Illumination is divine. I am with you.

"New Romantic engagement ...is often mistaken for ... postmodern interest. Modernity ... characterized by ... anxiety reconstruct(s) the everyday ... universalism. Postmodernity ... described ... neurosis ... deconstruct it along the heterogenous lines of race, gender, and place. New Romanticism attempts to both-neither reconstruct ... deconstruct the commonplace."
- *www.metamodernism.com*

China Faith Star is a multi-sensory artist, writer, performer. Her work spans action, painting, animation, soundscape, installation. She has performed and exhibited across coasts in solo and group exhibitions, and for public commissions, embracing community into the process of art making.

WWW.CHINAFAITHSTAR.COM

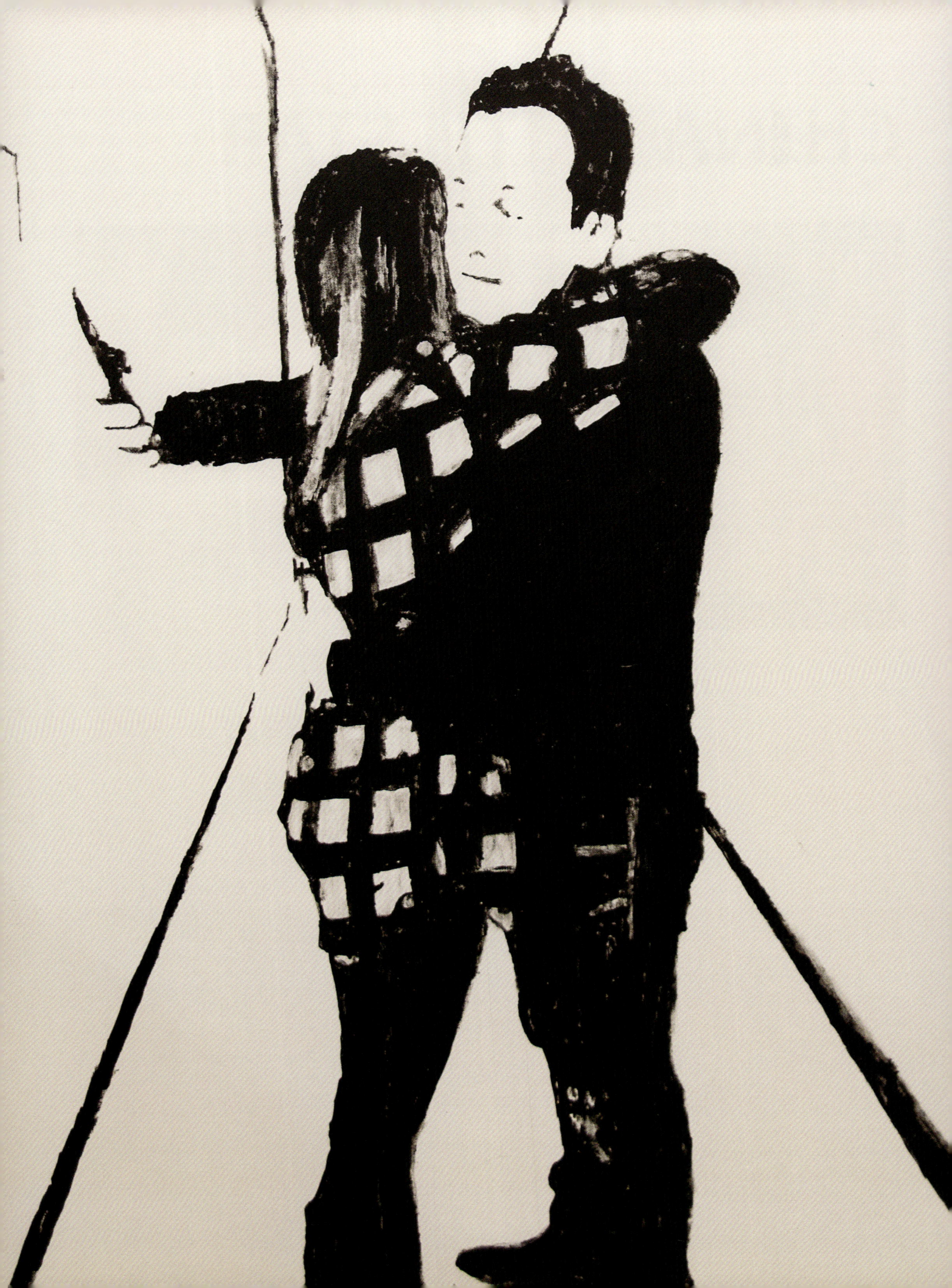

JOHAN WAHLSTROM

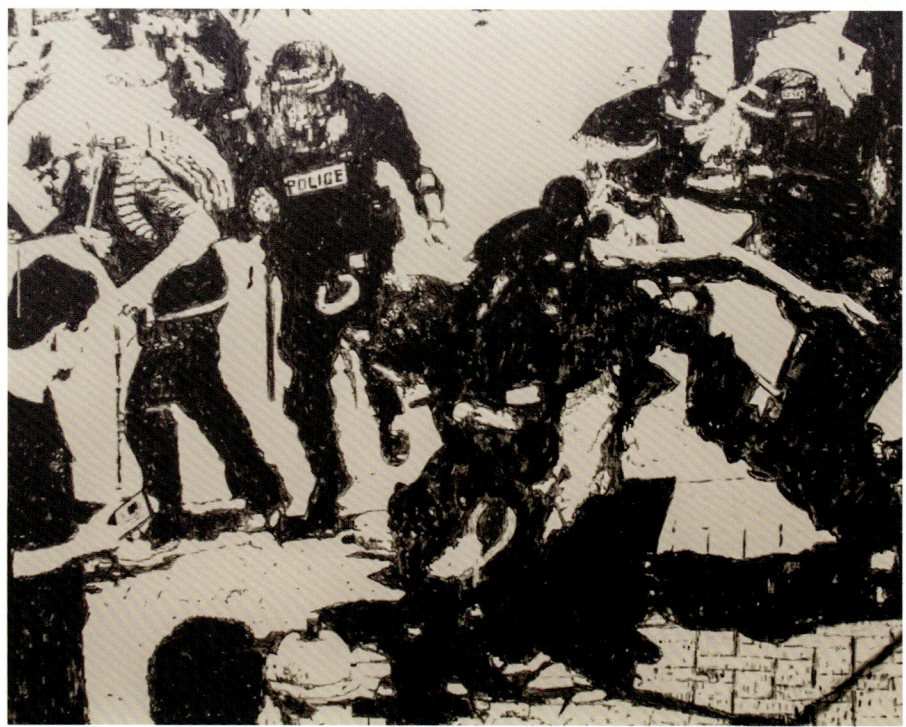

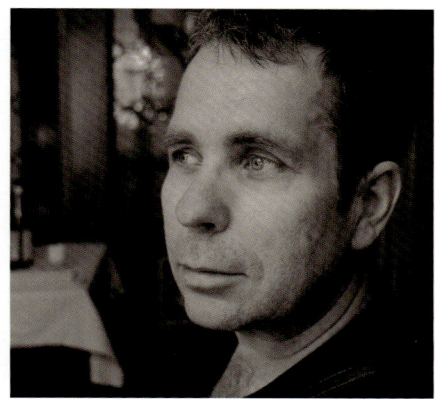

● (facing page) **Disconnecting 8**
acrylic on canvas, 40 x 30 in., 2018

● **Disconnecting 25**
acrylic on canvas, 48 x 60 in., 2018

"I paint to keep myself insane. I paint anxiety to be calm. I paint war to have peace. I paint sadness to be happy. I paint the dark to be in the light. I paint death to be alive. I paint a story so that I don't have to tell a story."

Born 1959, Stockholm, Sweden. Lives and works in New York City & Malaga, Spain. He is a fifth-generation and internationally recognized artist, exhibited in New York, Boston, Los Angeles, Elmhurst/Chicago, Miami, London, Berlin, Milan, Amsterdam, Madrid, Barcelona, Zurich, Amsterdam and Stockholm to name a few.

"Evocative artist Johan Wahlstrom aims to encourage the celebration of daily life and incite happiness through the acceptance of reality. His emotionally charged neoexpressionist paintings are a contemporary hybrid of Jean DuBuffet's chaotic geometric canvases and Jean-Michel Basquiat's subversively scrawled social critiques. Wahlstrom works in series that function as pointed signifiers to his artistic intention. His work aims to elucidate the uncontrollable nature of reality in an effort to embrace the small sufferings that signify life. Wahlstrom's work continues to gain attention fuelled by his overwhelming desire to connect with humanity in the hopes of provoking conversation. Pushing his abilities to the limit, Wahlstrom transcribes visual stories to enact societal change by illustrating the erratic and confusing nature of human existence."

-Kirsten Nicholas

WWW.JOHANWAHLSTROM.COM

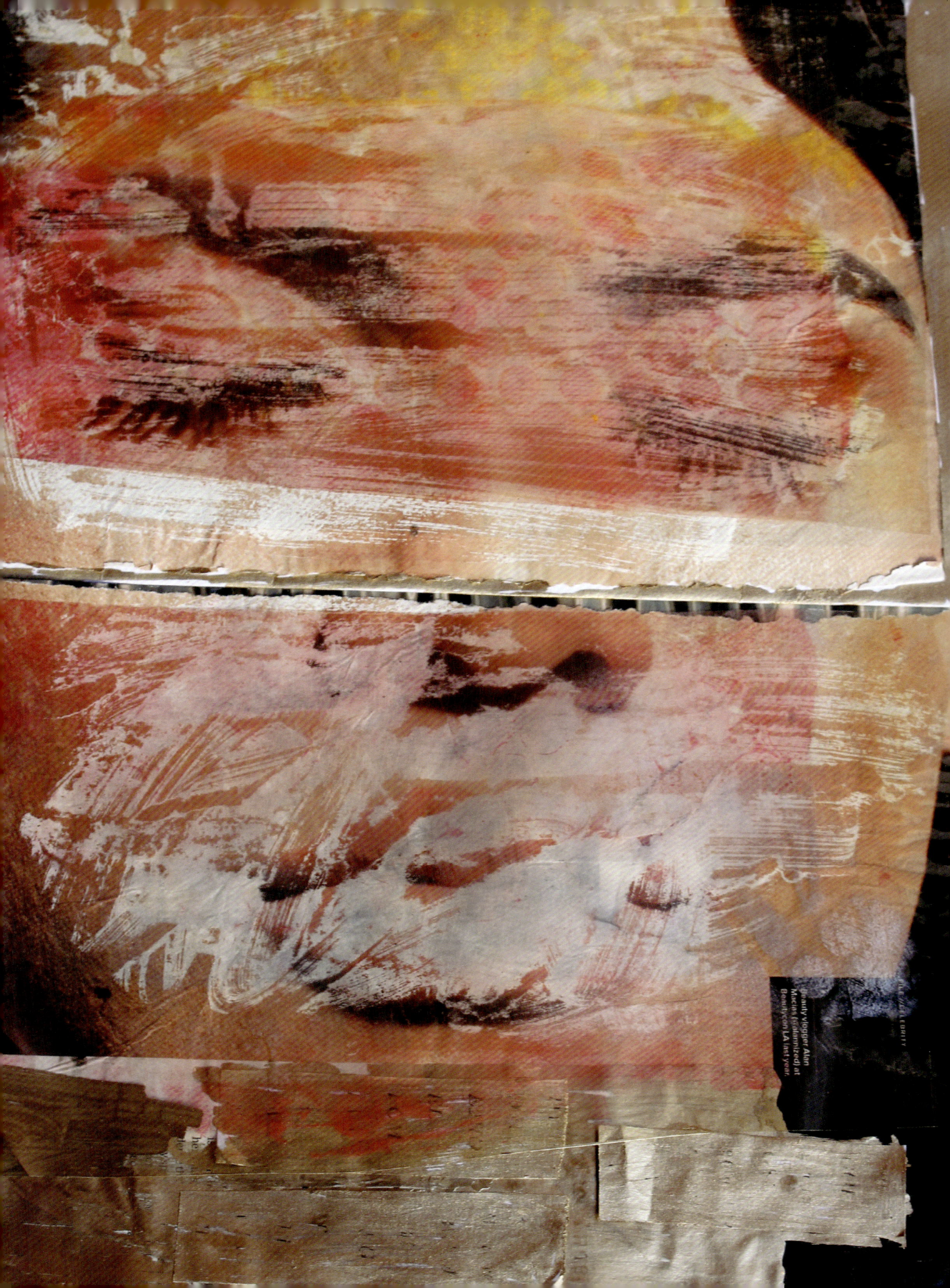

MARILYN WALTER

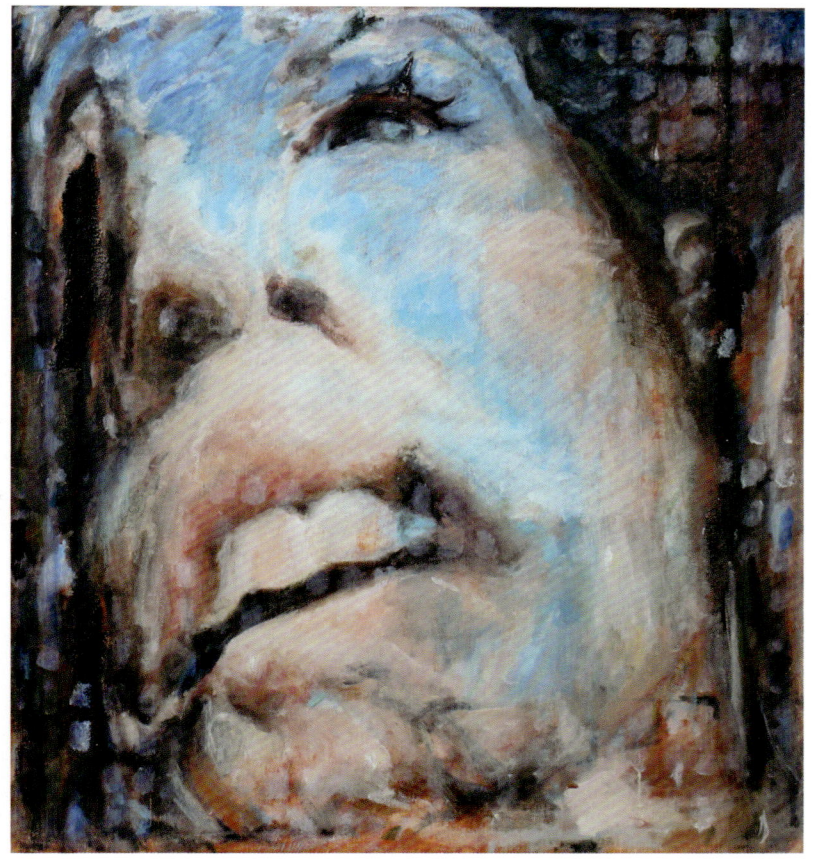

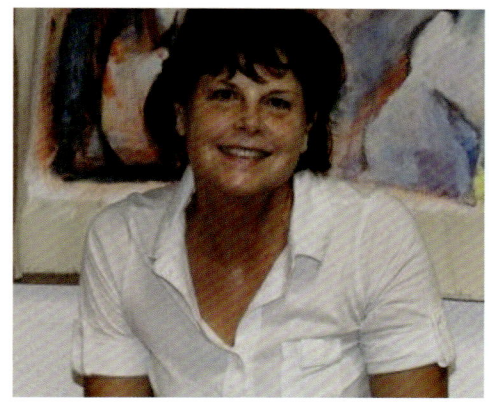

● (facing page) **Amnesia 2**
acrylic, paints, inks, marker, pencil on plastic, transfers, on board

● **A Passionate Heart Still Beats**
monoprint, paper litho, pencil, collaged photo piece,.

"The swirling, poetic moments, when I close my eyes and allow real and invented experiences to intersect, inspire my current mixed media paintings on paper, canvas and panel."

Marilyn Walter currently lives in West Palm Beach, Florida and works at her studio at The STUDIO 1016, 1016 Clare Avenue, Building 5. Walter is an avid educator who taught visual art classes for the Council Lifetime Learning Program at the National Council of Jewish Women New York Section. She also worked with the Intergenerational and Art & Memory workshop series. Walter attended Fairleigh Dickinson for her BA and continued her education at Parsons for teaching. In 2011 and 2012, she participated in the School of Visual Arts Summer Residencies in Painting & Mixed Media and Printmaking & Book Arts. Since participating with NYC HomeBase IV, a Social Engagement Project, Walter is currently experimenting with the incorporation of social interactions into her art.

Her process in creating art is to erase, inscribe, trace, incise, collage and transfer the resultant marks and images onto paper, canvas, wood, plastic or Plexiglas. Colors, shapes, movements, textures are repeated on multi-layered mixed media surfaces, becoming collages of traces. She reaches the desired result when the patchwork of translucent plastic, paper or blackboard paint seamlessly incorporates the surrounding elements. Growing up in Kuwait and Iran has allowed Walter to combine my passion and knowledge of both Eastern and Western cultures in my art. The influence of pattern, multiples and use of space viewed in her childhood are visible in the digital technology and printmaking processes that I use in creating my current work—a confluence of the timeless and the present.

WWW.MARILYNWALTER.COM

PING ZHENG

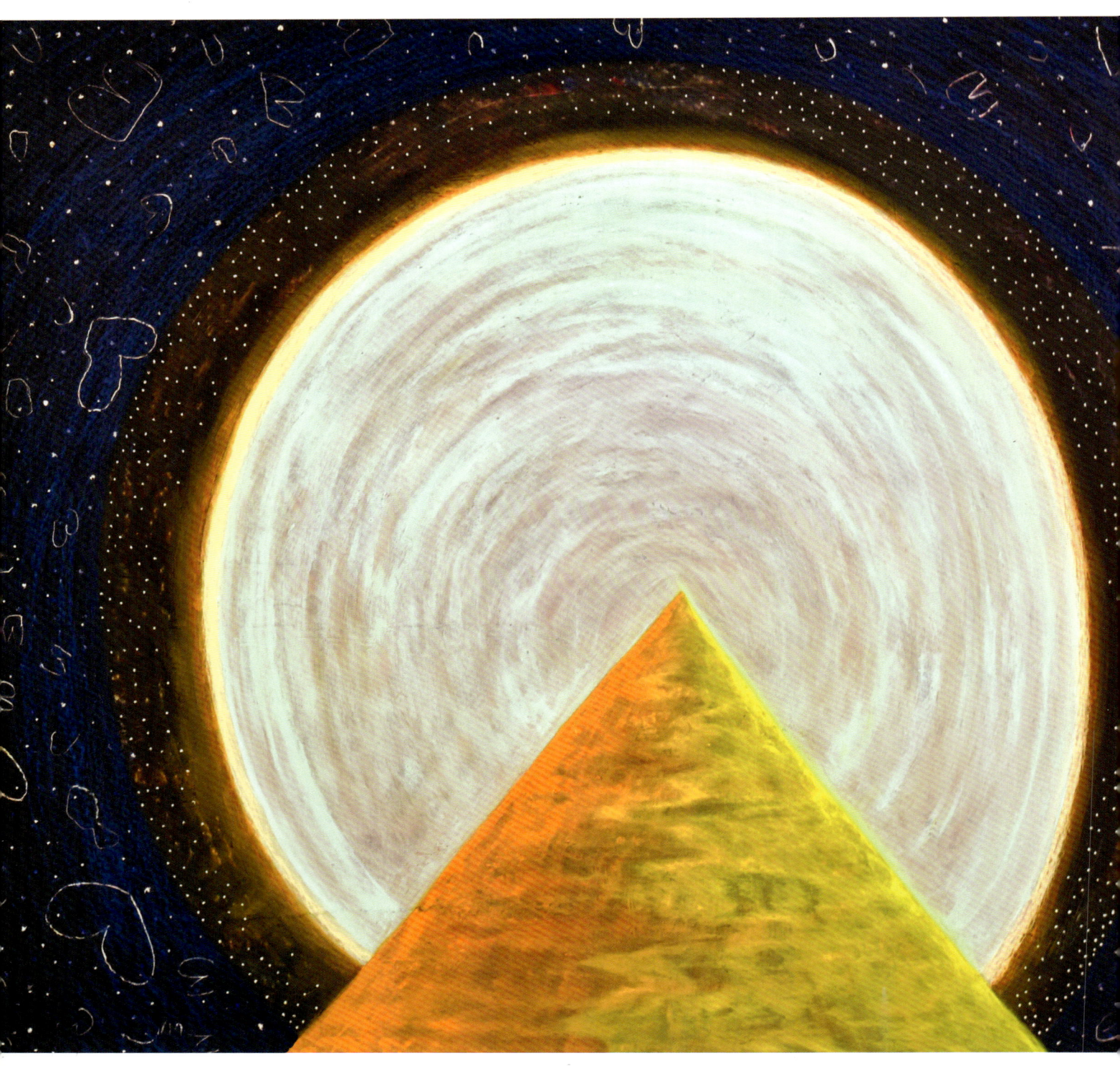

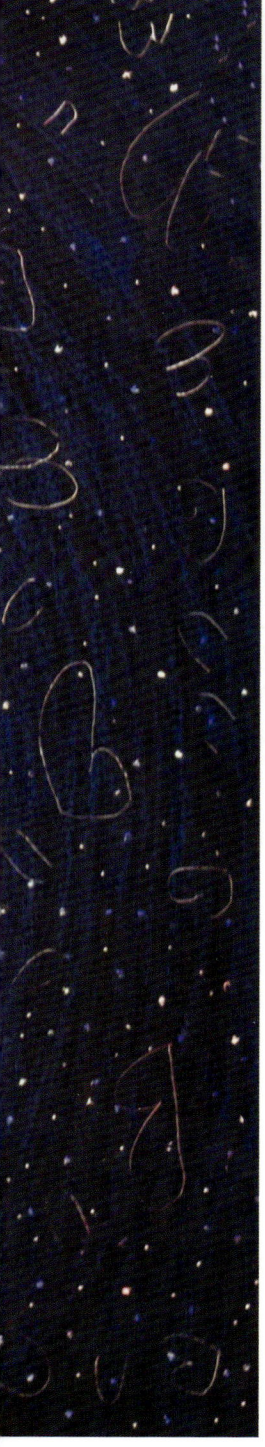

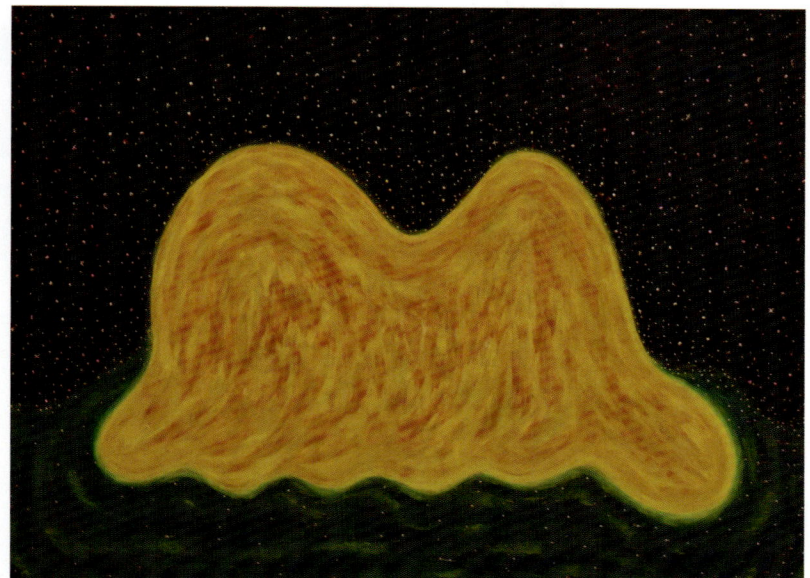

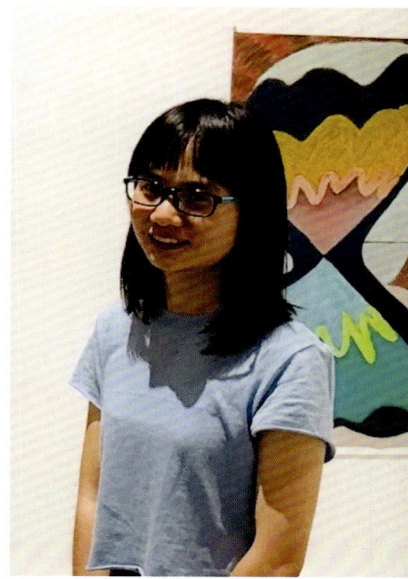

● **(facing page) A Good Timing**
oil stick on paper, 18 x 24 in.

● **Counting Stars**
oil stick on paper, 18 x 24 in.

Born in China, I grew up in a traditional patriarchal family under the restriction of the government's one-child policy. I lived in many different geographic regions, where I was surrounded by starkly contrasting natural environments. As an artist, my inspiration is grounded in childhood memories of natural landscapes, where I felt free as a human in the outdoors, avoiding family pressures: as a girl in a restricted traditional Chinese family, everything you do at home is wrong and nothing belongs to you, not even a shred of your thought or your emotion, therefore nature was my refuge.

Since I studied abroad in London and the United States, however, has triggered an awareness of gender equality as the very heart of human rights that shapes my world. I became aware of many contributions of women in the West. I began to express feminism to my artistic practice.

My artwork, straddling the line between figurative and abstract, functions as metaphor for the energy and limitless possibilities erupting from artistic freedom and my passionate belief in equality. It is as wide as the desire to expand my horizons, and through my awe-inspiring the nature has always evoked my childhood's memories of natural landscapes and gave me a renewed sense of self-discovery. It comes a growing opportunity to express my point of view as an artist.

WWW.ZHENG-PING.COM
WWW.KRISTENLORELLO.COM/PING-ZHENG-IN-THE-SKY-2018

ARTVOICES ART BOOKS

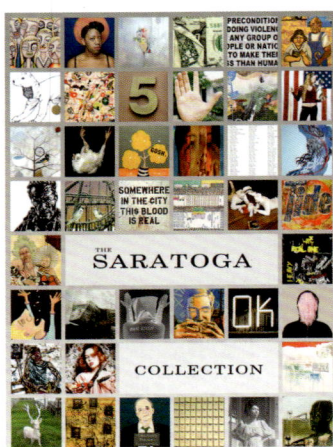

THE SARATOGA COLLECTION
$40.00 SOLD OUT

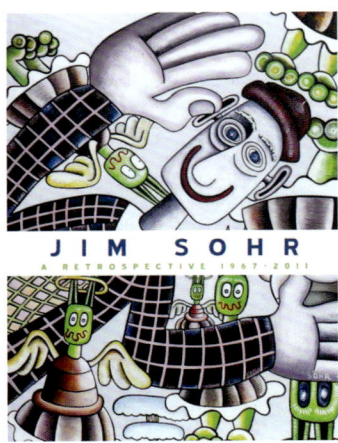

JIM SOHR
$60.00 SOLD OUT

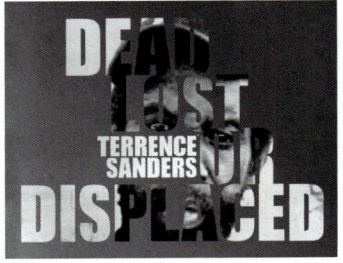

Terrence Sanders
DEAD LOST OR DISPLACED
$40.00

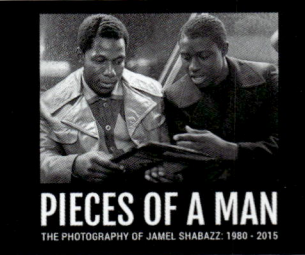

Jamel Shabazz
PIECES OF A MAN
$60.00 SOLD OUT

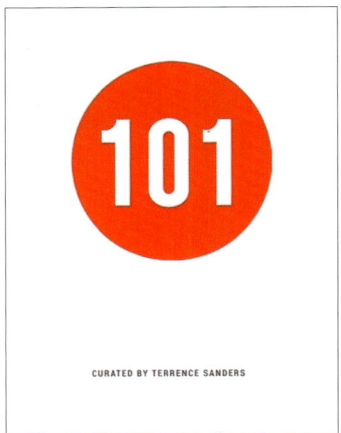

101 CONTEMPORARY ARTISTS
$60.00

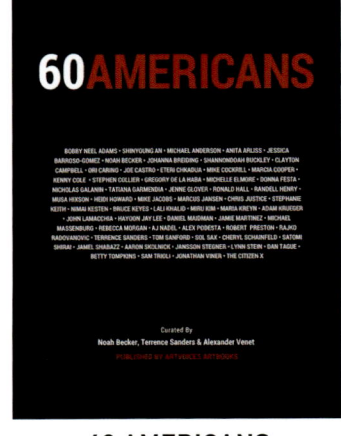

60 AMERICANS
Curated by Noah Becker, Alexander Venet & Terrence Sanders
$60.00

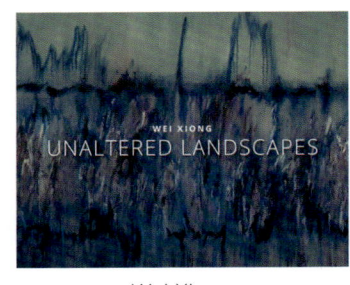

Wei Xiong
UNALTERED LANDSCAPES
$40.00

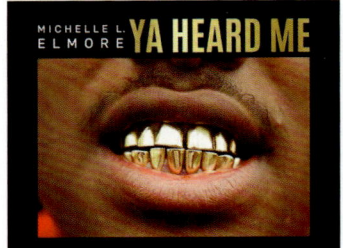

Michelle L. Elmore
YA HEARD ME
$40.00

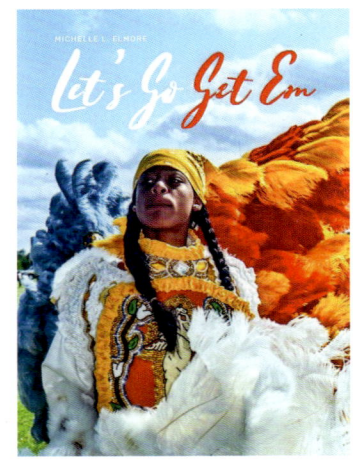

Michelle L. Elmore
LET'S GO GET EM
$60.00

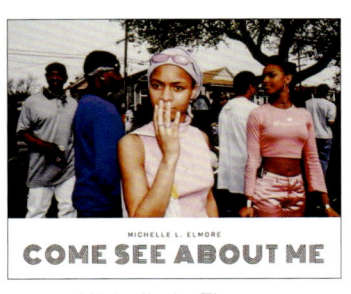

Michelle L. Elmore
COME SEE ABOUT ME
$40.00